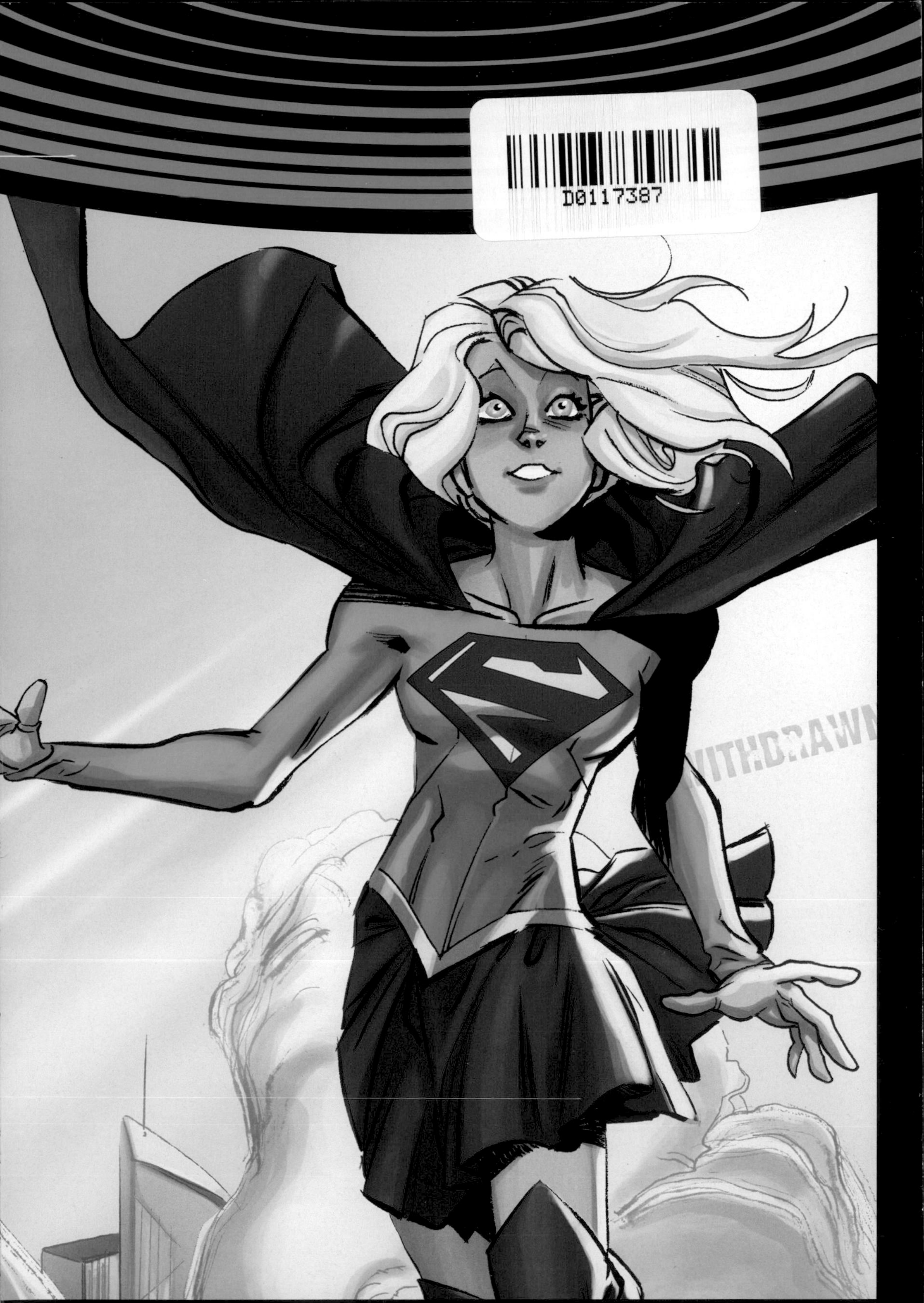

SUPERGIRL

VOL.2 ESCAPE FROM THE PHANTOM ZONE

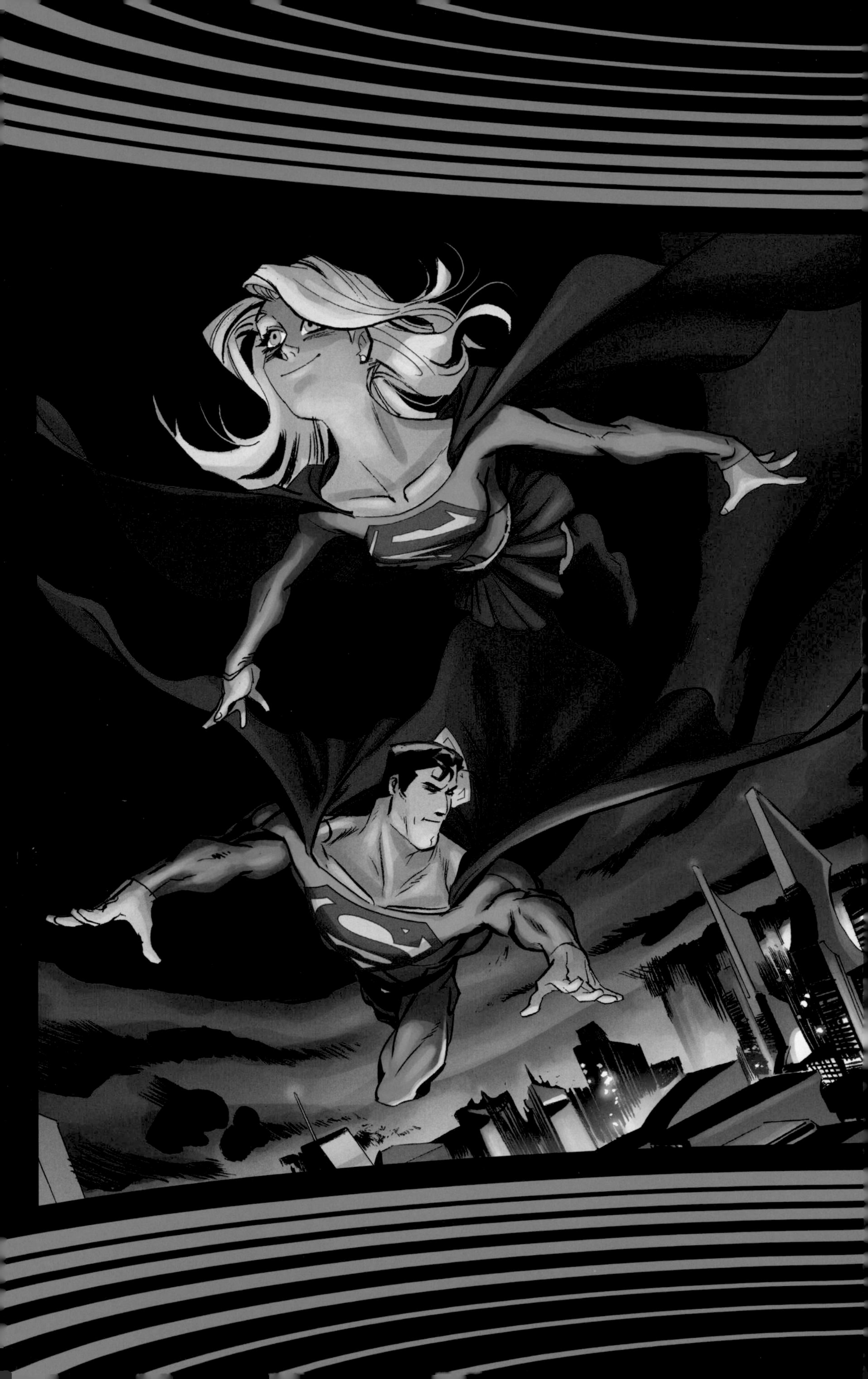

SUPERGIRL
VOL.2 ESCAPE FROM THE PHANTOM ZONE

STEVE ORLANDO * **HOPE LARSON**
writers

BRIAN CHING
MATIAS BERGARA
INAKI MIRANDA
artists

MICHAEL ATIYEH * **EVA DE LA CRUZ**
colorists

STEVE WANDS * **DERON BENNETT**
letterers

BRIAN CHING & MICHAEL ATIYEH
collection cover artists

SUPERMAN created by **JERRY SIEGEL** and **JOE SHUSTER**
SUPERGIRL based on characters created by **JERRY SIEGEL** and **JOE SHUSTER**
By special arrangement with the Jerry Siegel family
BATMAN created by **BOB KANE** with **BILL FINGER**

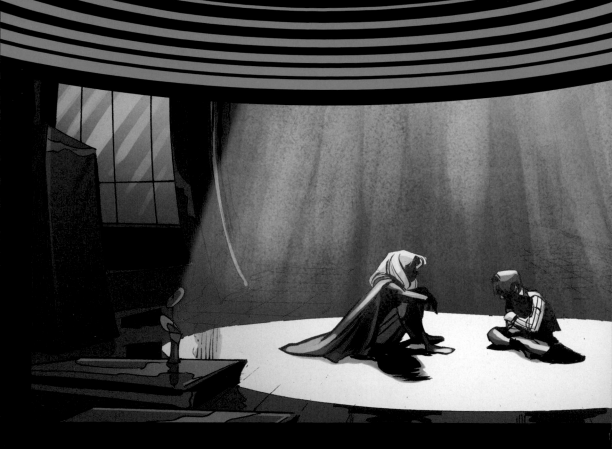

PAUL KAMINSKI Editor - Original Series * **ANDREW MARINO** Assistant Editor - Original Series
JEB WOODARD Group Editor - Collected Editions * **PAUL SANTOS** Editor - Collected Edition
STEVE COOK Design Director - Books * **MONIQUE NARBONETA** Publication Design

BOB HARRAS Senior VP - Editor-in-Chief, DC Comics
PAT McCALLUM Executive Editor, DC Comics

DIANE NELSON President * **DAN DiDIO** Publisher * **JIM LEE** Publisher * **GEOFF JOHNS** President & Chief Creative Officer
AMIT DESAI Executive VP - Business & Marketing Strategy, Direct to Consumer & Global Franchise Management
SAM ADES Senior VP & General Manager, Digital Services * **BOBBIE CHASE** VP & Executive Editor, Young Reader & Talent Development
MARK CHIARELLO Senior VP - Art, Design & Collected Editions * **JOHN CUNNINGHAM** Senior VP - Sales & Trade Marketing
ANNE DePIES Senior VP - Business Strategy, Finance & Administration * **DON FALLETTI** VP - Manufacturing Operations
LAWRENCE GANEM VP - Editorial Administration & Talent Relations * **ALISON GILL** Senior VP - Manufacturing & Operations
HANK KANALZ Senior VP - Editorial Strategy & Administration * **JAY KOGAN** VP - Legal Affairs * **JACK MAHAN** VP - Business Affairs
NICK J. NAPOLITANO VP - Manufacturing Administration * **EDDIE SCANNELL** VP - Consumer Marketing
COURTNEY SIMMONS Senior VP - Publicity & Communications * **JIM (SKI) SOKOLOWSKI** VP - Comic Book Specialty Sales & Trade Marketing
NANCY SPEARS VP - Mass, Book, Digital Sales & Trade Marketing * **MICHELE R. WELLS** VP - Content Strategy

SUPERGIRL VOL. 2 ESCAPE FROM THE PHANTOM ZONE

DC Comics, 2900 West Alameda Ave., Burbank, CA 91505
Printed by LSC Communications, Kendallville, IN, USA. 9/22/17. First Printing.
ISBN: 978-1-4012-7433-7

Library of Congress Cataloging-in-Publication Data is available.

PEFC Certified
Printed on paper from sustainably managed forests, controlled sources
PEFC/29-31-337
www.pefc.org

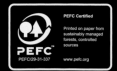

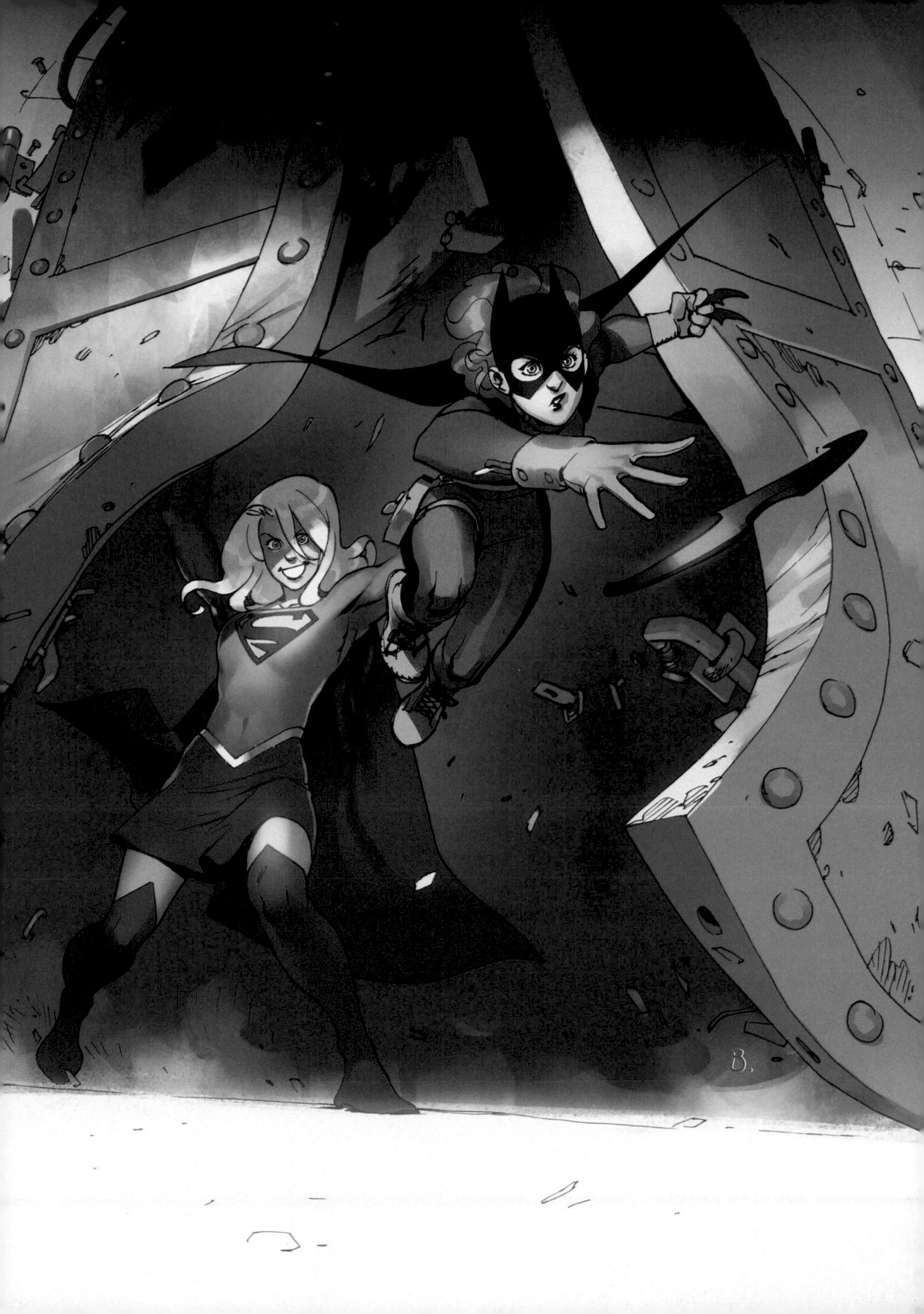

"WORLD'S FINEST"

HOPE LARSON writer * INAKI MIRANDA artist * EVA DE LA CRUZ colorist
cover by BENGAL

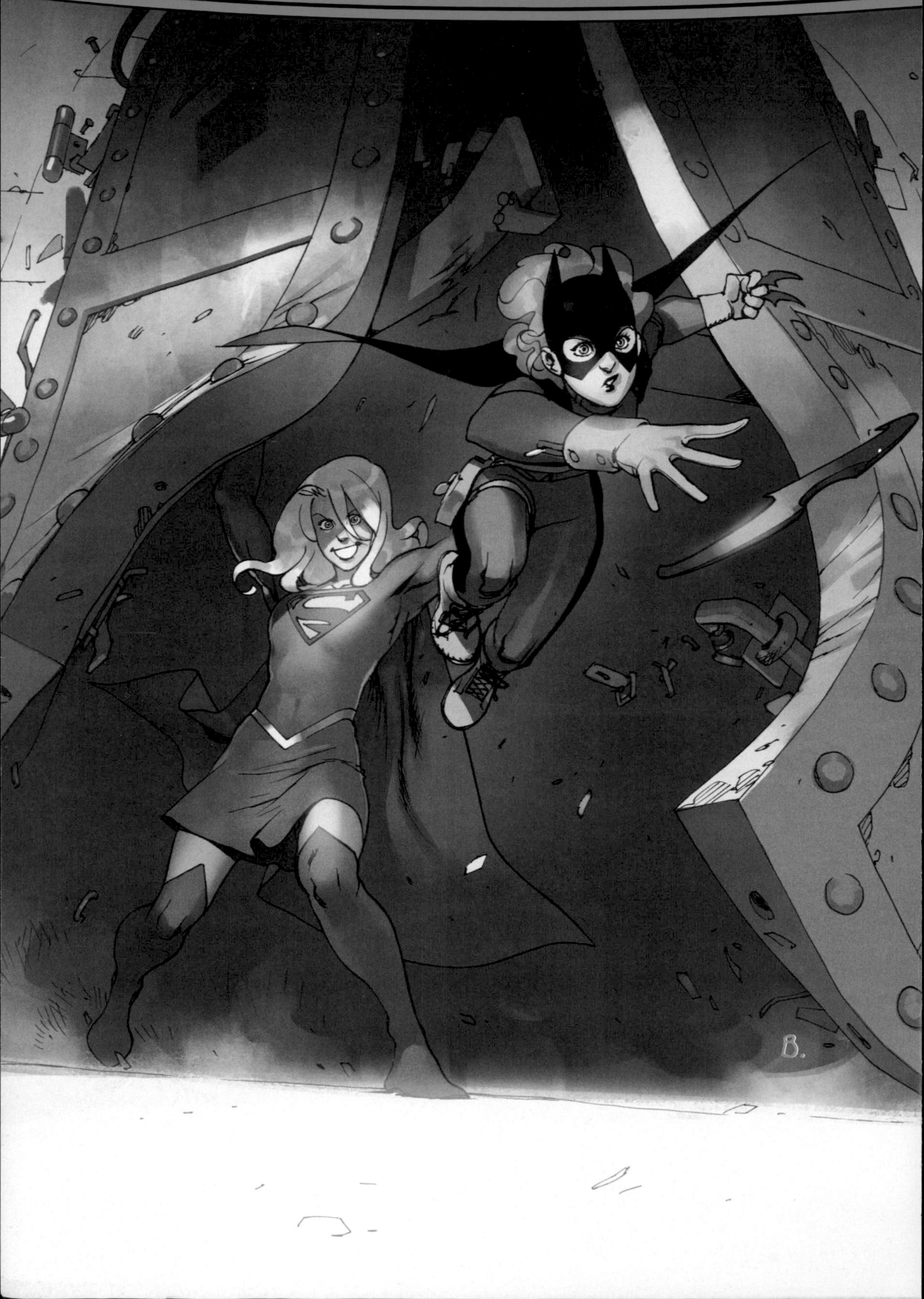

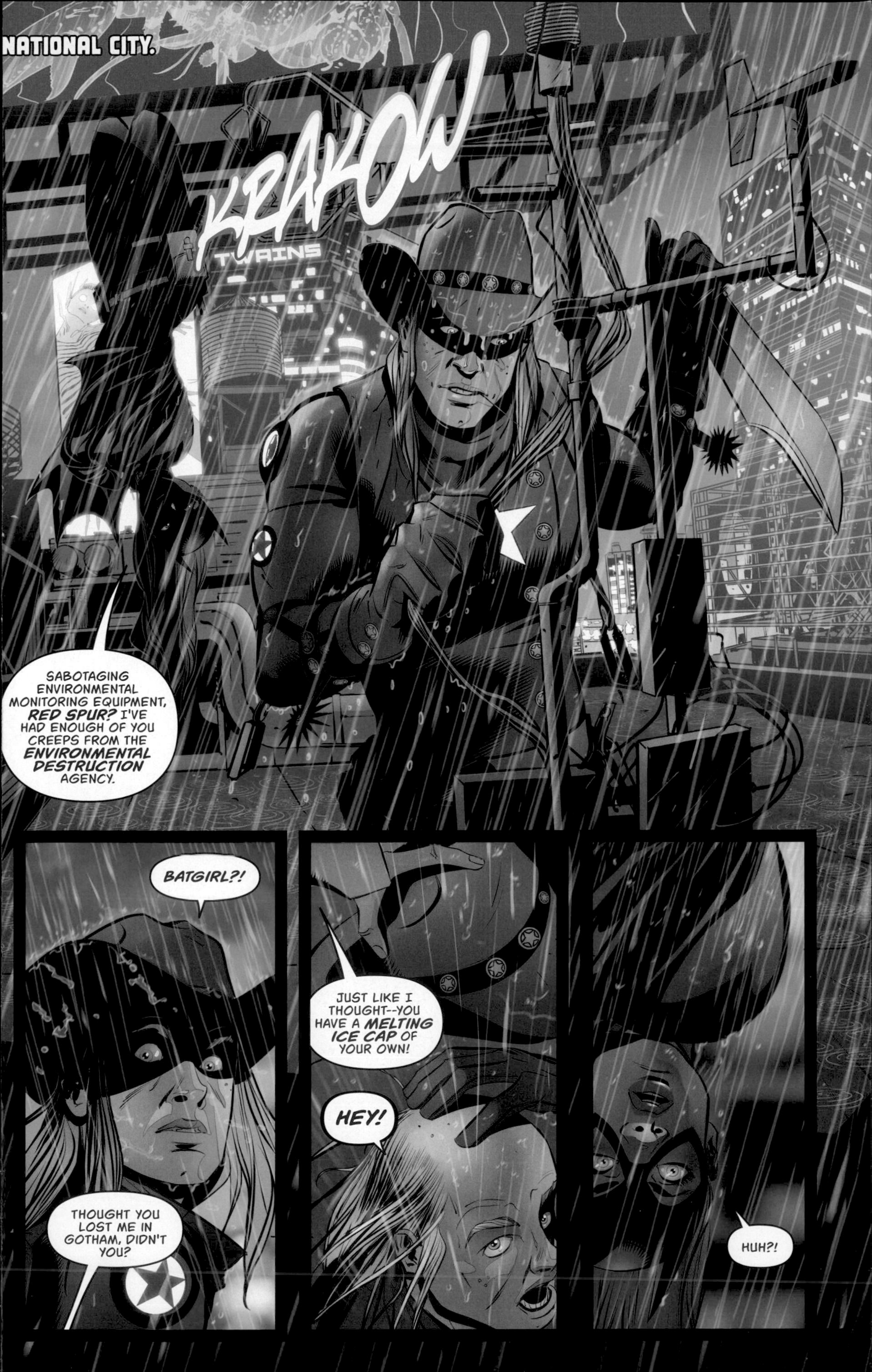
NATIONAL CITY.
KRAKOW
TWAINS
SABOTAGING ENVIRONMENTAL MONITORING EQUIPMENT, RED SPUR? I'VE HAD ENOUGH OF YOU CREEPS FROM THE ENVIRONMENTAL DESTRUCTION AGENCY.
BATGIRL?!
THOUGHT YOU LOST ME IN GOTHAM, DIDN'T YOU?
JUST LIKE I THOUGHT--YOU HAVE A MELTING ICE CAP OF YOUR OWN!
HEY!
HUH?!

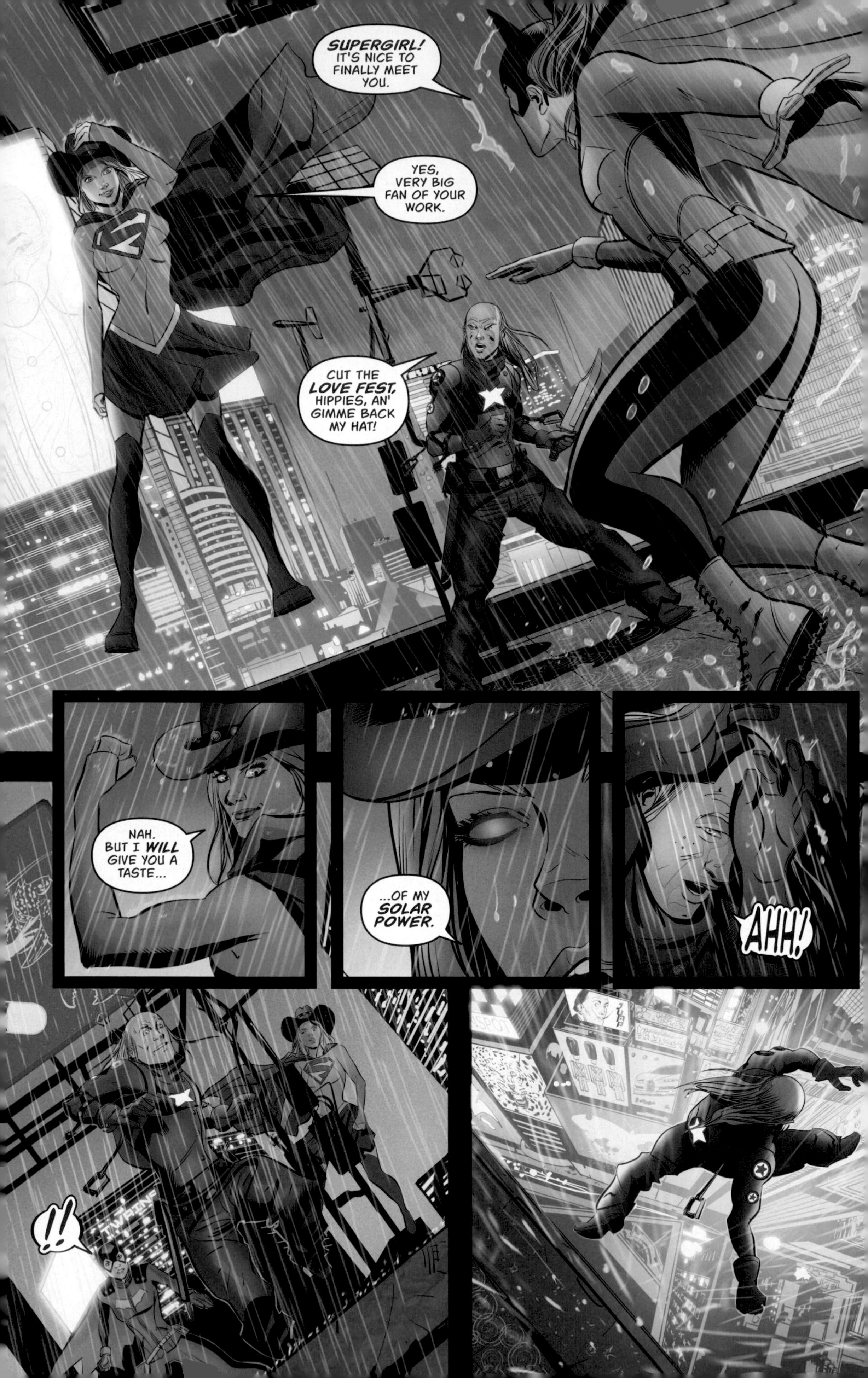
SUPERGIRL! IT'S NICE TO FINALLY MEET YOU.
YES, VERY BIG FAN OF YOUR WORK.
CUT THE LOVE FEST, HIPPIES, AN' GIMME BACK MY HAT!
NAH. BUT I WILL GIVE YOU A TASTE...
...OF MY SOLAR POWER.
AHH!
!!

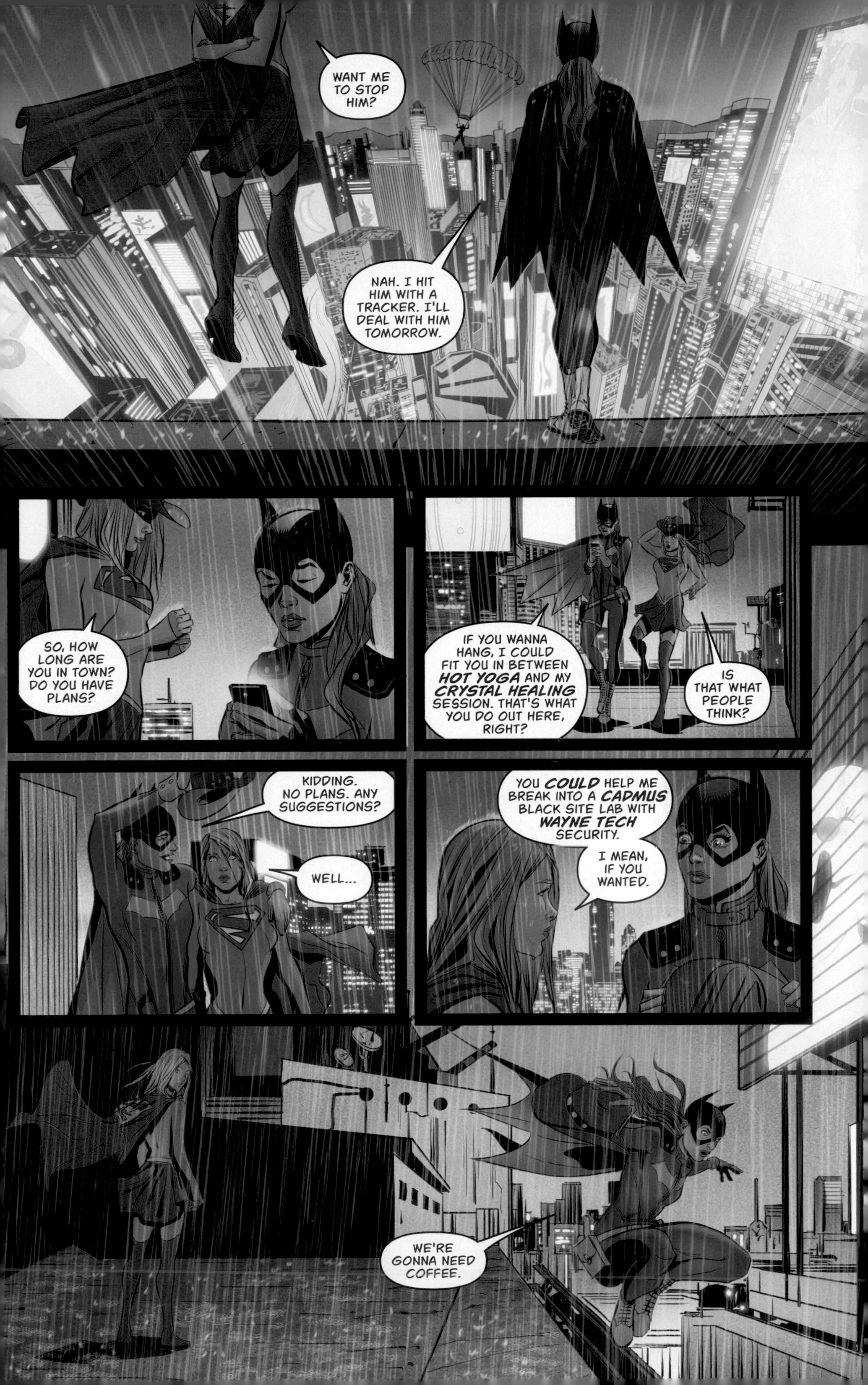
WANT ME TO STOP HIM?
NAH. I HIT HIM WITH A TRACKER. I'LL DEAL WITH HIM TOMORROW.
SO, HOW LONG ARE YOU IN TOWN? DO YOU HAVE PLANS?
IF YOU WANNA HANG, I COULD FIT YOU IN BETWEEN HOT YOGA AND MY CRYSTAL HEALING SESSION. THAT'S WHAT YOU DO OUT HERE, RIGHT?
IS THAT WHAT PEOPLE THINK?
KIDDING. NO PLANS. ANY SUGGESTIONS?
WELL...
YOU COULD HELP ME BREAK INTO A CADMUS BLACK SITE LAB WITH WAYNE TECH SECURITY.
I MEAN, IF YOU WANTED.
WE'RE GONNA NEED COFFEE.

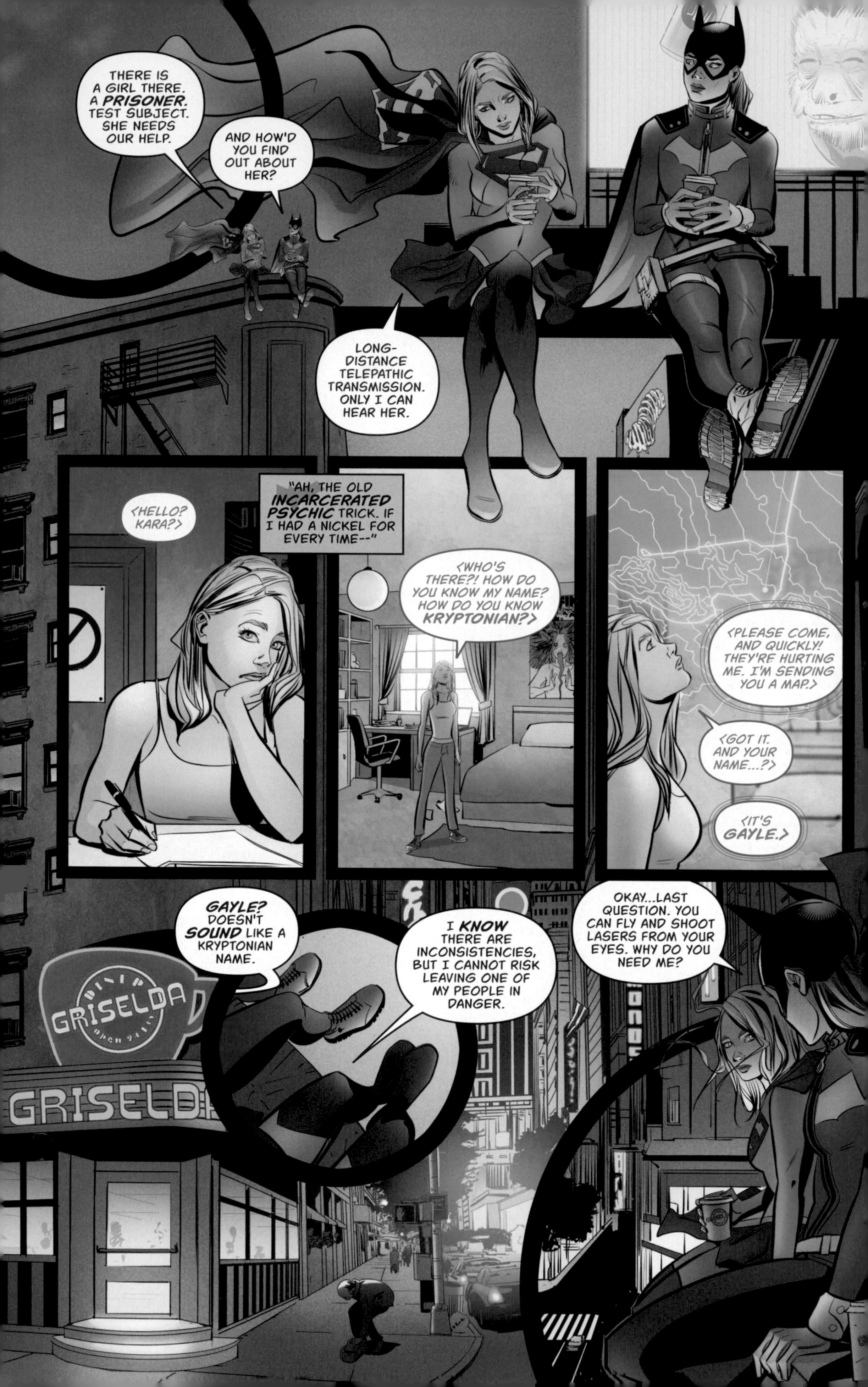

THERE IS A GIRL THERE. A PRISONER. TEST SUBJECT. SHE NEEDS OUR HELP.
AND HOW'D YOU FIND OUT ABOUT HER?
LONG-DISTANCE TELEPATHIC TRANSMISSION. ONLY I CAN HEAR HER.
<HELLO? KARA?>
"AH, THE OLD INCARCERATED PSYCHIC TRICK. IF I HAD A NICKEL FOR EVERY TIME--"
<WHO'S THERE?! HOW DO YOU KNOW MY NAME? HOW DO YOU KNOW KRYPTONIAN?>
<PLEASE COME, AND QUICKLY! THEY'RE HURTING ME. I'M SENDING YOU A MAP.>
<GOT IT. AND YOUR NAME...?>
<IT'S GAYLE.>
GAYLE? DOESN'T SOUND LIKE A KRYPTONIAN NAME.
I KNOW THERE ARE INCONSISTENCIES, BUT I CANNOT RISK LEAVING ONE OF MY PEOPLE IN DANGER.
OKAY...LAST QUESTION. YOU CAN FLY AND SHOOT LASERS FROM YOUR EYES. WHY DO YOU NEED ME?
GRISELDA
GRISELDA

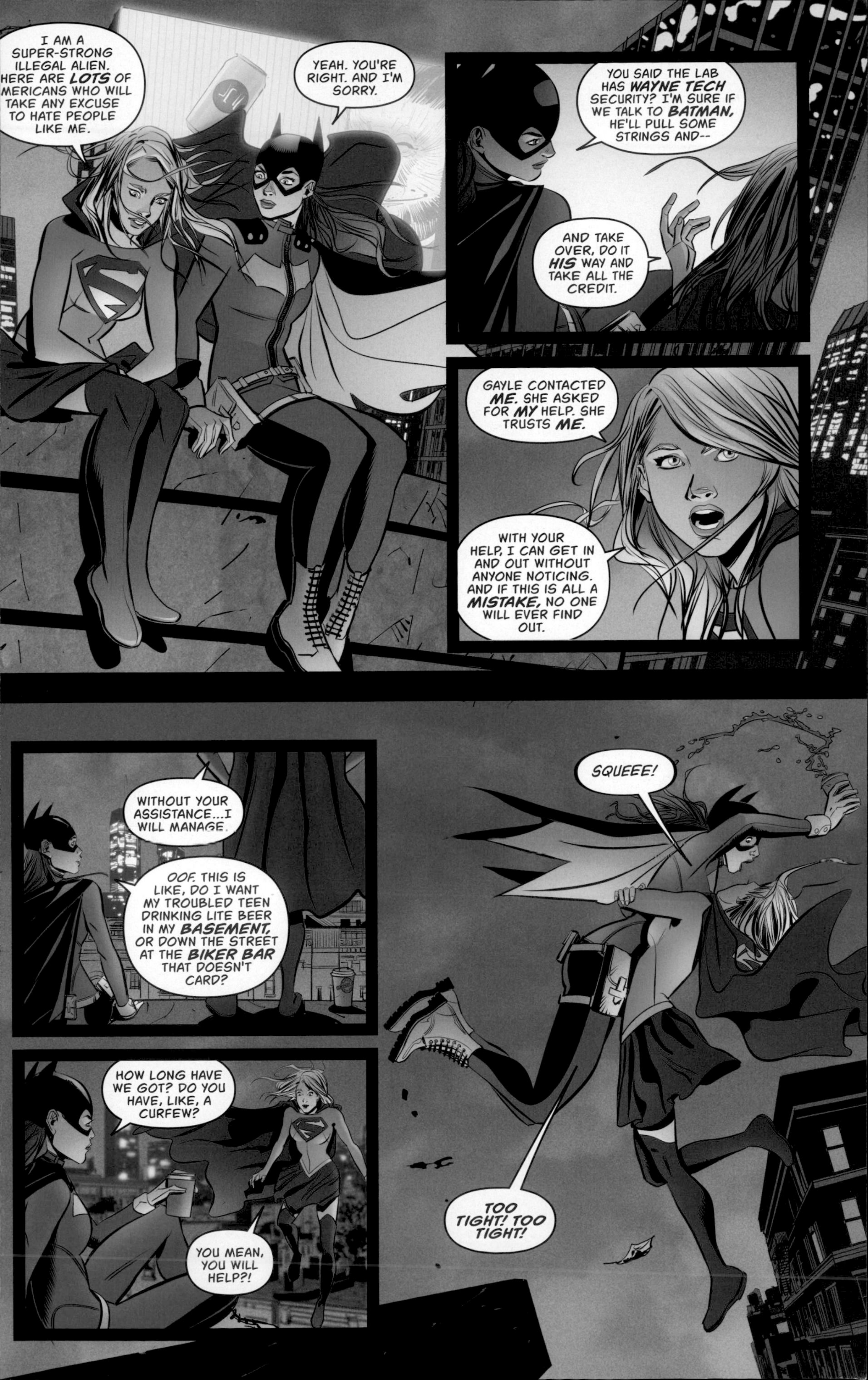
I AM A SUPER-STRONG ILLEGAL ALIEN. HERE ARE LOTS OF MERICANS WHO WILL TAKE ANY EXCUSE TO HATE PEOPLE LIKE ME.
YEAH. YOU'RE RIGHT. AND I'M SORRY.
YOU SAID THE LAB HAS WAYNE TECH SECURITY? I'M SURE IF WE TALK TO BATMAN, HE'LL PULL SOME STRINGS AND--
AND TAKE OVER, DO IT HIS WAY AND TAKE ALL THE CREDIT.
GAYLE CONTACTED ME. SHE ASKED FOR MY HELP. SHE TRUSTS ME.
WITH YOUR HELP, I CAN GET IN AND OUT WITHOUT ANYONE NOTICING. AND IF THIS IS ALL A MISTAKE, NO ONE WILL EVER FIND OUT.
WITHOUT YOUR ASSISTANCE...I WILL MANAGE.
OOF. THIS IS LIKE, DO I WANT MY TROUBLED TEEN DRINKING LITE BEER IN MY BASEMENT, OR DOWN THE STREET AT THE BIKER BAR THAT DOESN'T CARD?
HOW LONG HAVE WE GOT? DO YOU HAVE, LIKE, A CURFEW?
YOU MEAN, YOU WILL HELP?!
SQUEEE!
TOO TIGHT! TOO TIGHT!

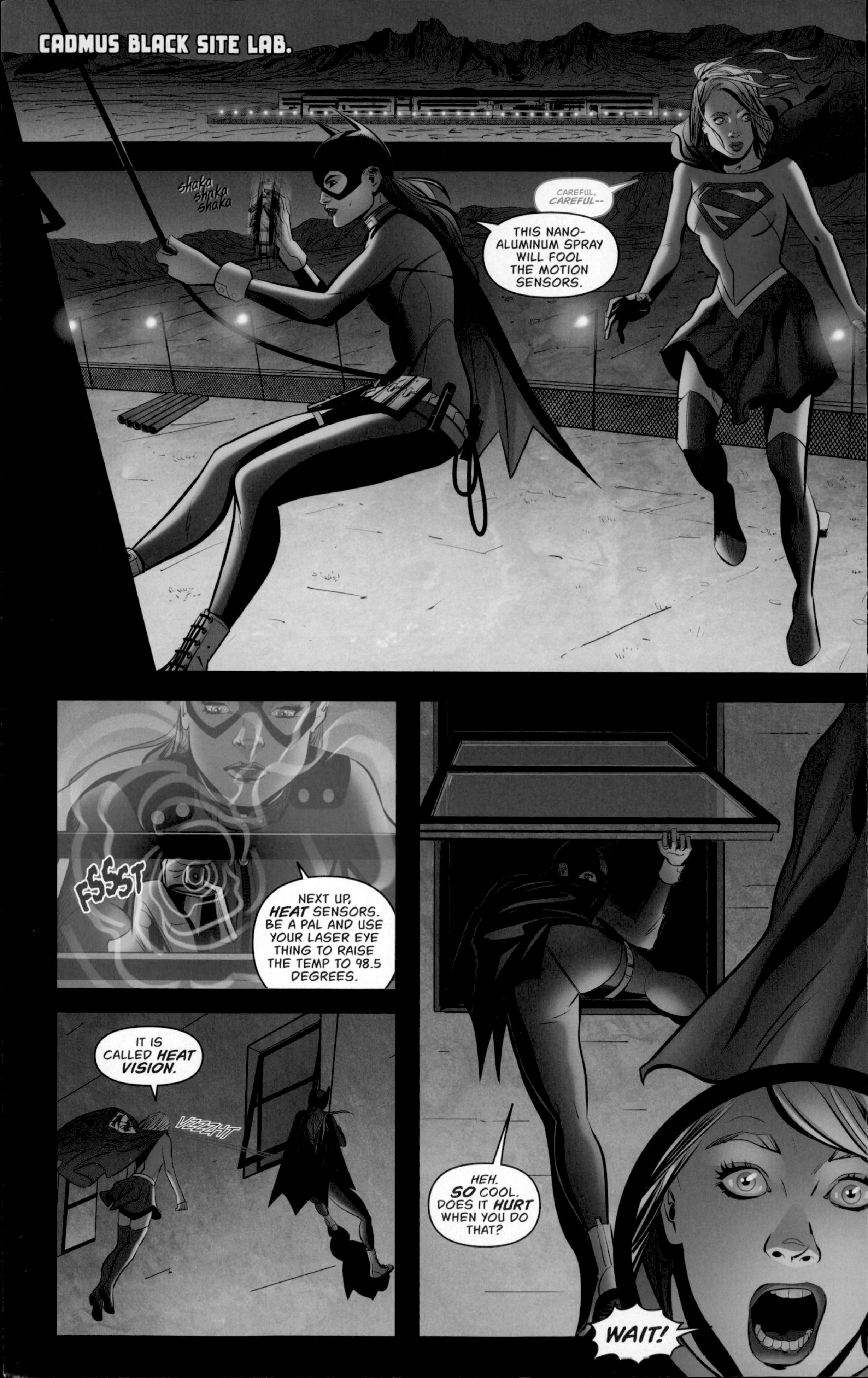
CADMUS BLACK SITE LAB.
shaka shaka shaka
CAREFUL, CAREFUL--
THIS NANO-ALUMINUM SPRAY WILL FOOL THE MOTION SENSORS.
FSSST
NEXT UP, HEAT SENSORS. BE A PAL AND USE YOUR LASER EYE THING TO RAISE THE TEMP TO 98.5 DEGREES.
IT IS CALLED HEAT VISION.
VZZZHT
HEH. SO COOL. DOES IT HURT WHEN YOU DO THAT?
WAIT!

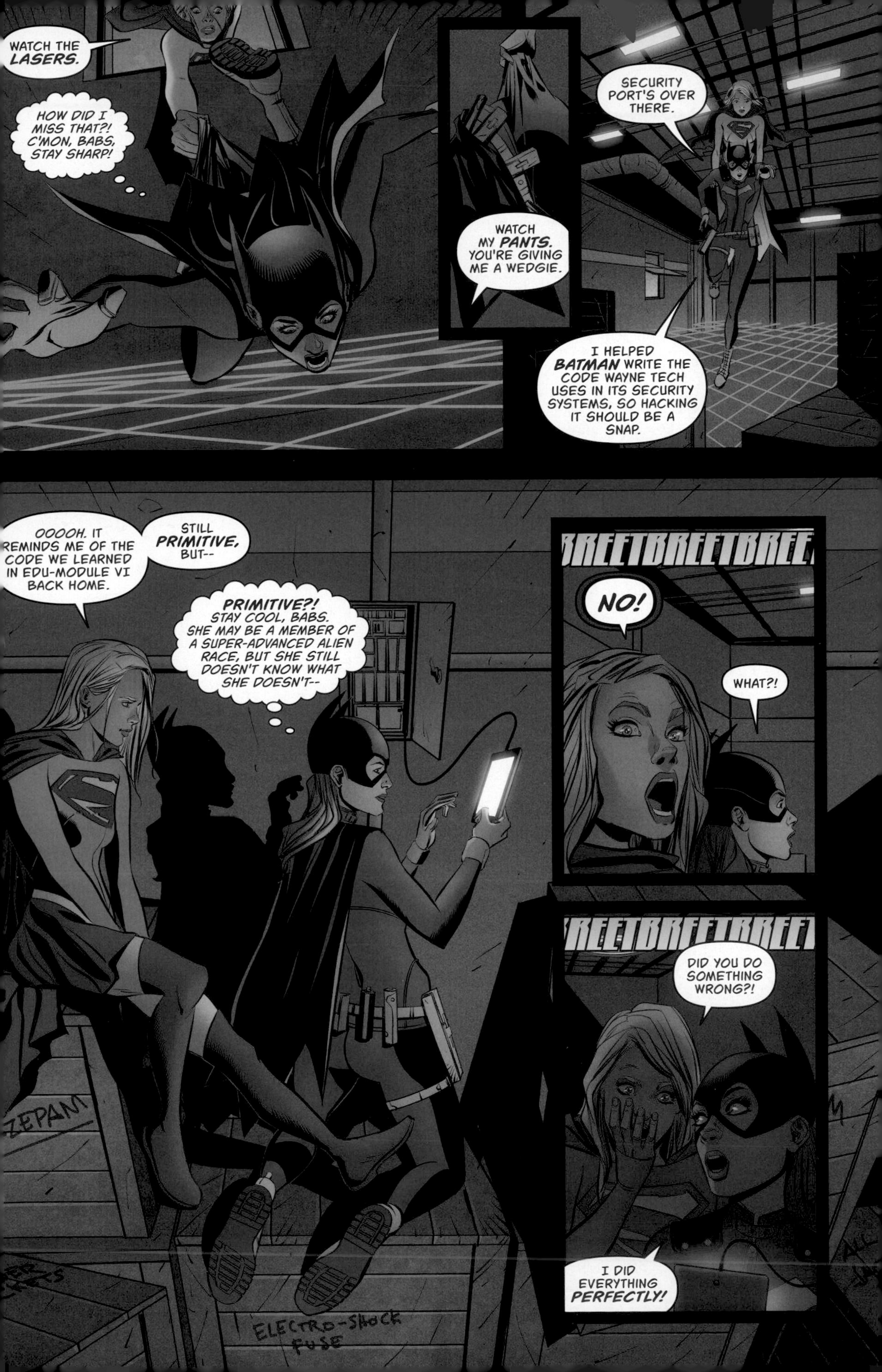
WATCH THE LASERS.
HOW DID I MISS THAT?! C'MON, BABS, STAY SHARP!
WATCH MY PANTS. YOU'RE GIVING ME A WEDGIE.
SECURITY PORT'S OVER THERE.
I HELPED BATMAN WRITE THE CODE WAYNE TECH USES IN ITS SECURITY SYSTEMS, SO HACKING IT SHOULD BE A SNAP.
OOOOH. IT REMINDS ME OF THE CODE WE LEARNED IN EDU-MODULE VI BACK HOME.
STILL PRIMITIVE, BUT--
PRIMITIVE?! STAY COOL, BABS. SHE MAY BE A MEMBER OF A SUPER-ADVANCED ALIEN RACE, BUT SHE STILL DOESN'T KNOW WHAT SHE DOESN'T--
BREETBREETBREE
NO!
WHAT?!
BREETBREETBREET
DID YOU DO SOMETHING WRONG?!
I DID EVERYTHING PERFECTLY!
ZEPAM
ELECTRO-SHOCK FUSE

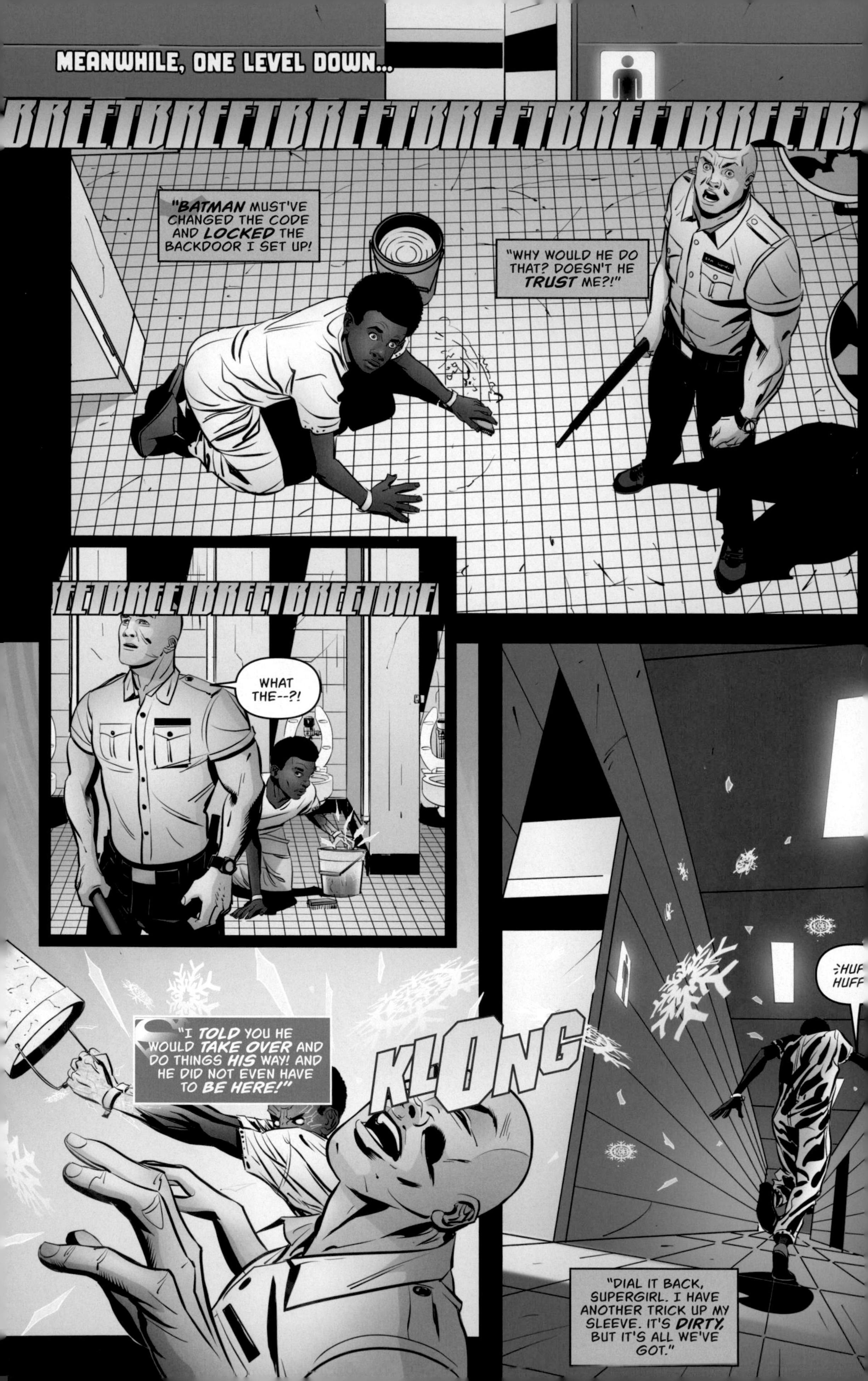
MEANWHILE, ONE LEVEL DOWN...
BREETBREETBREETBREETBREETBREETB
"BATMAN MUST'VE CHANGED THE CODE AND LOCKED THE BACKDOOR I SET UP!
"WHY WOULD HE DO THAT? DOESN'T HE TRUST ME?!"
EETBREETBREETBREETBRE
WHAT THE--?!
"I TOLD YOU HE WOULD TAKE OVER AND DO THINGS HIS WAY! AND HE DID NOT EVEN HAVE TO BE HERE!"
KLONG
HUF HUFF
"DIAL IT BACK, SUPERGIRL. I HAVE ANOTHER TRICK UP MY SLEEVE. IT'S DIRTY, BUT IT'S ALL WE'VE GOT."

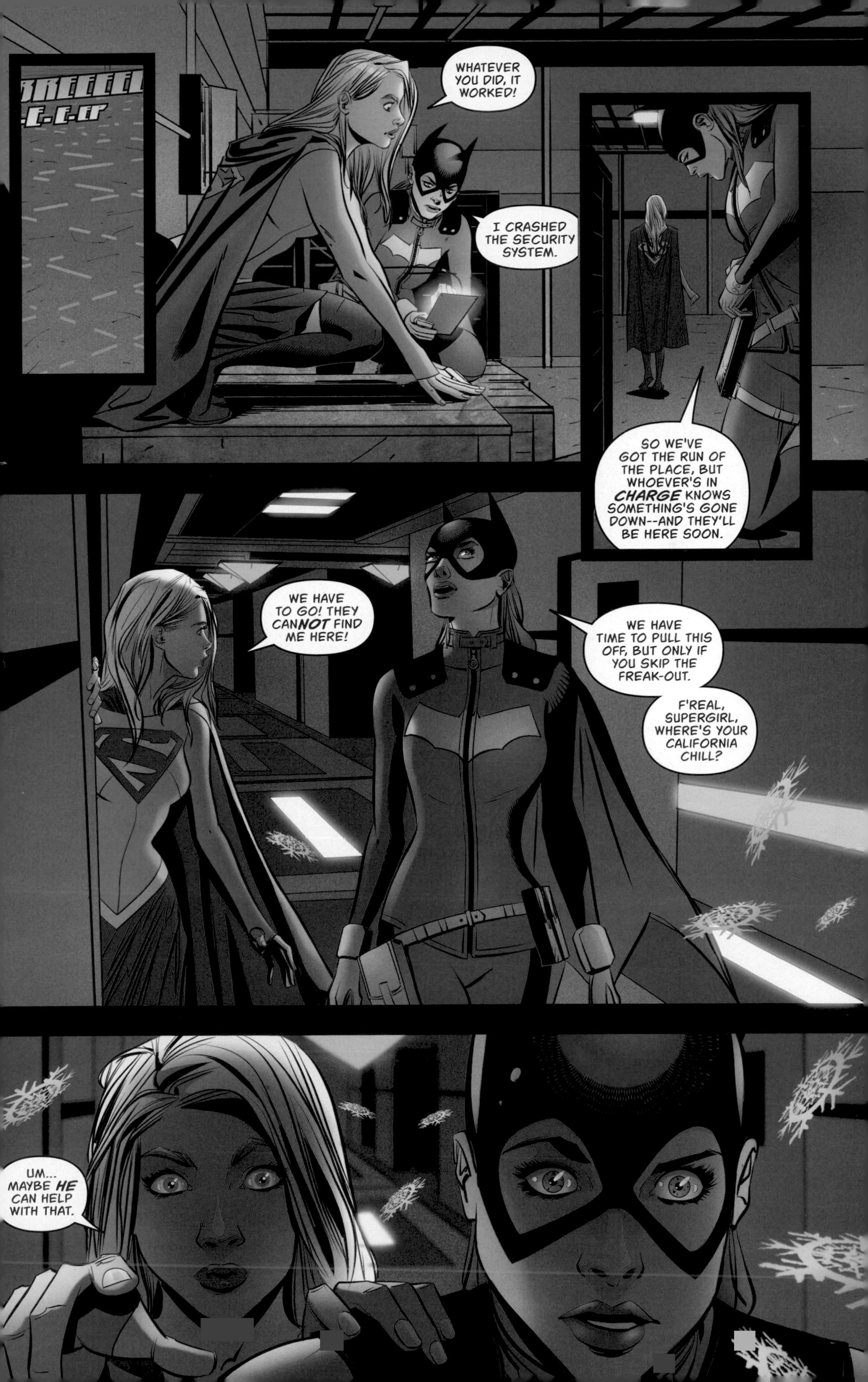
WHATEVER YOU DID, IT WORKED!
I CRASHED THE SECURITY SYSTEM.
SO WE'VE GOT THE RUN OF THE PLACE, BUT WHOEVER'S IN **CHARGE** KNOWS SOMETHING'S GONE DOWN--AND THEY'LL BE HERE SOON.
WE HAVE TO GO! THEY CAN**NOT** FIND ME HERE!
WE HAVE TIME TO PULL THIS OFF, BUT ONLY IF YOU SKIP THE FREAK-OUT.
F'REAL, SUPERGIRL, WHERE'S YOUR CALIFORNIA CHILL?
UM... MAYBE **HE** CAN HELP WITH THAT.

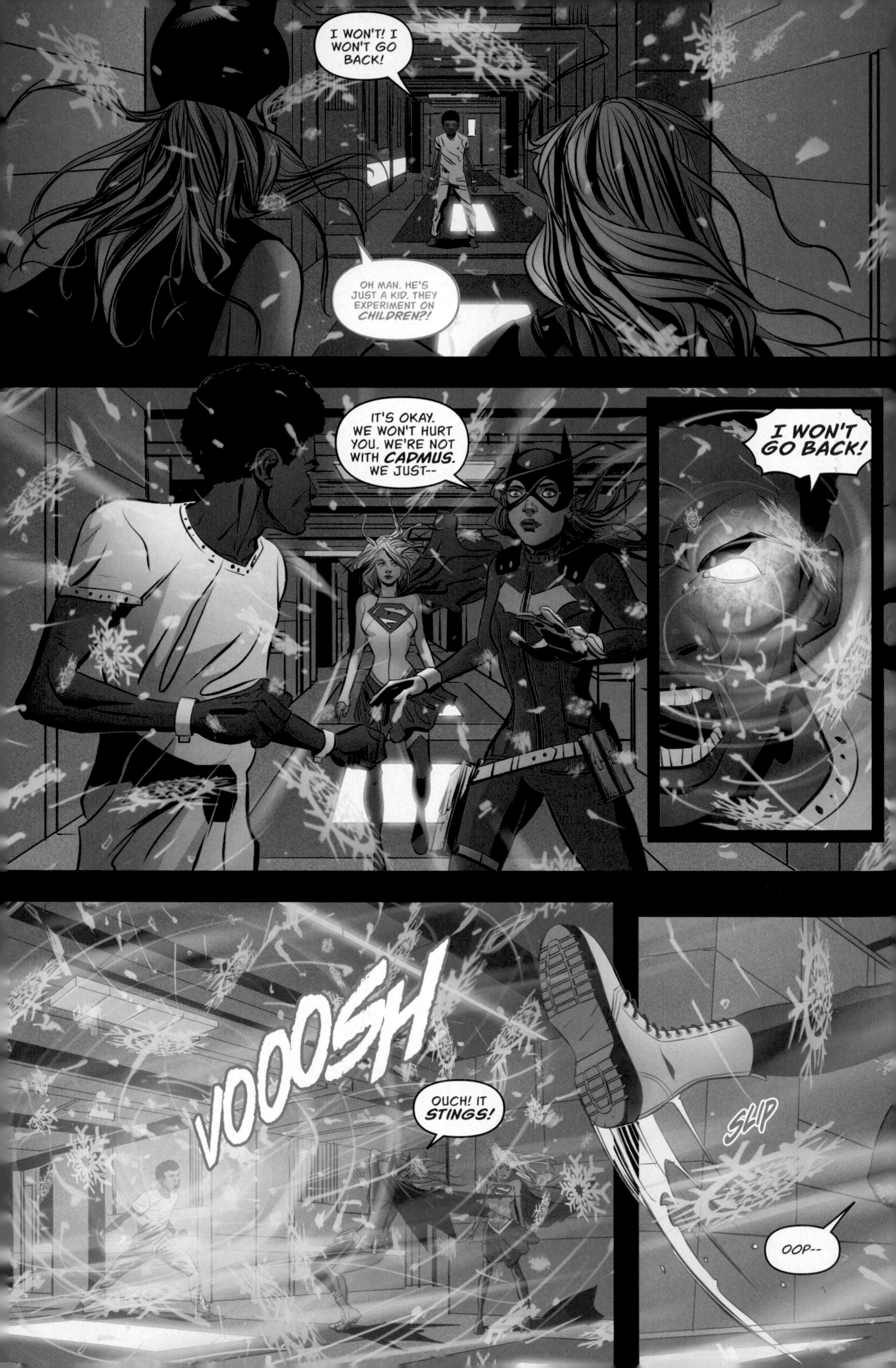
I WON'T! I WON'T GO BACK!
OH MAN. HE'S JUST A KID. THEY EXPERIMENT ON CHILDREN?!
IT'S OKAY. WE WON'T HURT YOU. WE'RE NOT WITH CADMUS. WE JUST--
I WON'T GO BACK!
VOOOSH
OUCH! IT STINGS!
SLIP
OOP--

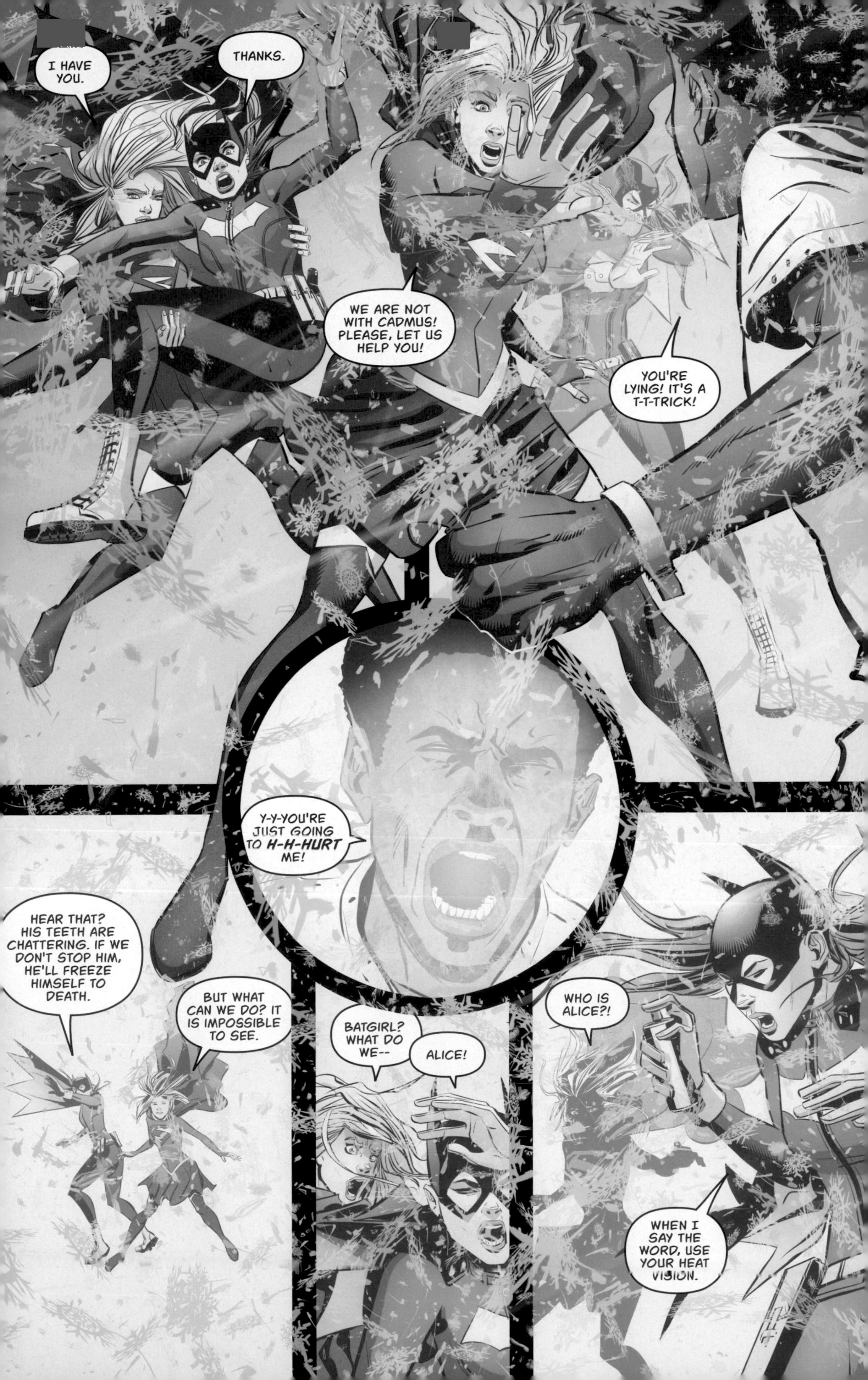
I HAVE YOU.
THANKS.
WE ARE NOT WITH CADMUS! PLEASE, LET US HELP YOU!
YOU'RE LYING! IT'S A T-T-TRICK!
Y-Y-YOU'RE JUST GOING TO **H-H-HURT** ME!
HEAR THAT? HIS TEETH ARE CHATTERING. IF WE DON'T STOP HIM, HE'LL FREEZE HIMSELF TO DEATH.
BUT WHAT CAN WE DO? IT IS IMPOSSIBLE TO SEE.
BATGIRL? WHAT DO WE--
ALICE!
WHO IS ALICE?!
WHEN I SAY THE WORD, USE YOUR HEAT VISION.

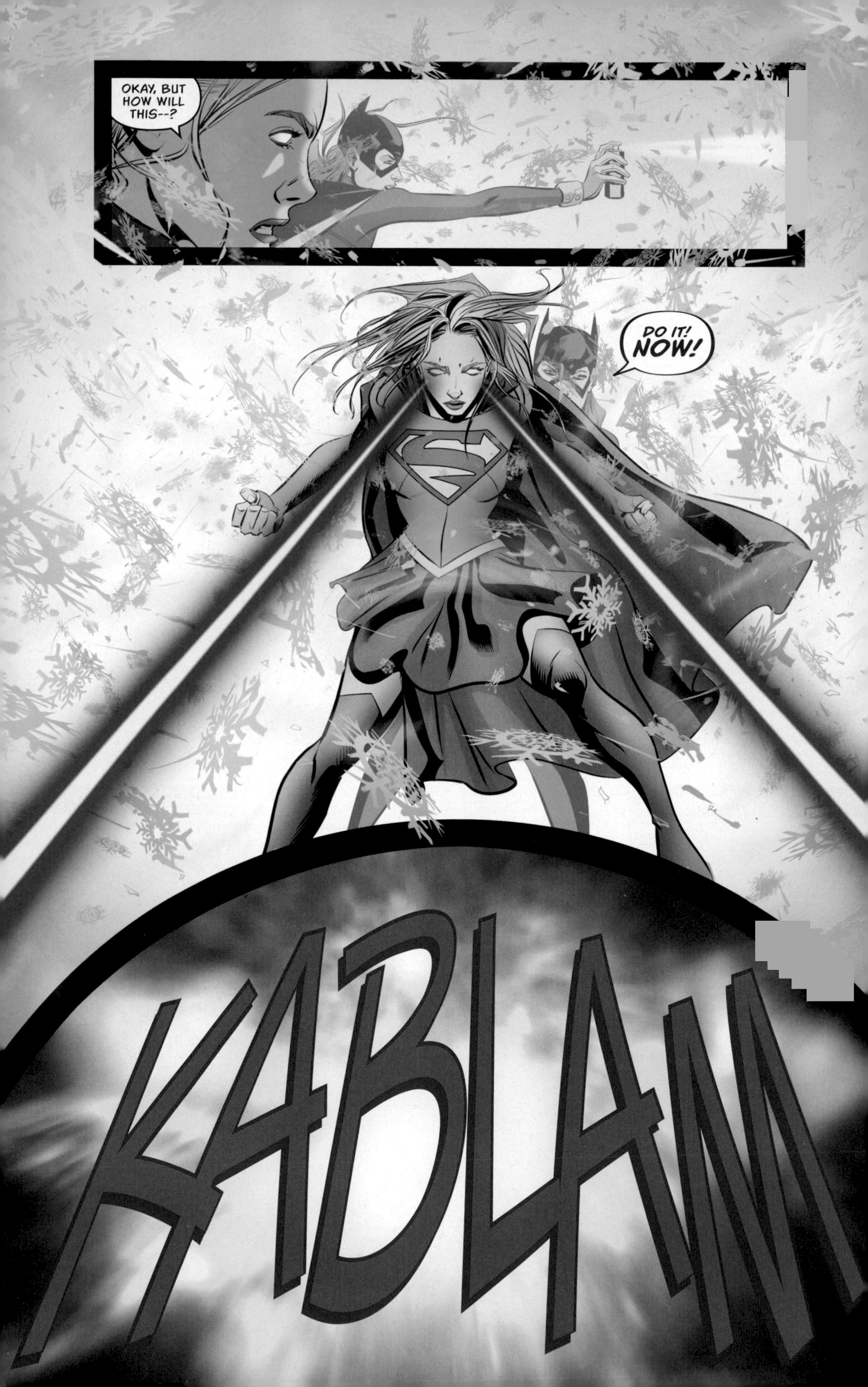
OKAY, BUT HOW WILL THIS--?
DO IT! NOW!
KABLAM

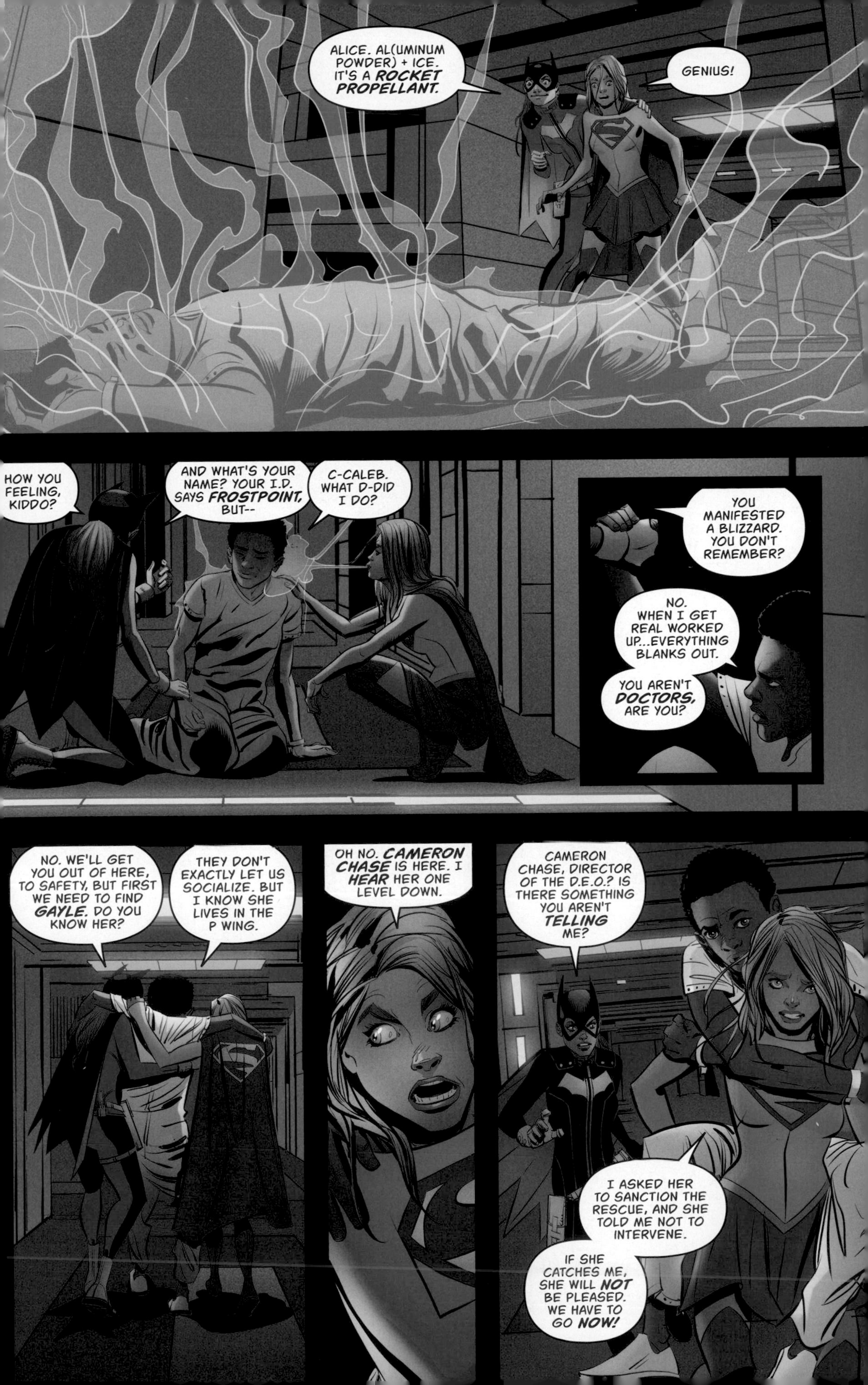

ALICE. AL(UMINUM POWDER) + ICE. IT'S A ROCKET PROPELLANT.
GENIUS!
HOW YOU FEELING, KIDDO?
AND WHAT'S YOUR NAME? YOUR I.D. SAYS FROSTPOINT, BUT--
C-CALEB. WHAT D-DID I DO?
YOU MANIFESTED A BLIZZARD. YOU DON'T REMEMBER?
NO. WHEN I GET REAL WORKED UP...EVERYTHING BLANKS OUT.
YOU AREN'T DOCTORS, ARE YOU?
NO. WE'LL GET YOU OUT OF HERE, TO SAFETY, BUT FIRST WE NEED TO FIND GAYLE. DO YOU KNOW HER?
THEY DON'T EXACTLY LET US SOCIALIZE. BUT I KNOW SHE LIVES IN THE P WING.
OH NO. CAMERON CHASE IS HERE. I HEAR HER ONE LEVEL DOWN.
CAMERON CHASE, DIRECTOR OF THE D.E.O.? IS THERE SOMETHING YOU AREN'T TELLING ME?
I ASKED HER TO SANCTION THE RESCUE, AND SHE TOLD ME NOT TO INTERVENE.
IF SHE CATCHES ME, SHE WILL NOT BE PLEASED. WE HAVE TO GO NOW!

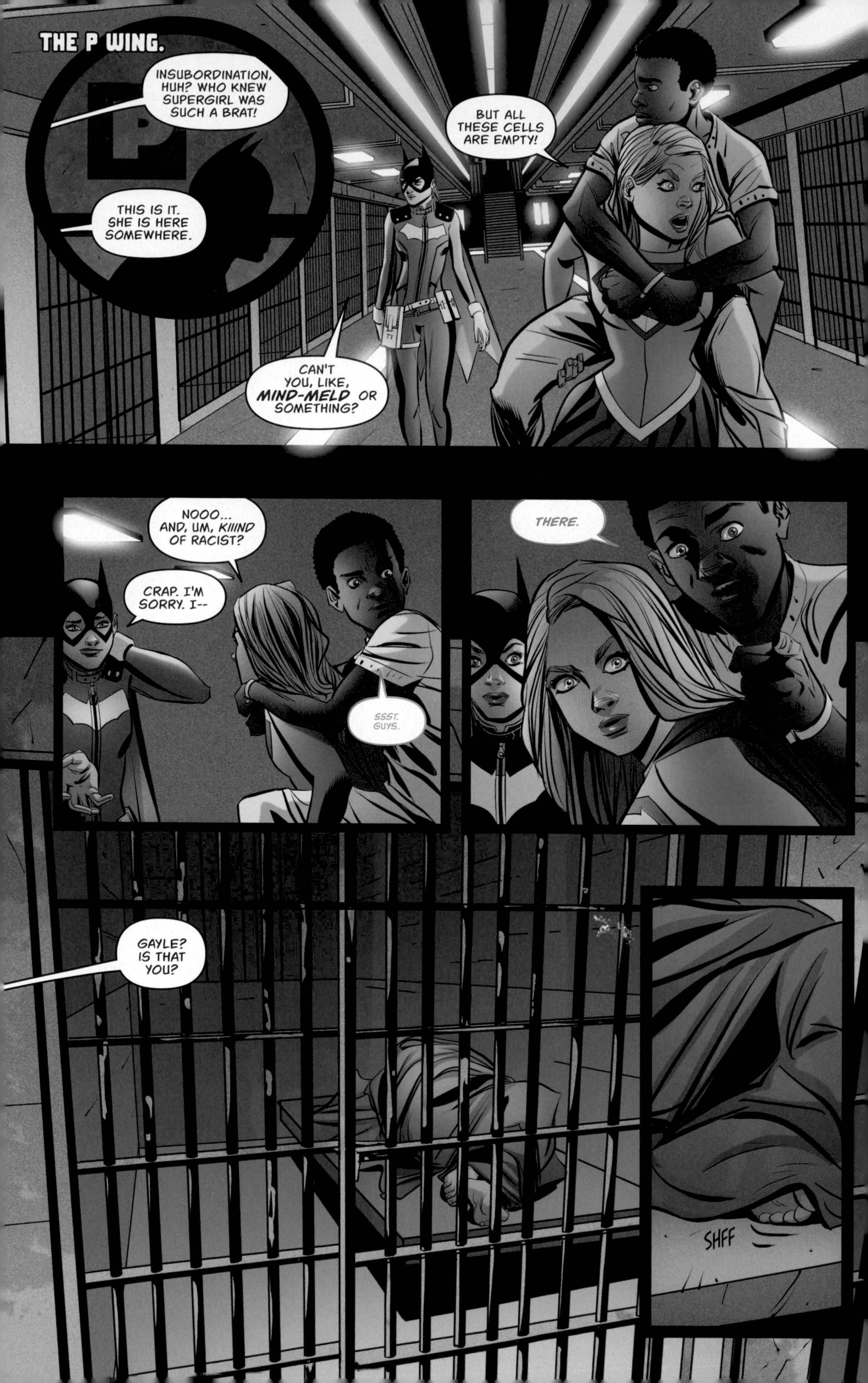
THE P WING.
INSUBORDINATION, HUH? WHO KNEW SUPERGIRL WAS SUCH A BRAT!
THIS IS IT. SHE IS HERE SOMEWHERE.
BUT ALL THESE CELLS ARE EMPTY!
CAN'T YOU, LIKE, MIND-MELD OR SOMETHING?
NOOO... AND, UM, KIIIND OF RACIST?
CRAP. I'M SORRY. I--
SSST. GUYS.
THERE.
GAYLE? IS THAT YOU?
SHFF

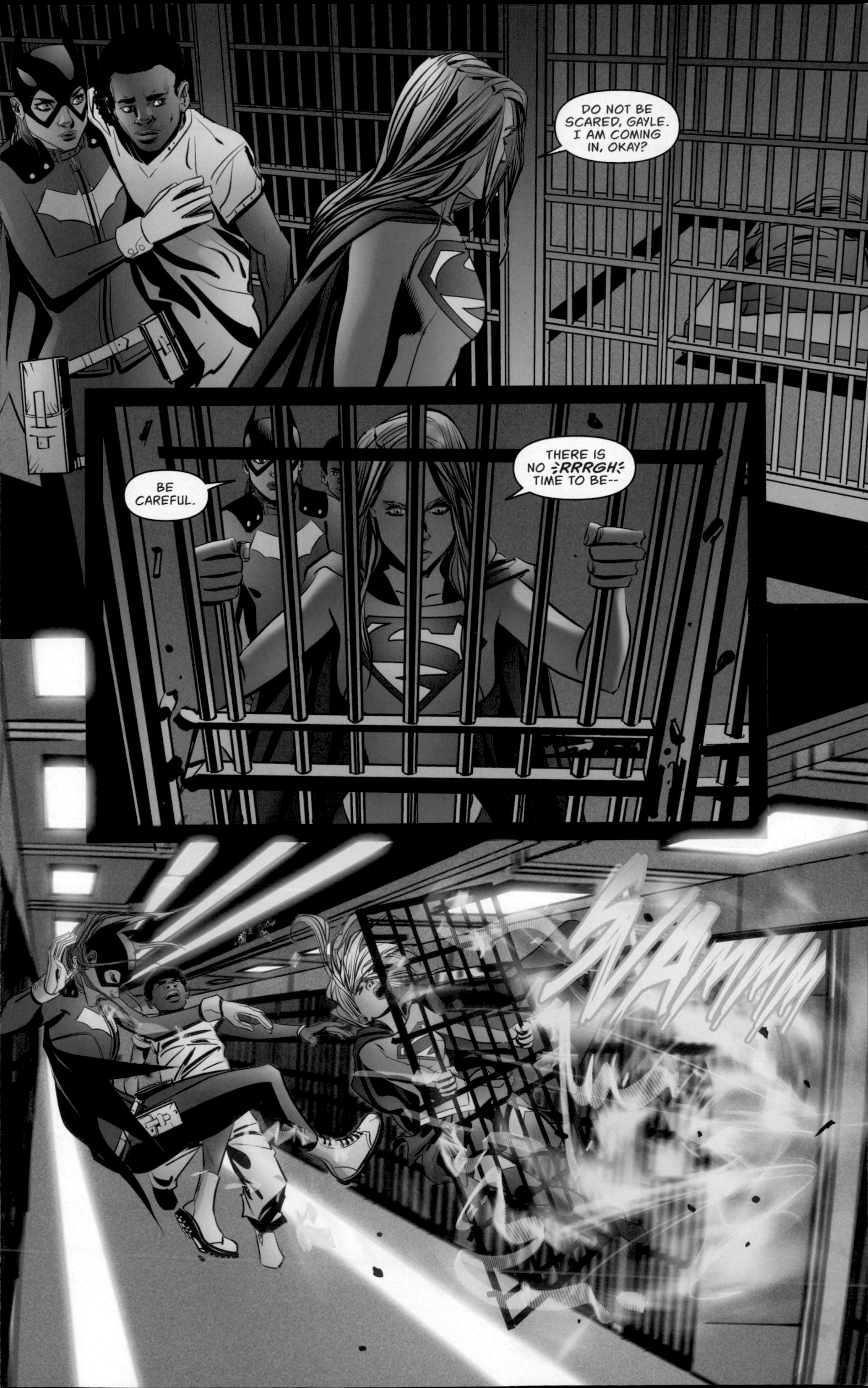
DO NOT BE SCARED, GAYLE. I AM COMING IN, OKAY?
BE CAREFUL.
THERE IS NO -RRRGH- TIME TO BE--
SLAMMM

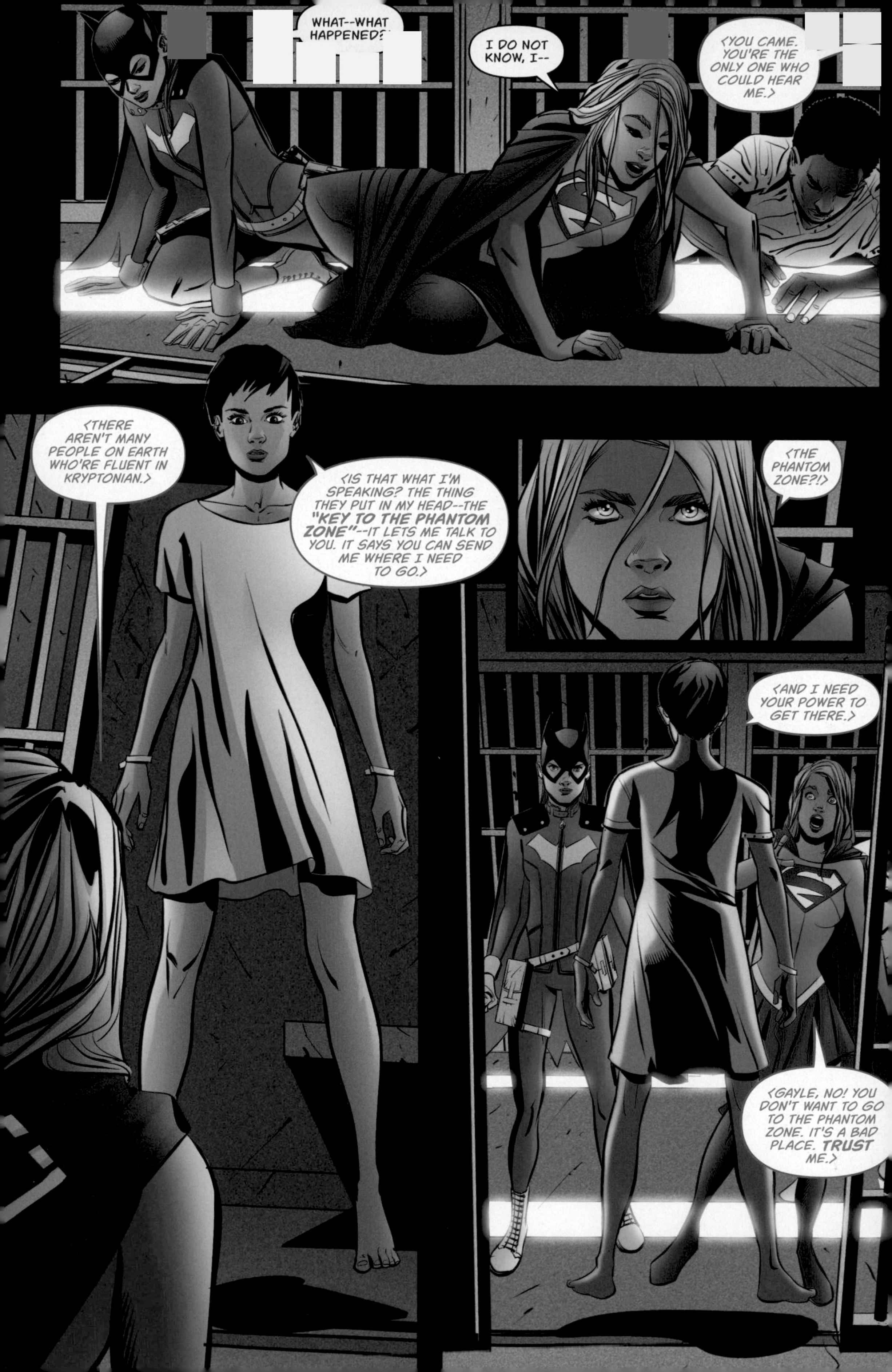
WHAT--WHAT HAPPENED?
I DO NOT KNOW, I--
<YOU CAME. YOU'RE THE ONLY ONE WHO COULD HEAR ME.>
<THERE AREN'T MANY PEOPLE ON EARTH WHO'RE FLUENT IN KRYPTONIAN.>
<IS THAT WHAT I'M SPEAKING? THE THING THEY PUT IN MY HEAD--THE "KEY TO THE PHANTOM ZONE"--IT LETS ME TALK TO YOU. IT SAYS YOU CAN SEND ME WHERE I NEED TO GO.>
<THE PHANTOM ZONE?!>
<AND I NEED YOUR POWER TO GET THERE.>
<GAYLE, NO! YOU DON'T WANT TO GO TO THE PHANTOM ZONE. IT'S A BAD PLACE. TRUST ME.>

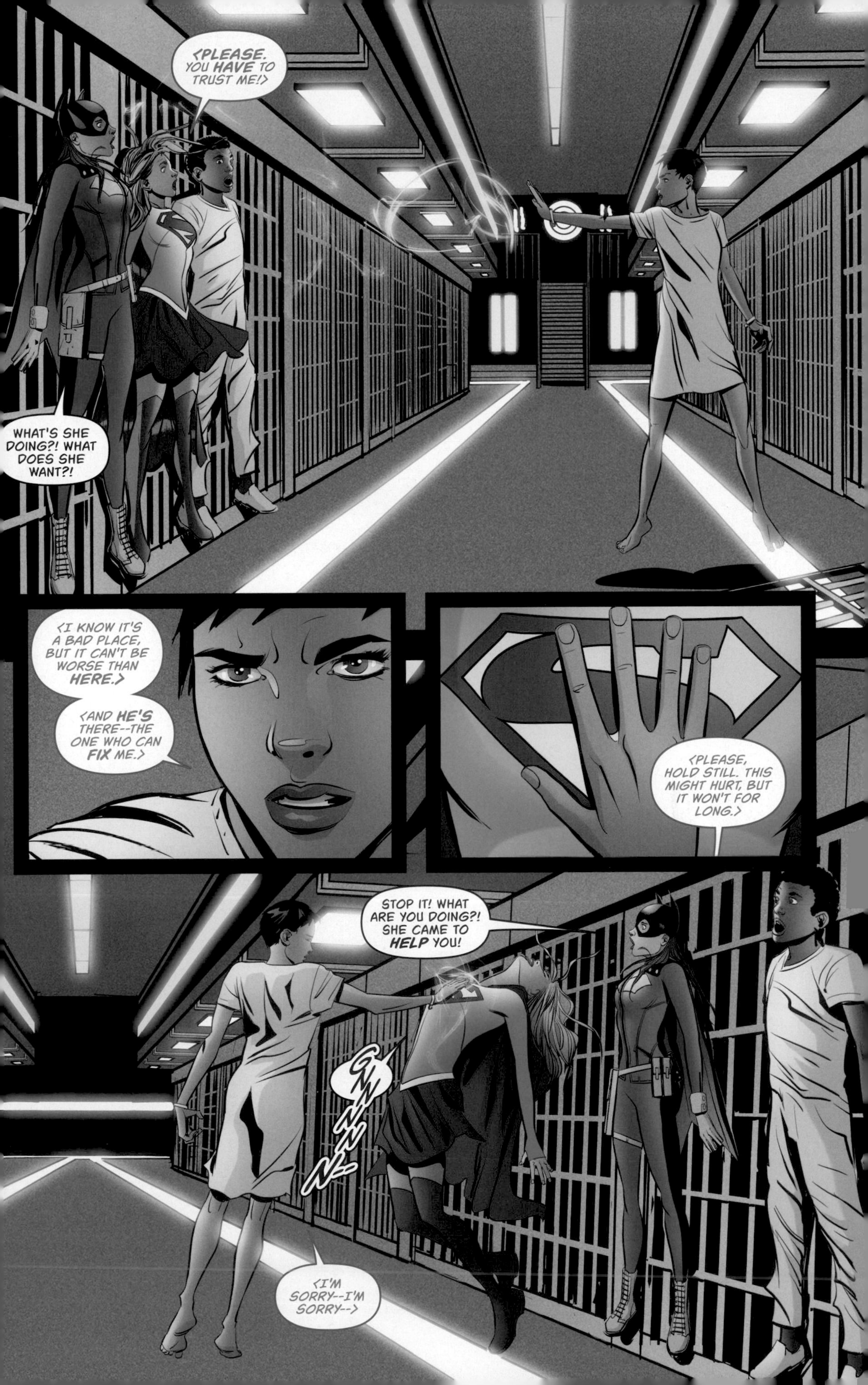
<PLEASE. YOU **HAVE** TO TRUST ME!>
WHAT'S SHE DOING?! WHAT DOES SHE WANT?!
<I KNOW IT'S A BAD PLACE, BUT IT CAN'T BE WORSE THAN **HERE.**>
<AND **HE'S** THERE--THE ONE WHO CAN **FIX** ME.>
<PLEASE, HOLD STILL. THIS MIGHT HURT, BUT IT WON'T FOR LONG.>
STOP IT! WHAT ARE YOU DOING?! SHE CAME TO **HELP** YOU!
GNNNNN-
<I'M SORRY--I'M SORRY-->

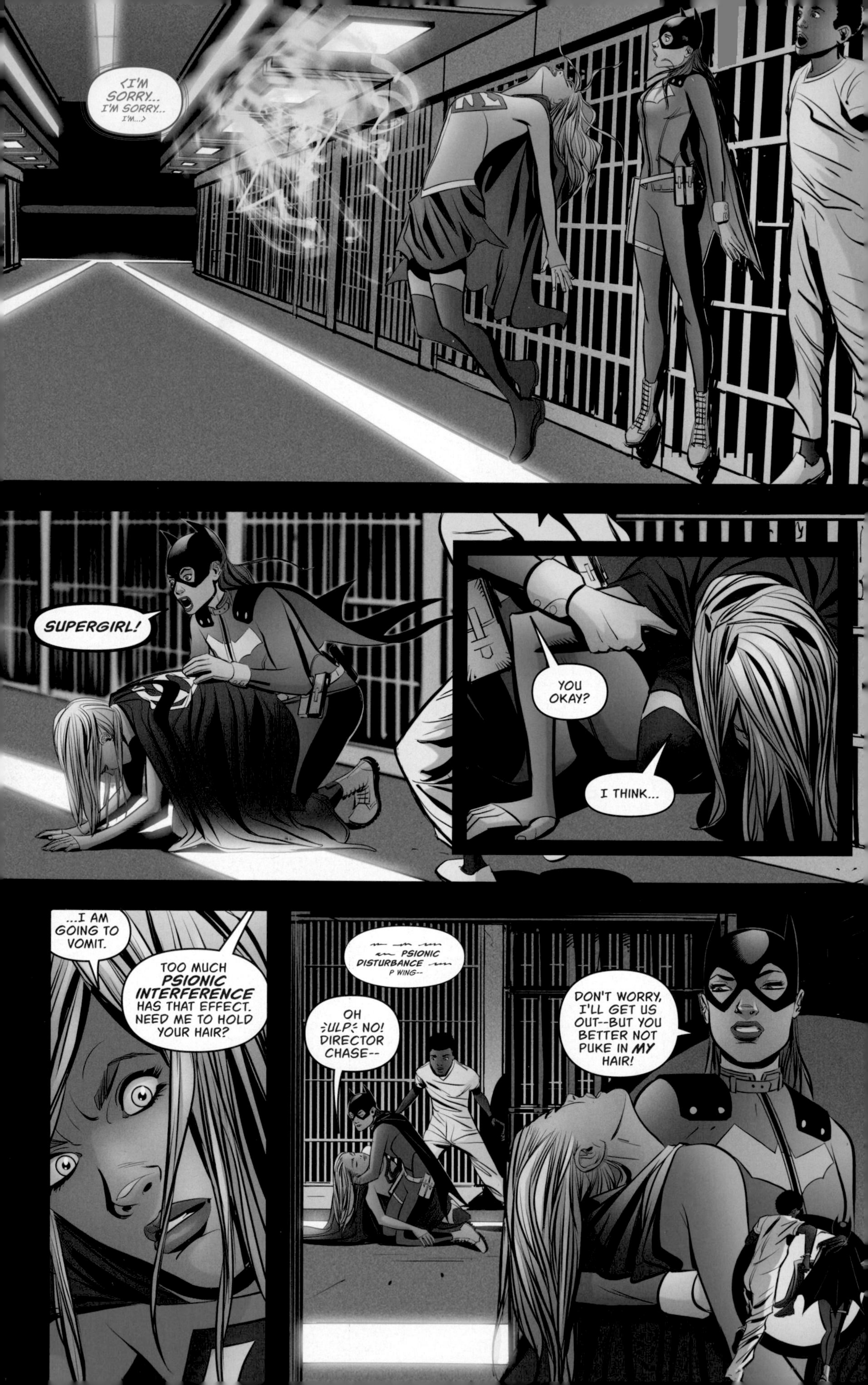

<I'M SORRY... I'M SORRY... I'M...>
SUPERGIRL!
YOU OKAY?
I THINK...
...I AM GOING TO VOMIT.
TOO MUCH PSIONIC INTERFERENCE HAS THAT EFFECT. NEED ME TO HOLD YOUR HAIR?
PSIONIC DISTURBANCE P WING--
OH -ULP- NO! DIRECTOR CHASE--
DON'T WORRY, I'LL GET US OUT--BUT YOU BETTER NOT PUKE IN MY HAIR!

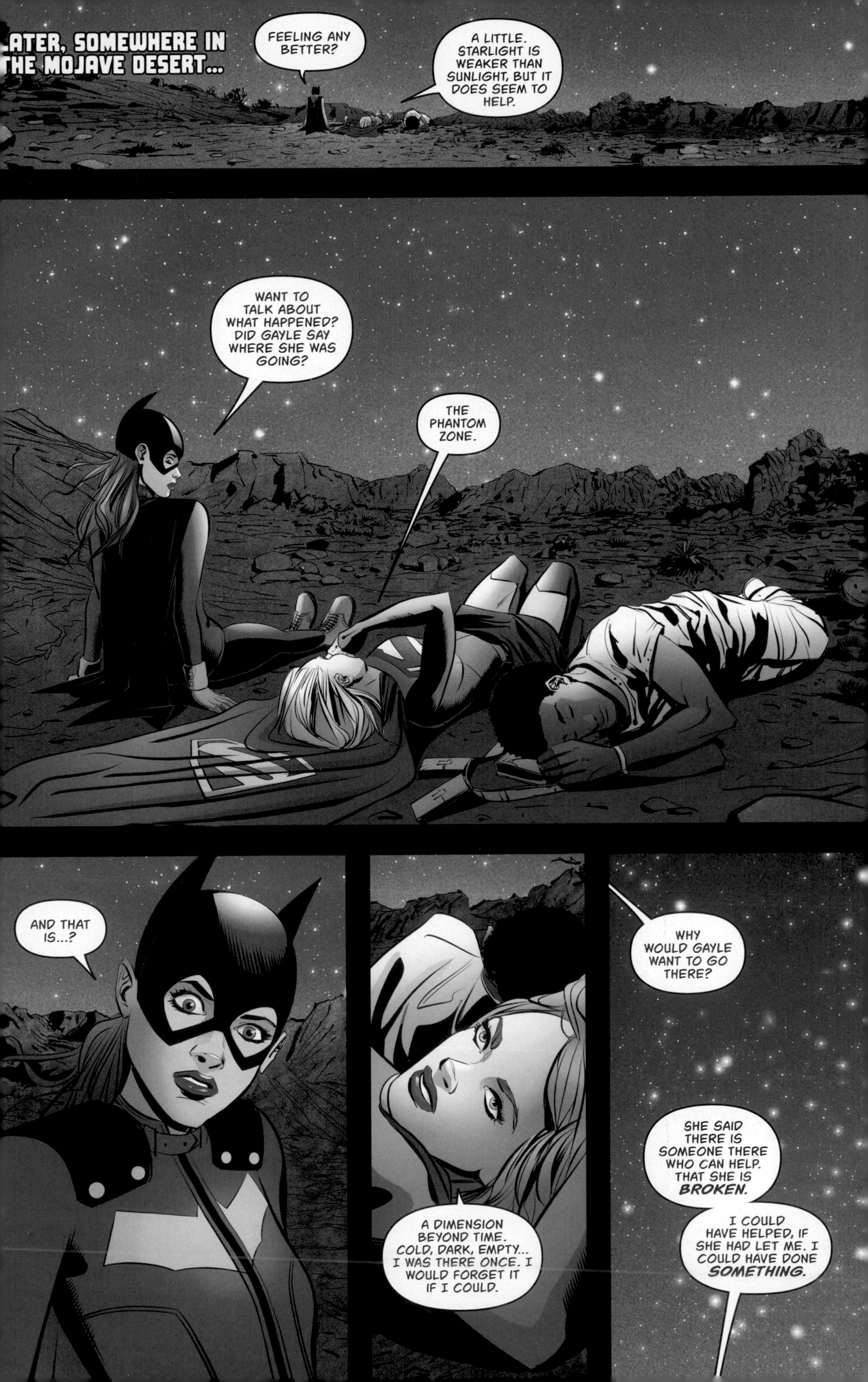
LATER, SOMEWHERE IN THE MOJAVE DESERT...
FEELING ANY BETTER?
A LITTLE. STARLIGHT IS WEAKER THAN SUNLIGHT, BUT IT DOES SEEM TO HELP.
WANT TO TALK ABOUT WHAT HAPPENED? DID GAYLE SAY WHERE SHE WAS GOING?
THE PHANTOM ZONE.
AND THAT IS...?
A DIMENSION BEYOND TIME. COLD, DARK, EMPTY... I WAS THERE ONCE. I WOULD FORGET IT IF I COULD.
WHY WOULD GAYLE WANT TO GO THERE?
SHE SAID THERE IS SOMEONE THERE WHO CAN HELP. THAT SHE IS BROKEN.
I COULD HAVE HELPED, IF SHE HAD LET ME. I COULD HAVE DONE SOMETHING.

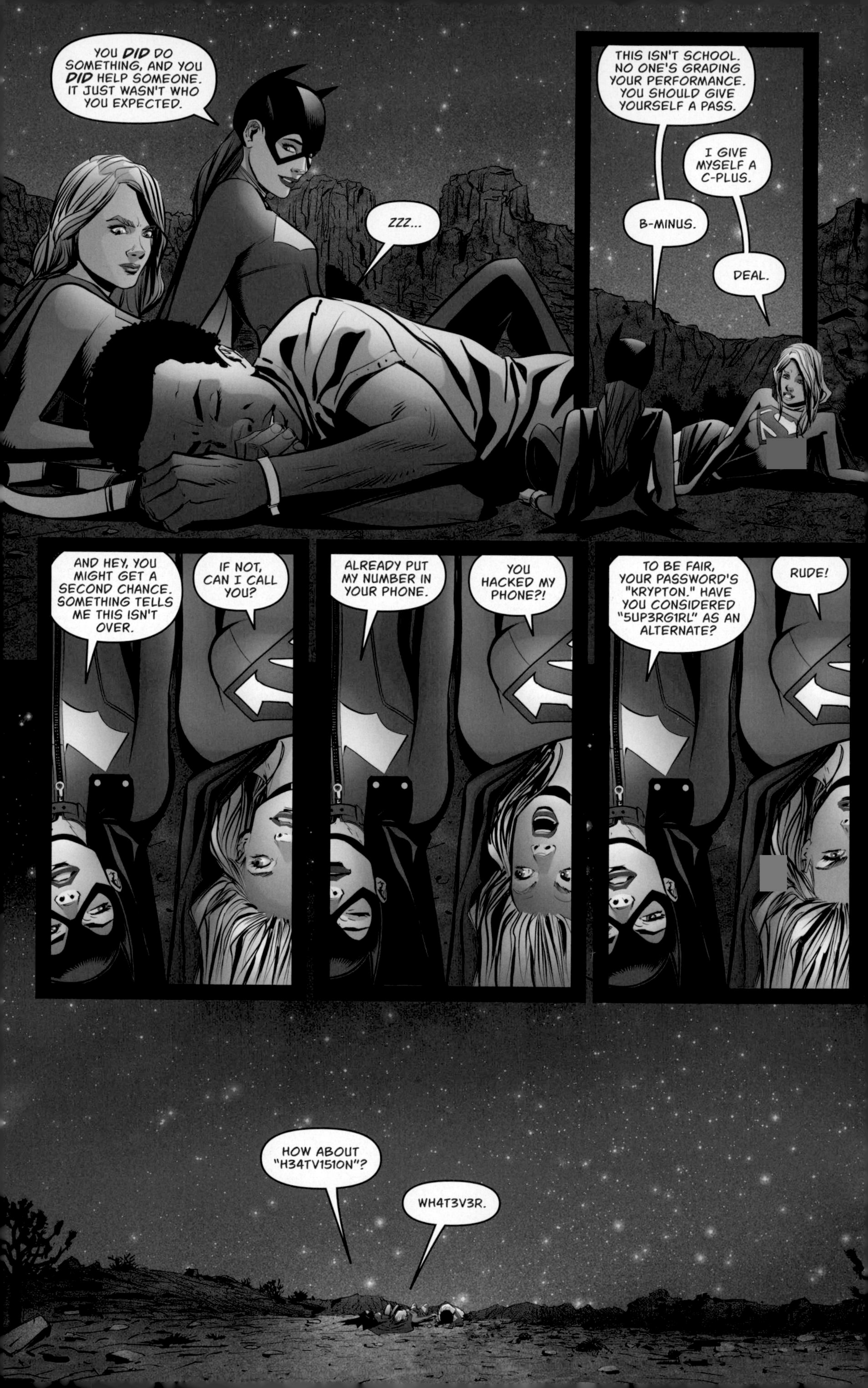
YOU *DID* DO SOMETHING, AND YOU *DID* HELP SOMEONE. IT JUST WASN'T WHO YOU EXPECTED.
ZZZ...
THIS ISN'T SCHOOL. NO ONE'S GRADING YOUR PERFORMANCE. YOU SHOULD GIVE YOURSELF A PASS.
I GIVE MYSELF A C-PLUS.
B-MINUS.
DEAL.
AND HEY, YOU MIGHT GET A SECOND CHANCE. SOMETHING TELLS ME THIS ISN'T OVER.
IF NOT, CAN I CALL YOU?
ALREADY PUT MY NUMBER IN YOUR PHONE.
YOU HACKED MY PHONE?!
TO BE FAIR, YOUR PASSWORD'S "KRYPTON." HAVE YOU CONSIDERED "5UP3RG1RL" AS AN ALTERNATE?
RUDE!
HOW ABOUT "H34TV1510N"?
WH4T3V3R.

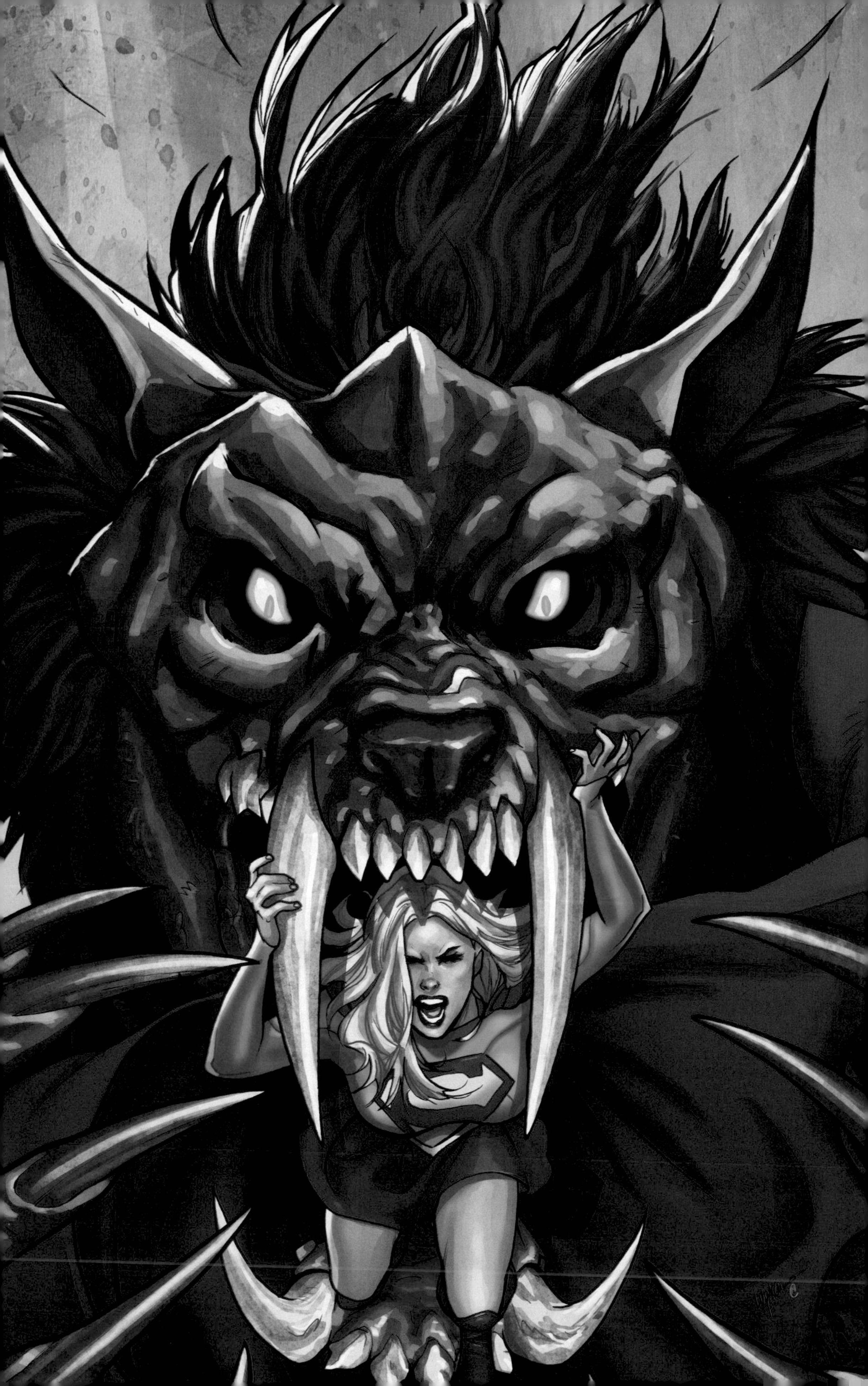

"MISSION: MIND"

STEVE ORLANDO writer * MATIAS BERGARA artist * MICHAEL ATIYEH colorist
cover by EMANUELA LUPACCHINO and MICHAEL ATIYEH

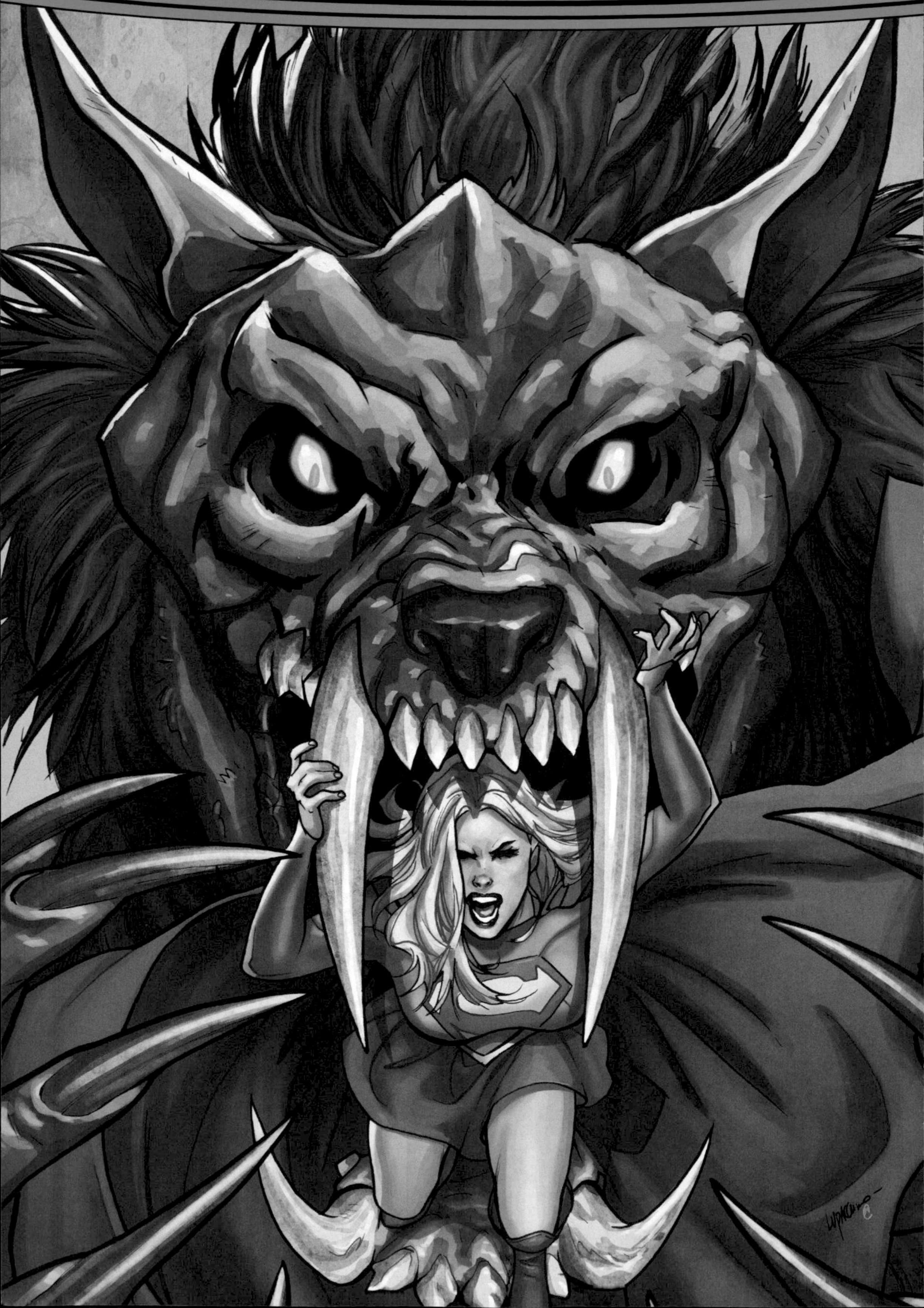

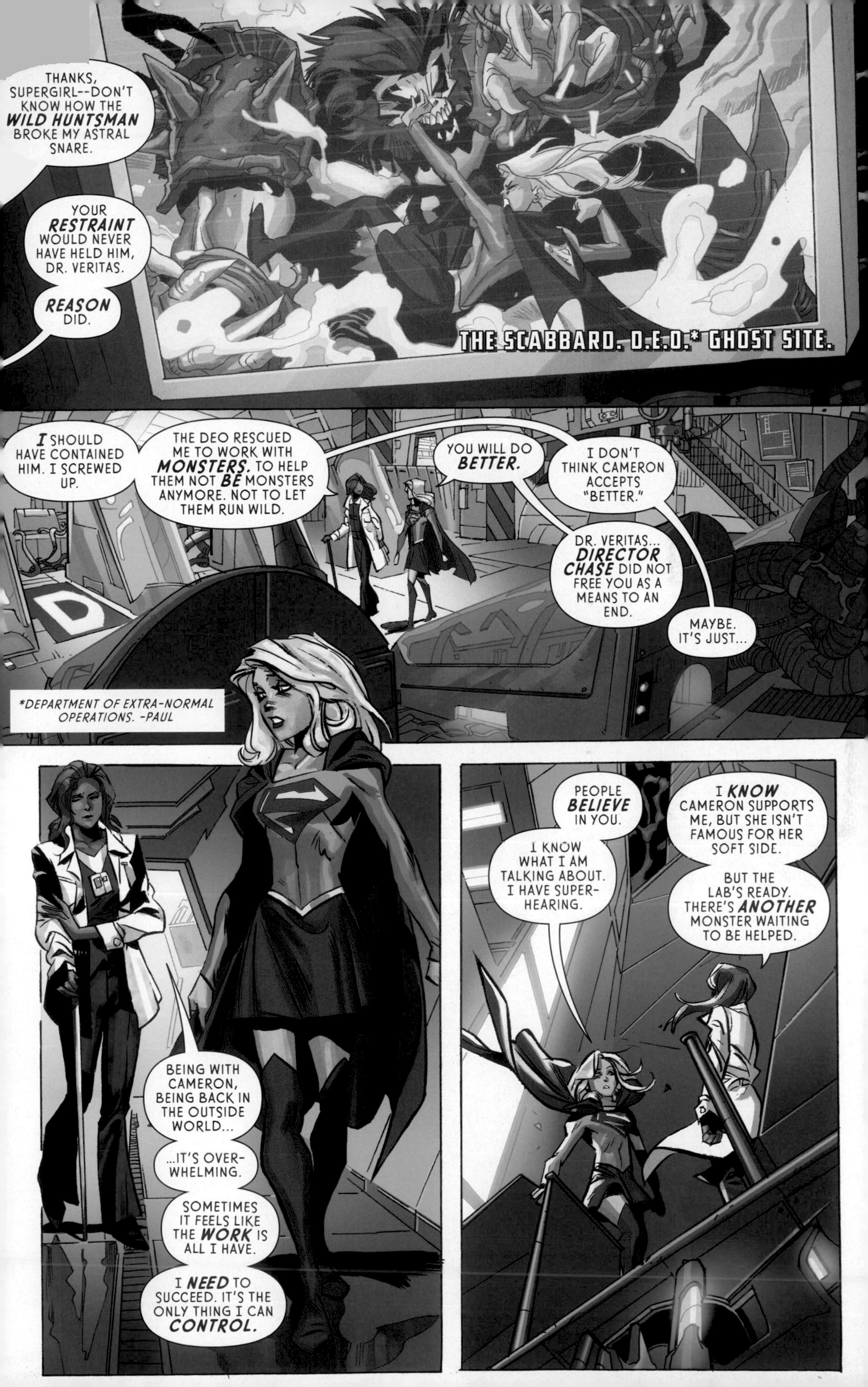
THANKS, SUPERGIRL--DON'T KNOW HOW THE WILD HUNTSMAN BROKE MY ASTRAL SNARE.
YOUR RESTRAINT WOULD NEVER HAVE HELD HIM, DR. VERITAS.
REASON DID.
THE SCABBARD. D.E.O.* GHOST SITE.
I SHOULD HAVE CONTAINED HIM. I SCREWED UP.
THE DEO RESCUED ME TO WORK WITH MONSTERS. TO HELP THEM NOT BE MONSTERS ANYMORE. NOT TO LET THEM RUN WILD.
YOU WILL DO BETTER.
I DON'T THINK CAMERON ACCEPTS "BETTER."
DR. VERITAS... DIRECTOR CHASE DID NOT FREE YOU AS A MEANS TO AN END.
MAYBE. IT'S JUST...
*DEPARTMENT OF EXTRA-NORMAL OPERATIONS. -PAUL
BEING WITH CAMERON, BEING BACK IN THE OUTSIDE WORLD...
...IT'S OVER-WHELMING.
SOMETIMES IT FEELS LIKE THE WORK IS ALL I HAVE.
I NEED TO SUCCEED. IT'S THE ONLY THING I CAN CONTROL.
PEOPLE BELIEVE IN YOU.
I KNOW WHAT I AM TALKING ABOUT. I HAVE SUPER-HEARING.
I KNOW CAMERON SUPPORTS ME, BUT SHE ISN'T FAMOUS FOR HER SOFT SIDE.
BUT THE LAB'S READY. THERE'S ANOTHER MONSTER WAITING TO BE HELPED.

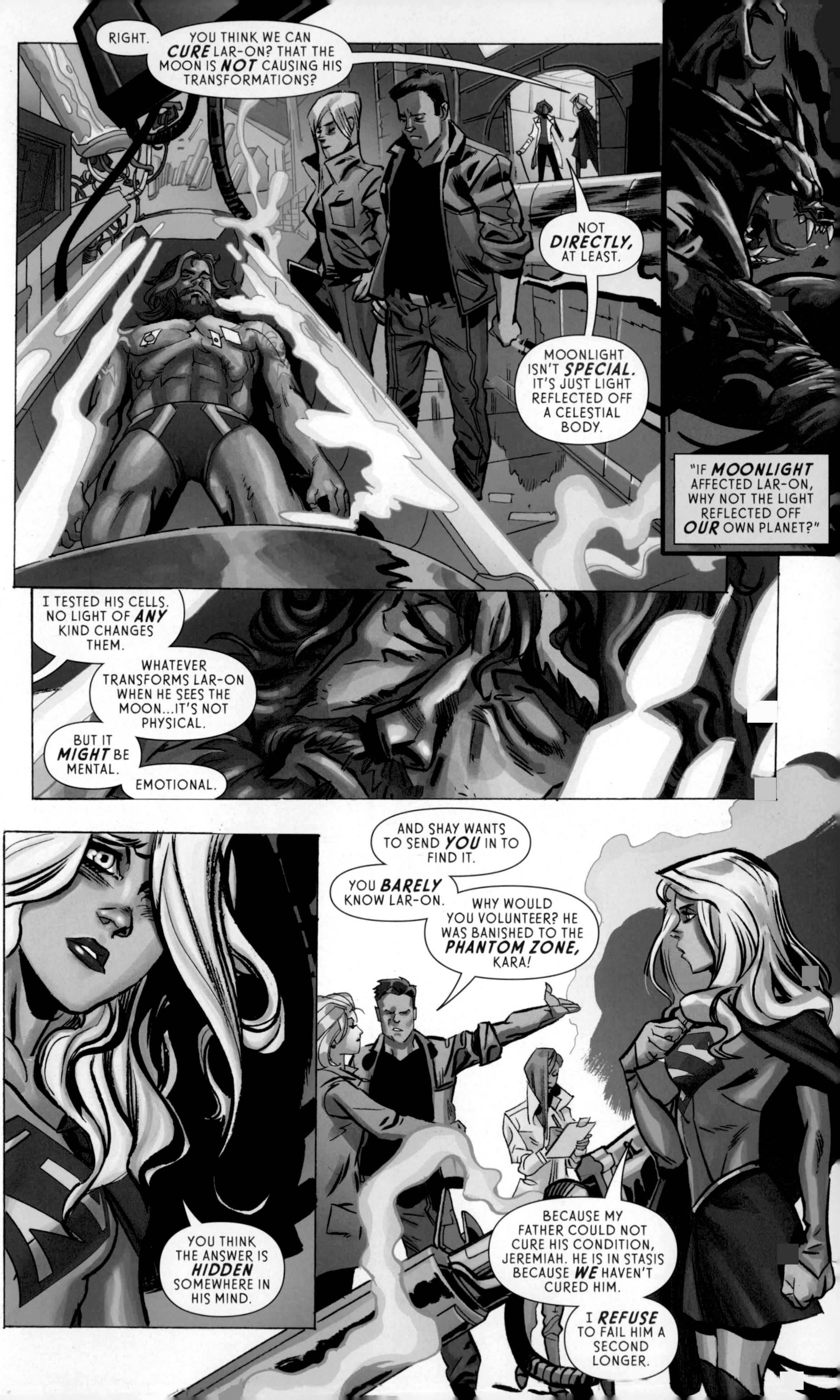
RIGHT.
YOU THINK WE CAN CURE LAR-ON? THAT THE MOON IS NOT CAUSING HIS TRANSFORMATIONS?
NOT DIRECTLY, AT LEAST.
MOONLIGHT ISN'T SPECIAL. IT'S JUST LIGHT REFLECTED OFF A CELESTIAL BODY.
"IF MOONLIGHT AFFECTED LAR-ON, WHY NOT THE LIGHT REFLECTED OFF OUR OWN PLANET?"
I TESTED HIS CELLS. NO LIGHT OF ANY KIND CHANGES THEM.
WHATEVER TRANSFORMS LAR-ON WHEN HE SEES THE MOON...IT'S NOT PHYSICAL.
BUT IT MIGHT BE MENTAL.
EMOTIONAL.
YOU THINK THE ANSWER IS HIDDEN SOMEWHERE IN HIS MIND.
AND SHAY WANTS TO SEND YOU IN TO FIND IT.
YOU BARELY KNOW LAR-ON.
WHY WOULD YOU VOLUNTEER? HE WAS BANISHED TO THE PHANTOM ZONE, KARA!
BECAUSE MY FATHER COULD NOT CURE HIS CONDITION, JEREMIAH. HE IS IN STASIS BECAUSE WE HAVEN'T CURED HIM.
I REFUSE TO FAIL HIM A SECOND LONGER.

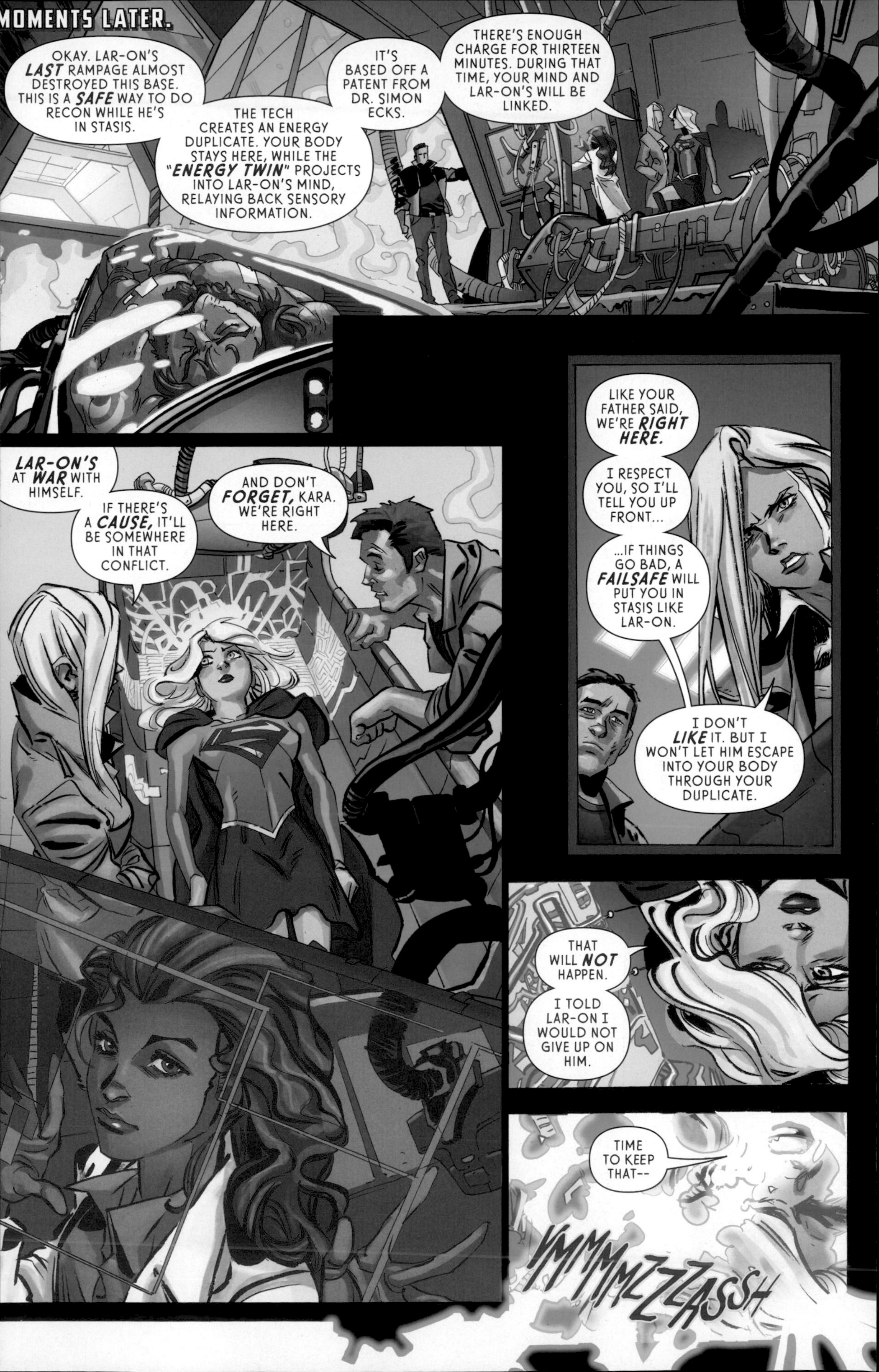
MOMENTS LATER.
OKAY. LAR-ON'S LAST RAMPAGE ALMOST DESTROYED THIS BASE. THIS IS A SAFE WAY TO DO RECON WHILE HE'S IN STASIS.
THE TECH CREATES AN ENERGY DUPLICATE. YOUR BODY STAYS HERE, WHILE THE "ENERGY TWIN" PROJECTS INTO LAR-ON'S MIND, RELAYING BACK SENSORY INFORMATION.
IT'S BASED OFF A PATENT FROM DR. SIMON ECKS.
THERE'S ENOUGH CHARGE FOR THIRTEEN MINUTES. DURING THAT TIME, YOUR MIND AND LAR-ON'S WILL BE LINKED.
LAR-ON'S AT WAR WITH HIMSELF.
IF THERE'S A CAUSE, IT'LL BE SOMEWHERE IN THAT CONFLICT.
AND DON'T FORGET, KARA. WE'RE RIGHT HERE.
LIKE YOUR FATHER SAID, WE'RE RIGHT HERE.
I RESPECT YOU, SO I'LL TELL YOU UP FRONT...
...IF THINGS GO BAD, A FAILSAFE WILL PUT YOU IN STASIS LIKE LAR-ON.
I DON'T LIKE IT. BUT I WON'T LET HIM ESCAPE INTO YOUR BODY THROUGH YOUR DUPLICATE.
THAT WILL NOT HAPPEN.
I TOLD LAR-ON I WOULD NOT GIVE UP ON HIM.
TIME TO KEEP THAT--
VMMMMZZZASSH

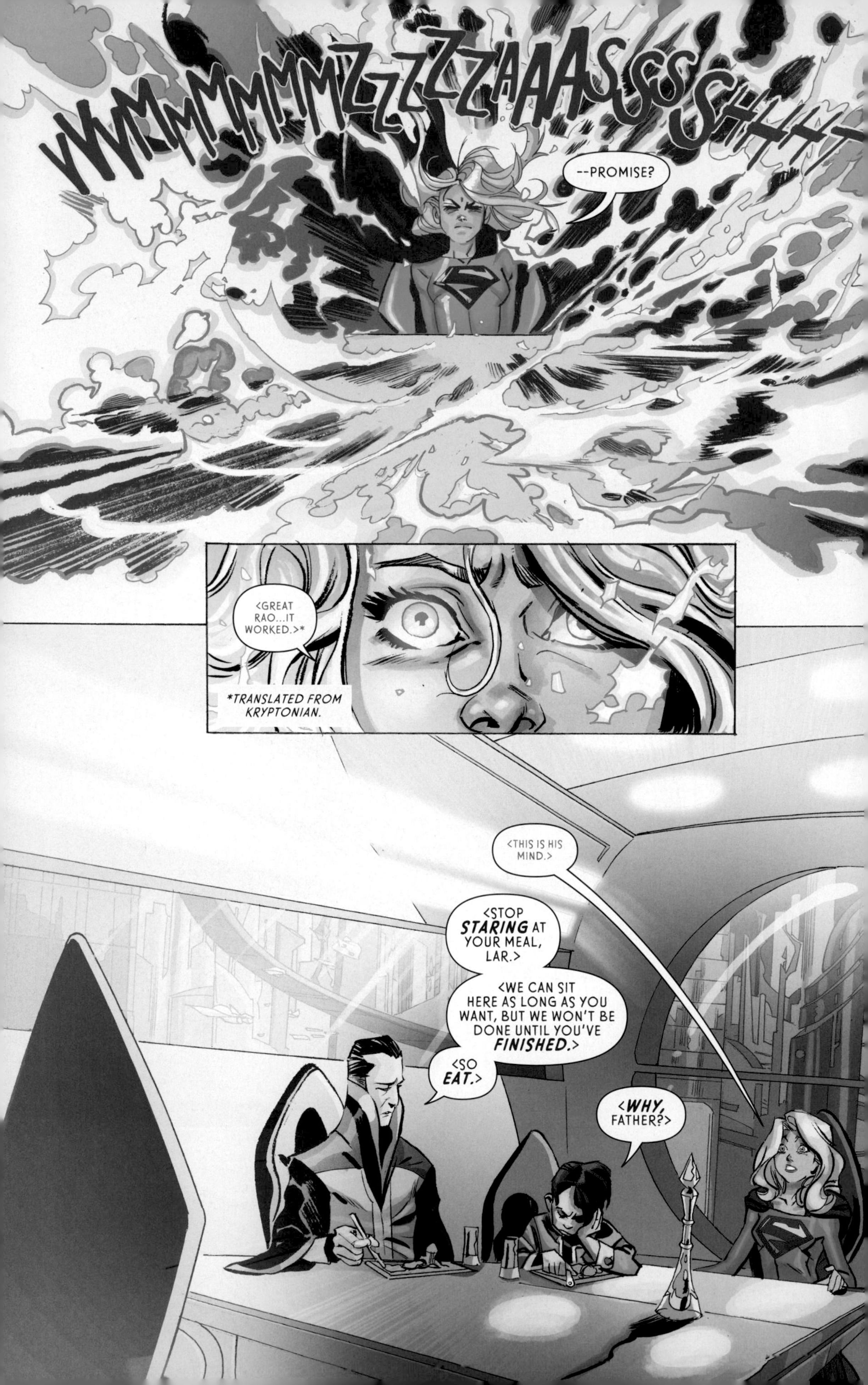
YVMMMMMMZZZZZAAASSSSHHHT
--PROMISE?
<GREAT RAO...IT WORKED.>*
*TRANSLATED FROM KRYPTONIAN.
<THIS IS HIS MIND.>
<STOP **STARING** AT YOUR MEAL, LAR.>
<WE CAN SIT HERE AS LONG AS YOU WANT, BUT WE WON'T BE DONE UNTIL YOU'VE **FINISHED.**>
<SO **EAT.**>
<**WHY,** FATHER?>

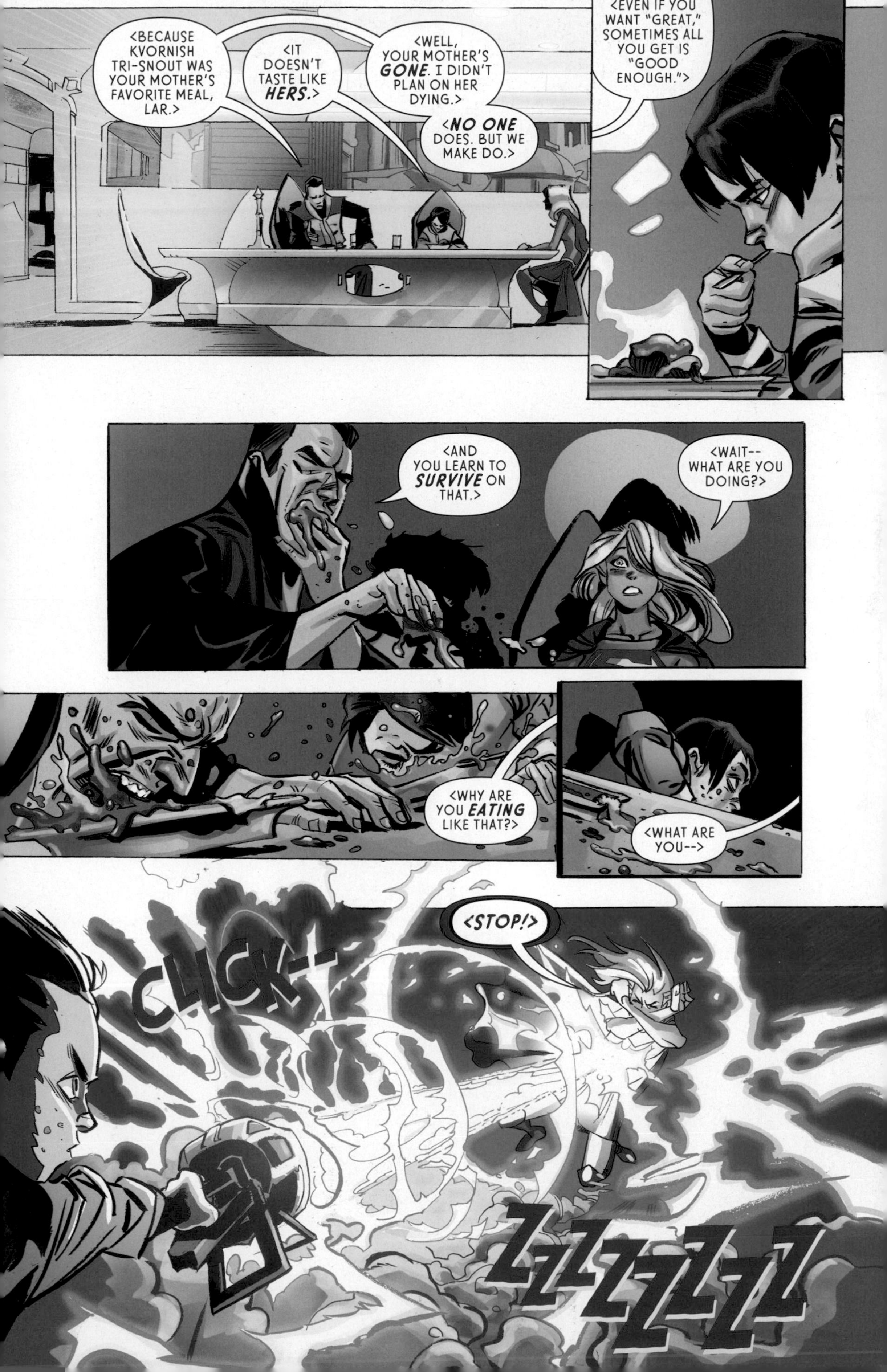

<BECAUSE KVORNISH TRI-SNOUT WAS YOUR MOTHER'S FAVORITE MEAL, LAR.>
<IT DOESN'T TASTE LIKE HERS.>
<WELL, YOUR MOTHER'S GONE. I DIDN'T PLAN ON HER DYING.>
<NO ONE DOES. BUT WE MAKE DO.>
<EVEN IF YOU WANT "GREAT," SOMETIMES ALL YOU GET IS "GOOD ENOUGH.">
<AND YOU LEARN TO SURVIVE ON THAT.>
<WAIT-- WHAT ARE YOU DOING?>
<WHY ARE YOU EATING LIKE THAT?>
<WHAT ARE YOU-->
<STOP!>
CLICK--
ZZZZZZZ

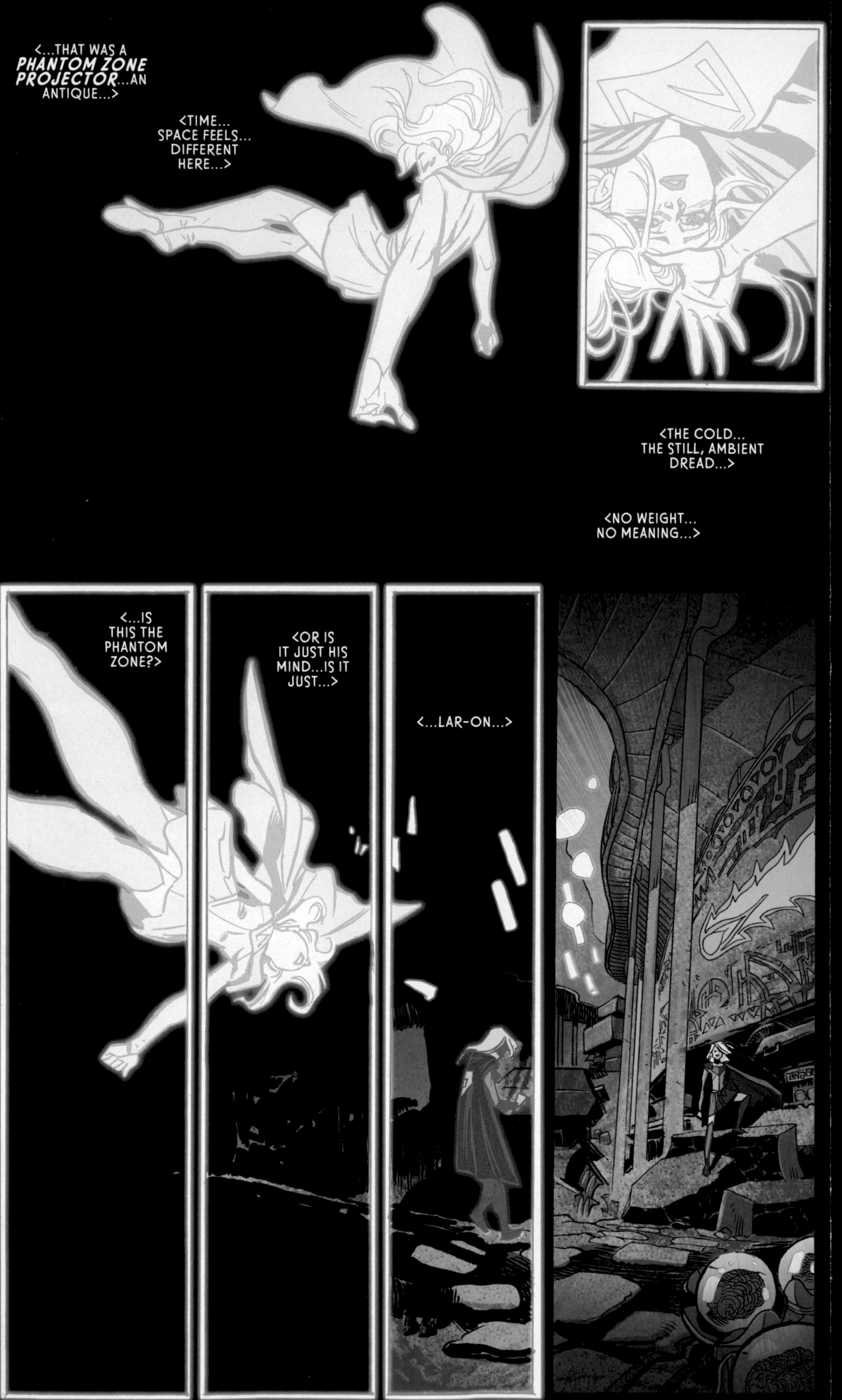
<...THAT WAS A *PHANTOM ZONE PROJECTOR*...AN ANTIQUE...>
<TIME... SPACE FEELS... DIFFERENT HERE...>
<THE COLD... THE STILL, AMBIENT DREAD...>
<NO WEIGHT... NO MEANING...>
<...IS THIS THE PHANTOM ZONE?>
<OR IS IT JUST HIS MIND...IS IT JUST...>
<...LAR-ON...>

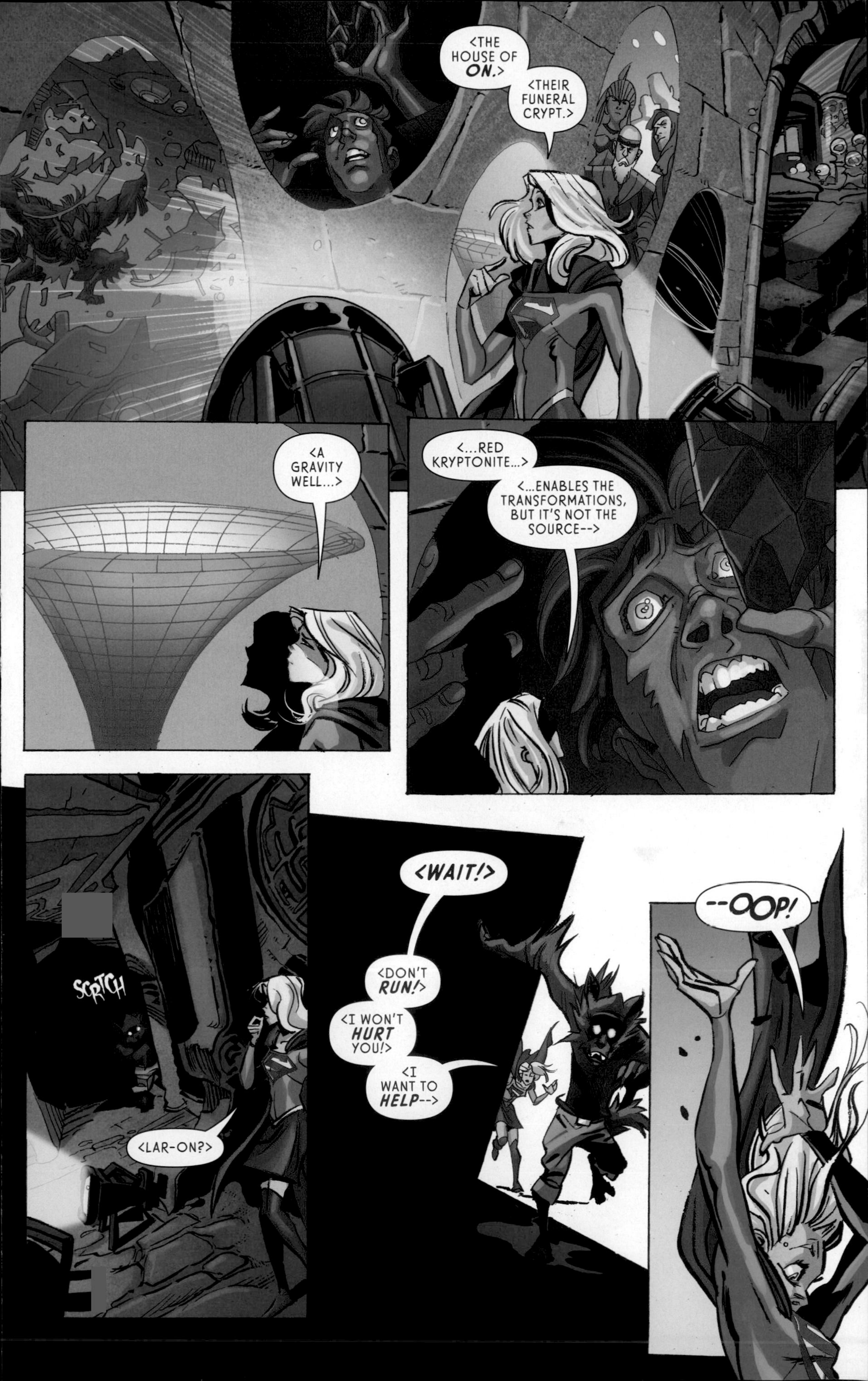
<THE HOUSE OF ON.>
<THEIR FUNERAL CRYPT.>
<A GRAVITY WELL...>
<...RED KRYPTONITE...>
<...ENABLES THE TRANSFORMATIONS, BUT IT'S NOT THE SOURCE-->
SCRTCH
<LAR-ON?>
<WAIT!>
<DON'T RUN!>
<I WON'T HURT YOU!>
<I WANT TO HELP-->
--OOP!

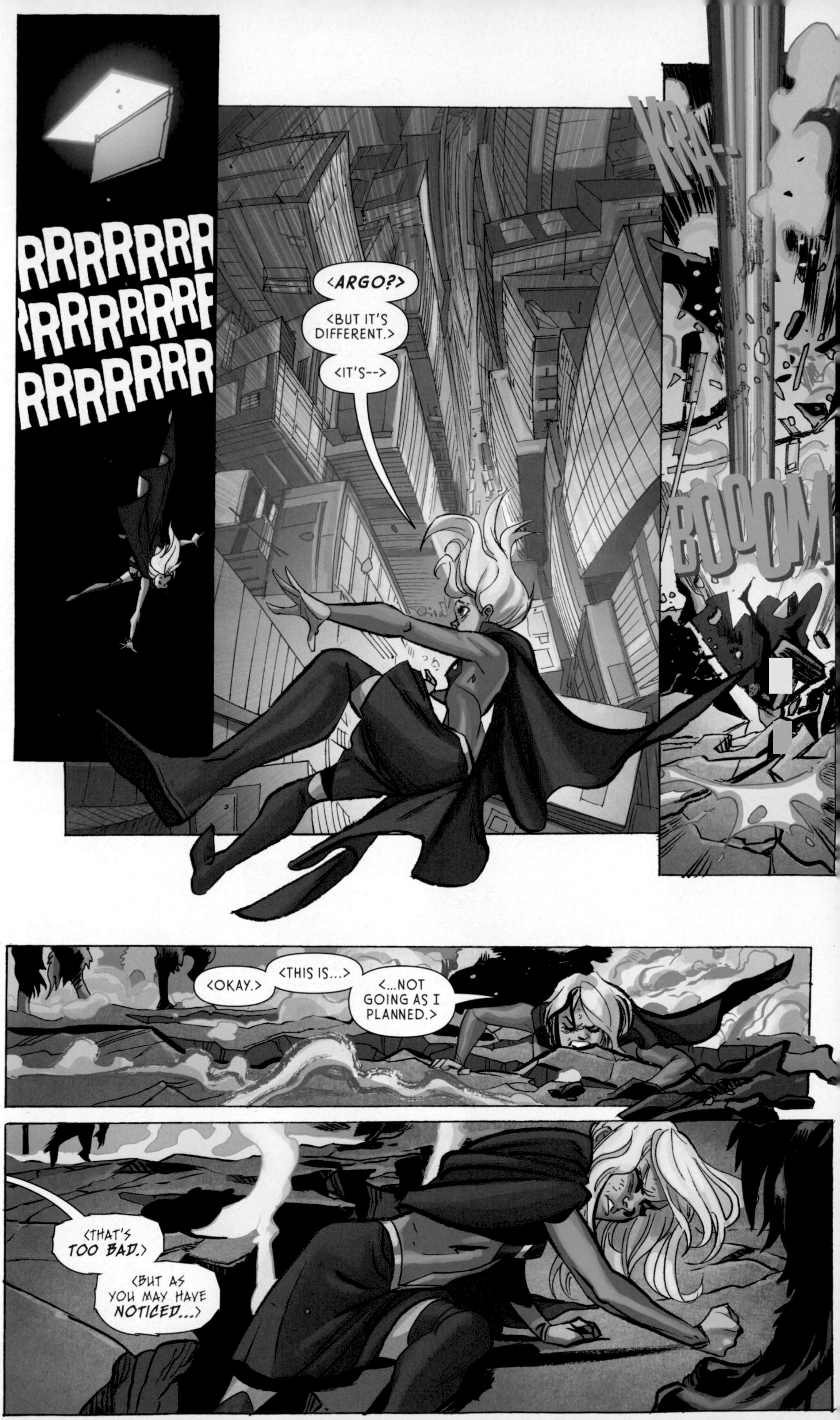

RRRRRRRR
RRRRRRRR
RRRRRRRR
<ARGO?>
<BUT IT'S DIFFERENT.>
<IT'S-->
KRA-
BOOOM
<OKAY.>
<THIS IS...>
<...NOT GOING AS I PLANNED.>
<THAT'S TOO BAD.>
<BUT AS YOU MAY HAVE NOTICED...>

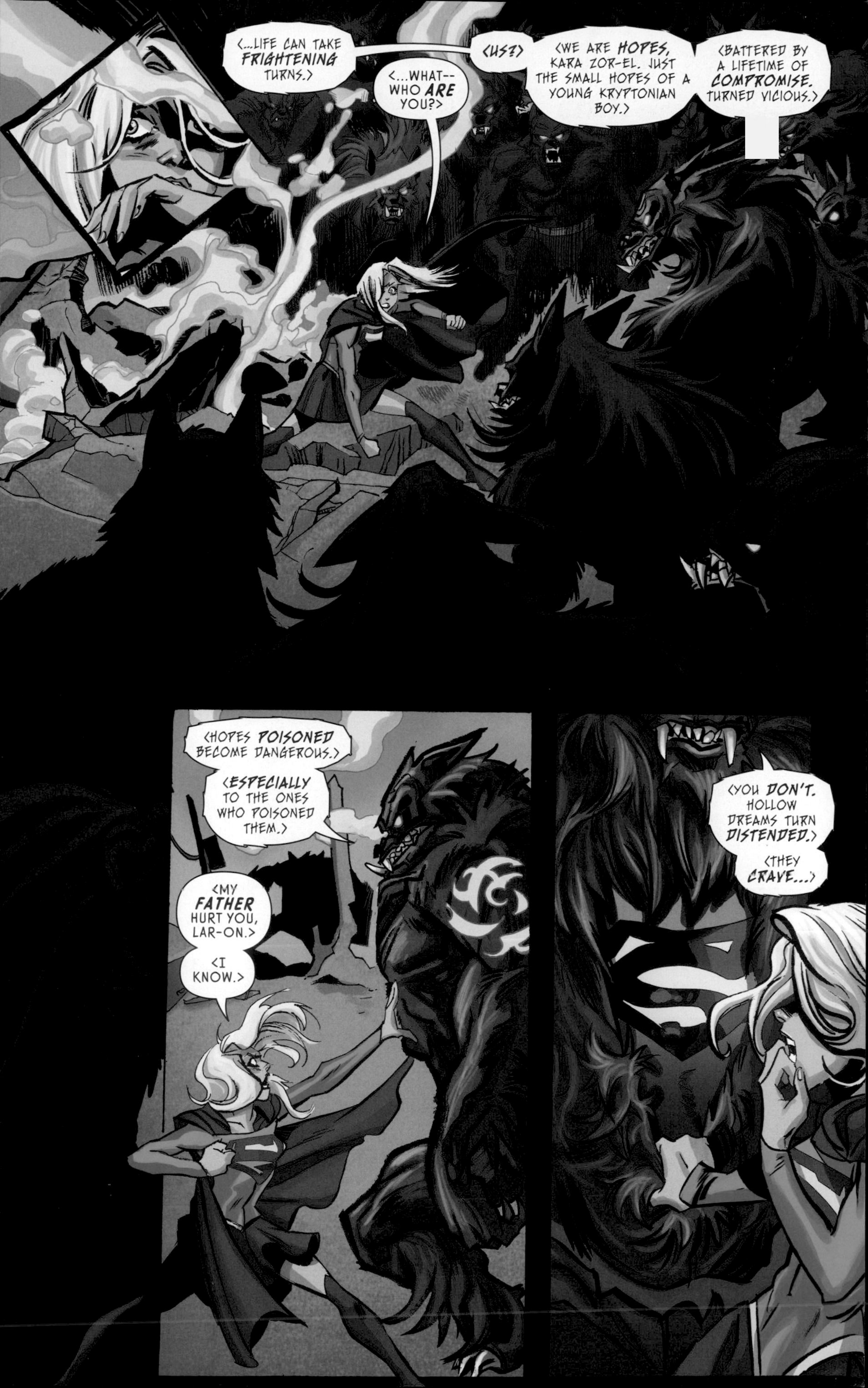

<...LIFE CAN TAKE FRIGHTENING TURNS.>
<...WHAT--WHO ARE YOU?>
<US?>
<WE ARE HOPES, KARA ZOR-EL. JUST THE SMALL HOPES OF A YOUNG KRYPTONIAN BOY.>
<BATTERED BY A LIFETIME OF COMPROMISE. TURNED VICIOUS.>
<HOPES POISONED BECOME DANGEROUS.>
<ESPECIALLY TO THE ONES WHO POISONED THEM.>
<MY FATHER HURT YOU, LAR-ON.>
<I KNOW.>
<YOU DON'T. HOLLOW DREAMS TURN DISTENDED.>
<THEY CRAVE...>

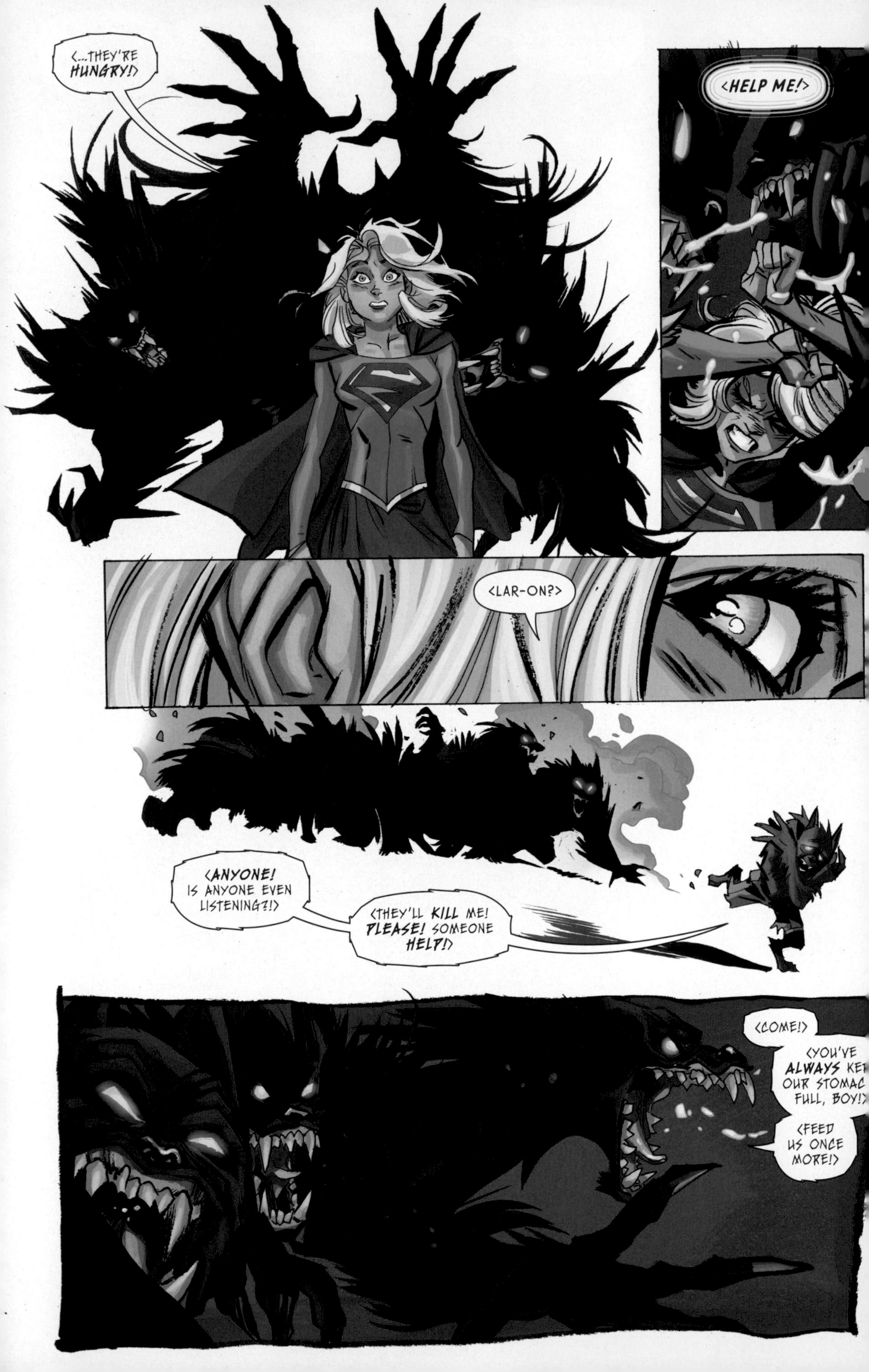

<...THEY'RE HUNGRY!>
<HELP ME!>
<LAR-ON?>
<ANYONE! IS ANYONE EVEN LISTENING?!>
<THEY'LL KILL ME! PLEASE! SOMEONE HELP!>
<COME!>
<YOU'VE ALWAYS KE
OUR STOMAC
FULL, BOY!>
<FEED US ONCE MORE!>

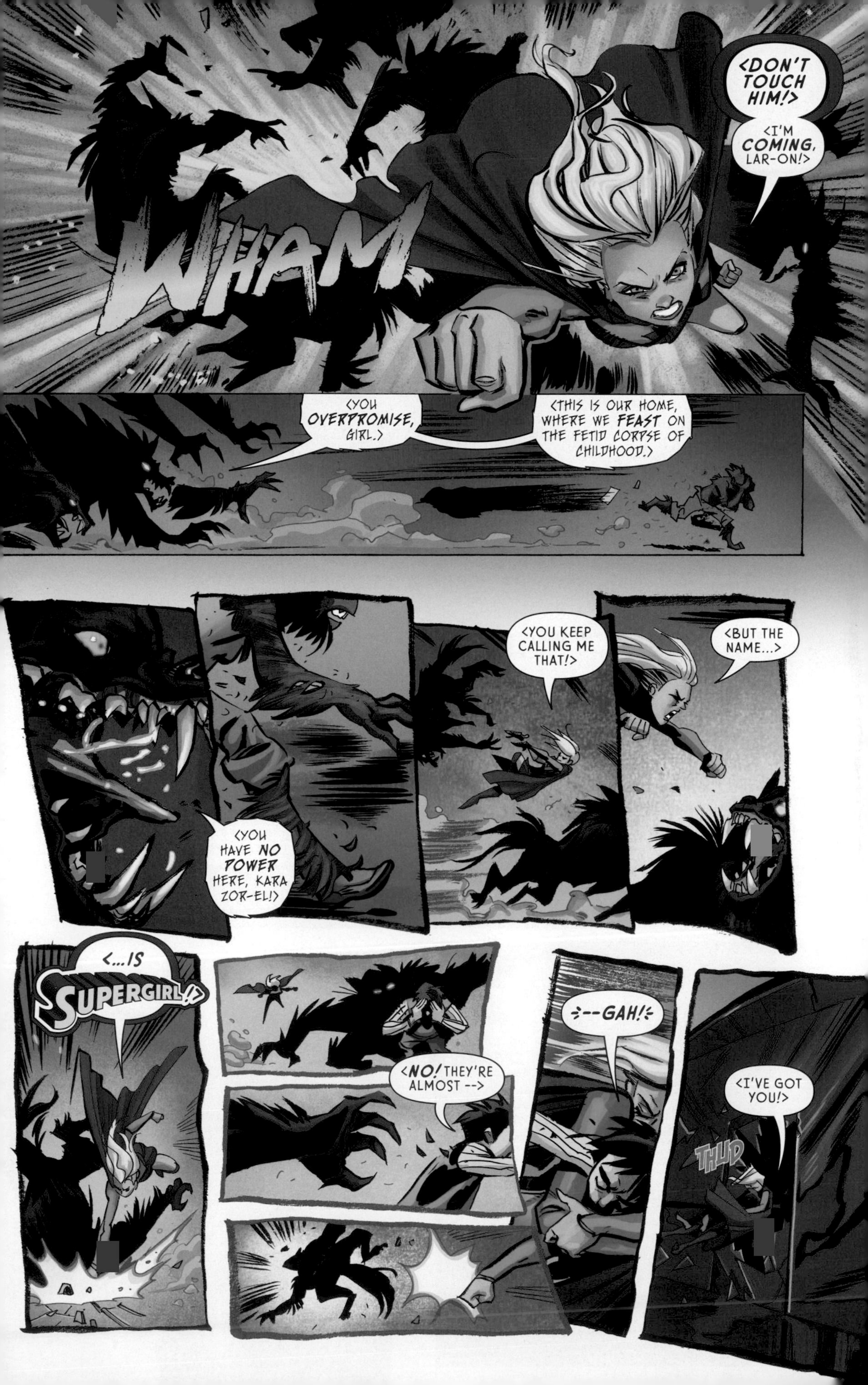
<DON'T TOUCH HIM!>
<I'M COMING, LAR-ON!>
WHAM
<YOU OVERPROMISE, GIRL.>
<THIS IS OUR HOME, WHERE WE FEAST ON THE FETID CORPSE OF CHILDHOOD.>
<YOU HAVE NO POWER HERE, KARA ZOR-EL!>
<YOU KEEP CALLING ME THAT!>
<BUT THE NAME...>
<...IS SUPERGIRL!>
<NO! THEY'RE ALMOST -->
--GAH!
THUD
<I'VE GOT YOU!>

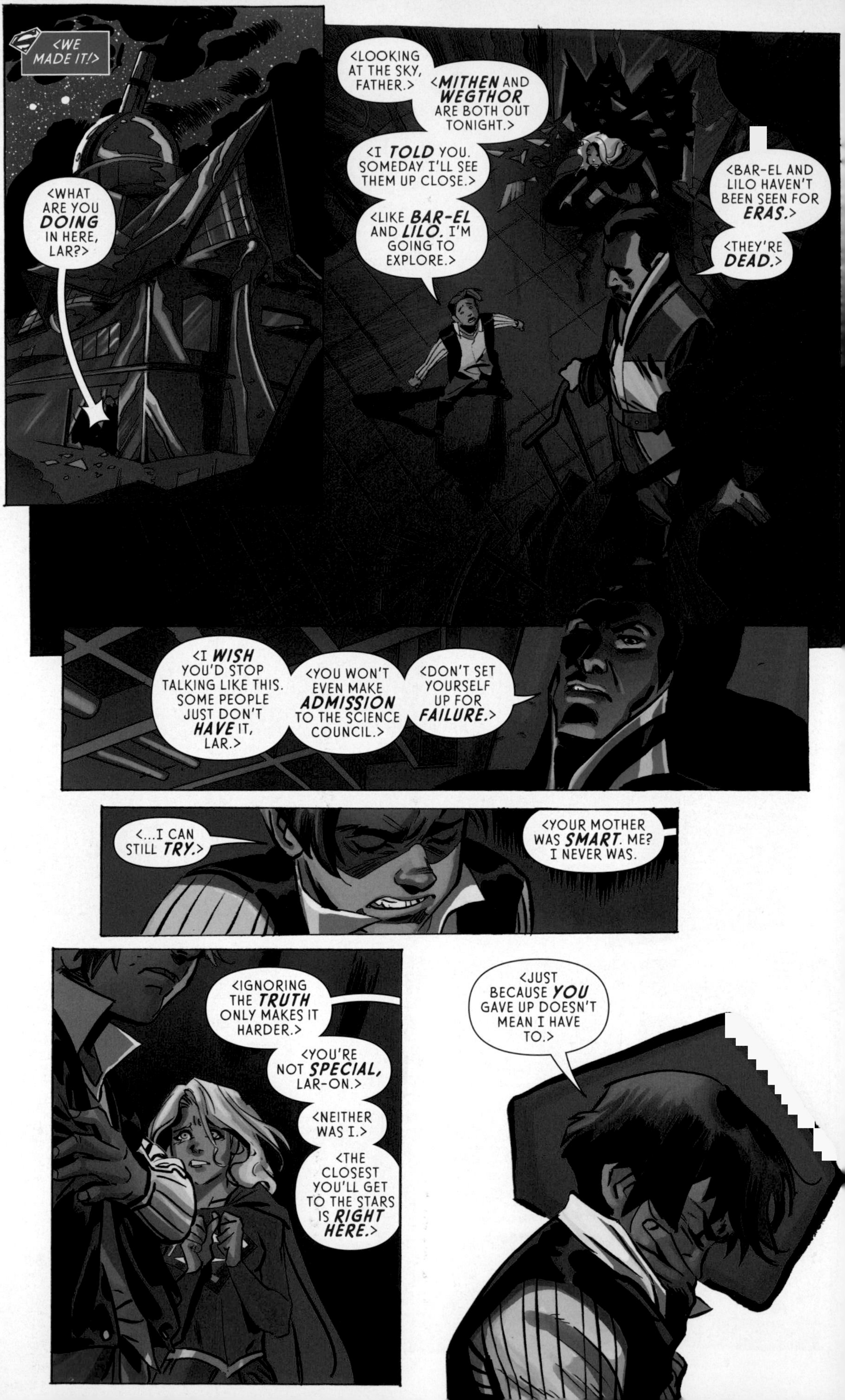
<WE MADE IT!>
<WHAT ARE YOU DOING IN HERE, LAR?>
<LOOKING AT THE SKY, FATHER.>
<MITHEN AND WEGTHOR ARE BOTH OUT TONIGHT.>
<I TOLD YOU. SOMEDAY I'LL SEE THEM UP CLOSE.>
<LIKE BAR-EL AND LILO. I'M GOING TO EXPLORE.>
<BAR-EL AND LILO HAVEN'T BEEN SEEN FOR ERAS.>
<THEY'RE DEAD.>
<DON'T SET YOURSELF UP FOR FAILURE.>
<YOU WON'T EVEN MAKE ADMISSION TO THE SCIENCE COUNCIL.>
<I WISH YOU'D STOP TALKING LIKE THIS. SOME PEOPLE JUST DON'T HAVE IT, LAR.>
<YOUR MOTHER WAS SMART. ME? I NEVER WAS.
<...I CAN STILL TRY.>
<IGNORING THE TRUTH ONLY MAKES IT HARDER.>
<YOU'RE NOT SPECIAL, LAR-ON.>
<NEITHER WAS I.>
<THE CLOSEST YOU'LL GET TO THE STARS IS RIGHT HERE.>
<JUST BECAUSE YOU GAVE UP DOESN'T MEAN I HAVE TO.>

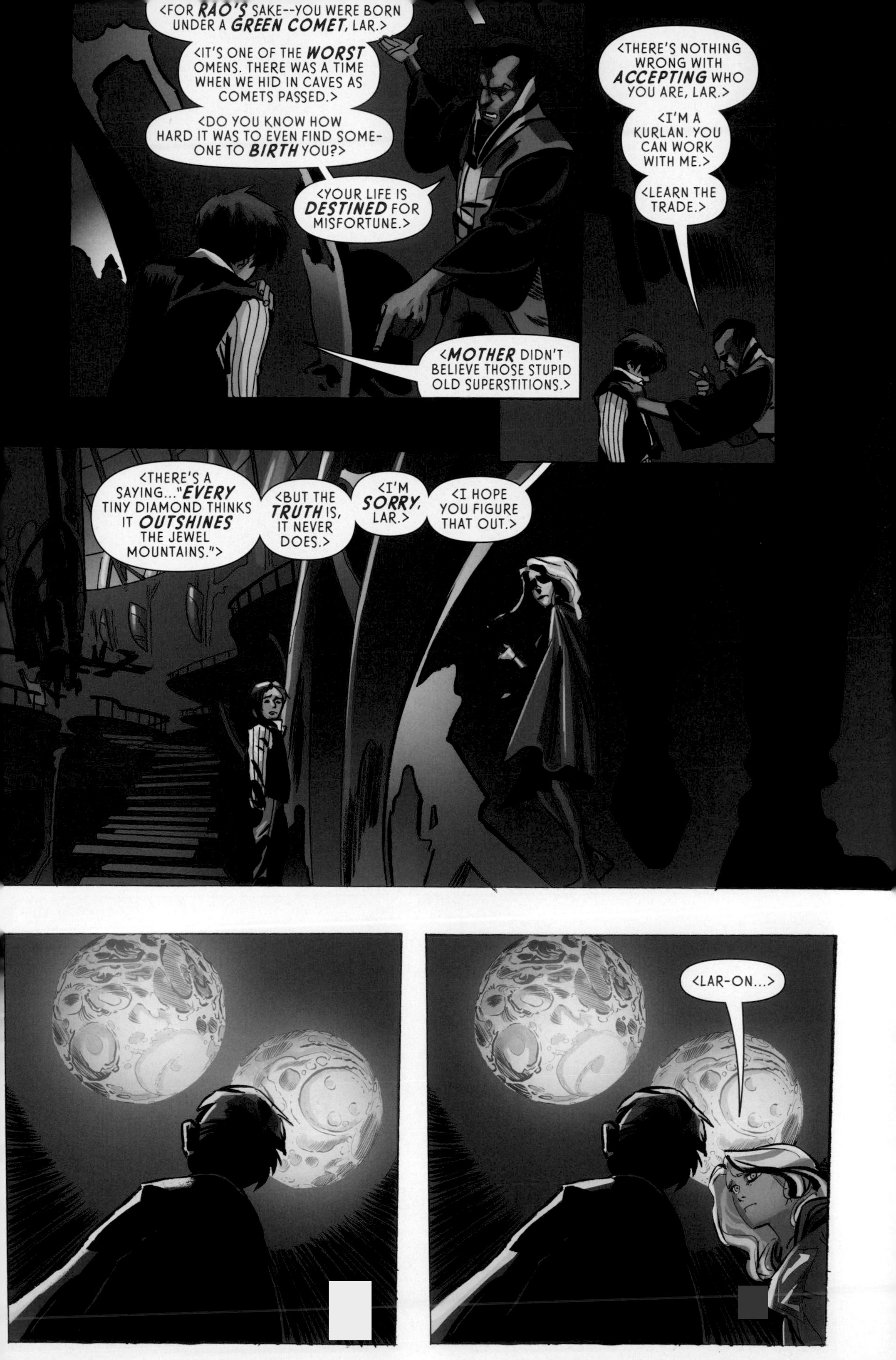
<FOR RAO'S SAKE--YOU WERE BORN UNDER A GREEN COMET, LAR.>
<IT'S ONE OF THE WORST OMENS. THERE WAS A TIME WHEN WE HID IN CAVES AS COMETS PASSED.>
<DO YOU KNOW HOW HARD IT WAS TO EVEN FIND SOME-ONE TO BIRTH YOU?>
<YOUR LIFE IS DESTINED FOR MISFORTUNE.>
<MOTHER DIDN'T BELIEVE THOSE STUPID OLD SUPERSTITIONS.>
<THERE'S NOTHING WRONG WITH ACCEPTING WHO YOU ARE, LAR.>
<I'M A KURLAN. YOU CAN WORK WITH ME.>
<LEARN THE TRADE.>
<THERE'S A SAYING..."EVERY TINY DIAMOND THINKS IT OUTSHINES THE JEWEL MOUNTAINS.">
<BUT THE TRUTH IS, IT NEVER DOES.>
<I'M SORRY, LAR.>
<I HOPE YOU FIGURE THAT OUT.>
<LAR-ON...>

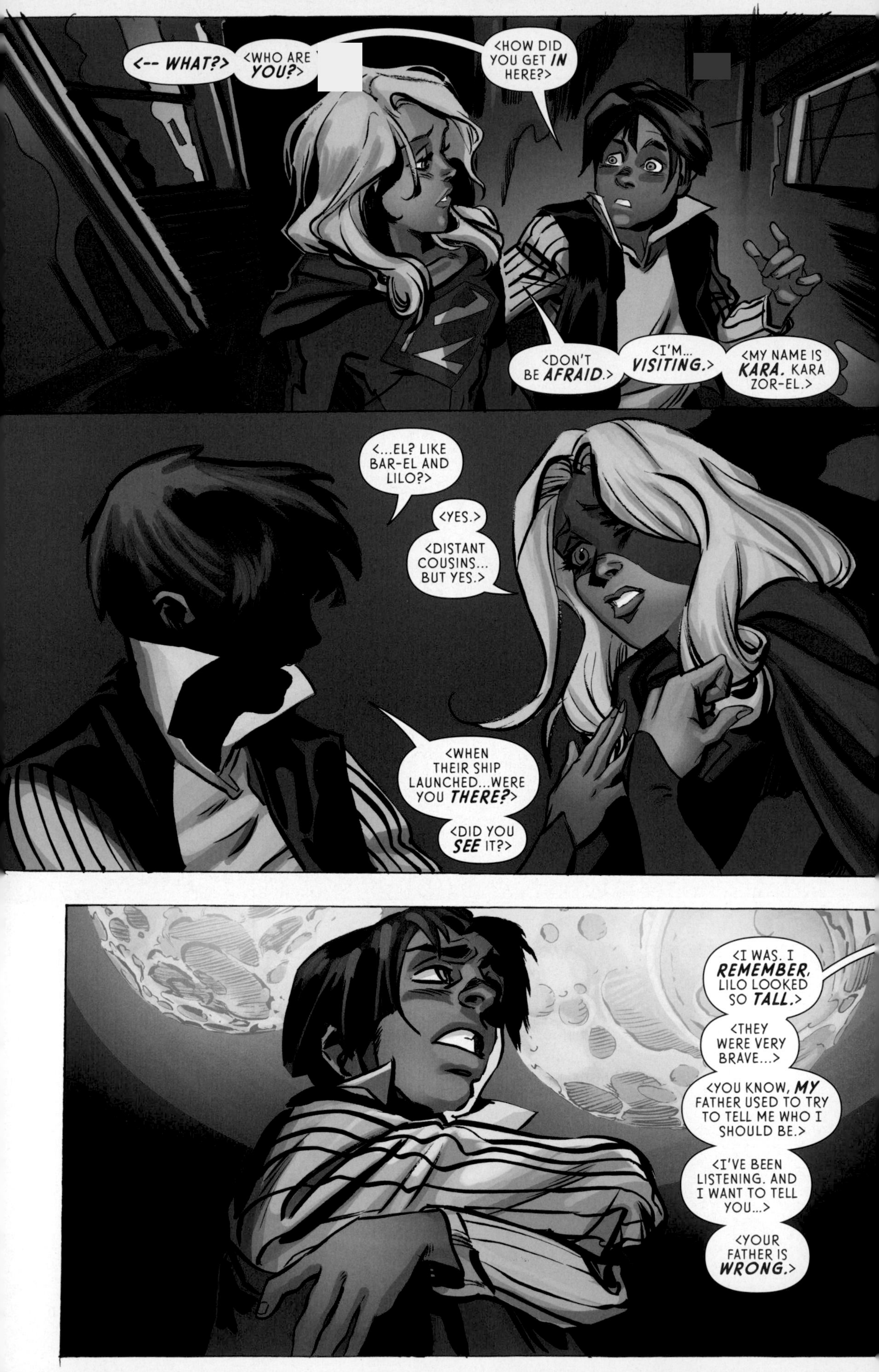
<-- WHAT?>
<WHO ARE YOU?>
<HOW DID YOU GET IN HERE?>
<DON'T BE AFRAID.>
<I'M... VISITING.>
<MY NAME IS KARA. KARA ZOR-EL.>
<...EL? LIKE BAR-EL AND LILO?>
<YES.>
<DISTANT COUSINS... BUT YES.>
<WHEN THEIR SHIP LAUNCHED...WERE YOU THERE?>
<DID YOU SEE IT?>
<I WAS. I REMEMBER. LILO LOOKED SO TALL.>
<THEY WERE VERY BRAVE...>
<YOU KNOW, MY FATHER USED TO TRY TO TELL ME WHO I SHOULD BE.>
<I'VE BEEN LISTENING. AND I WANT TO TELL YOU...>
<YOUR FATHER IS WRONG.>

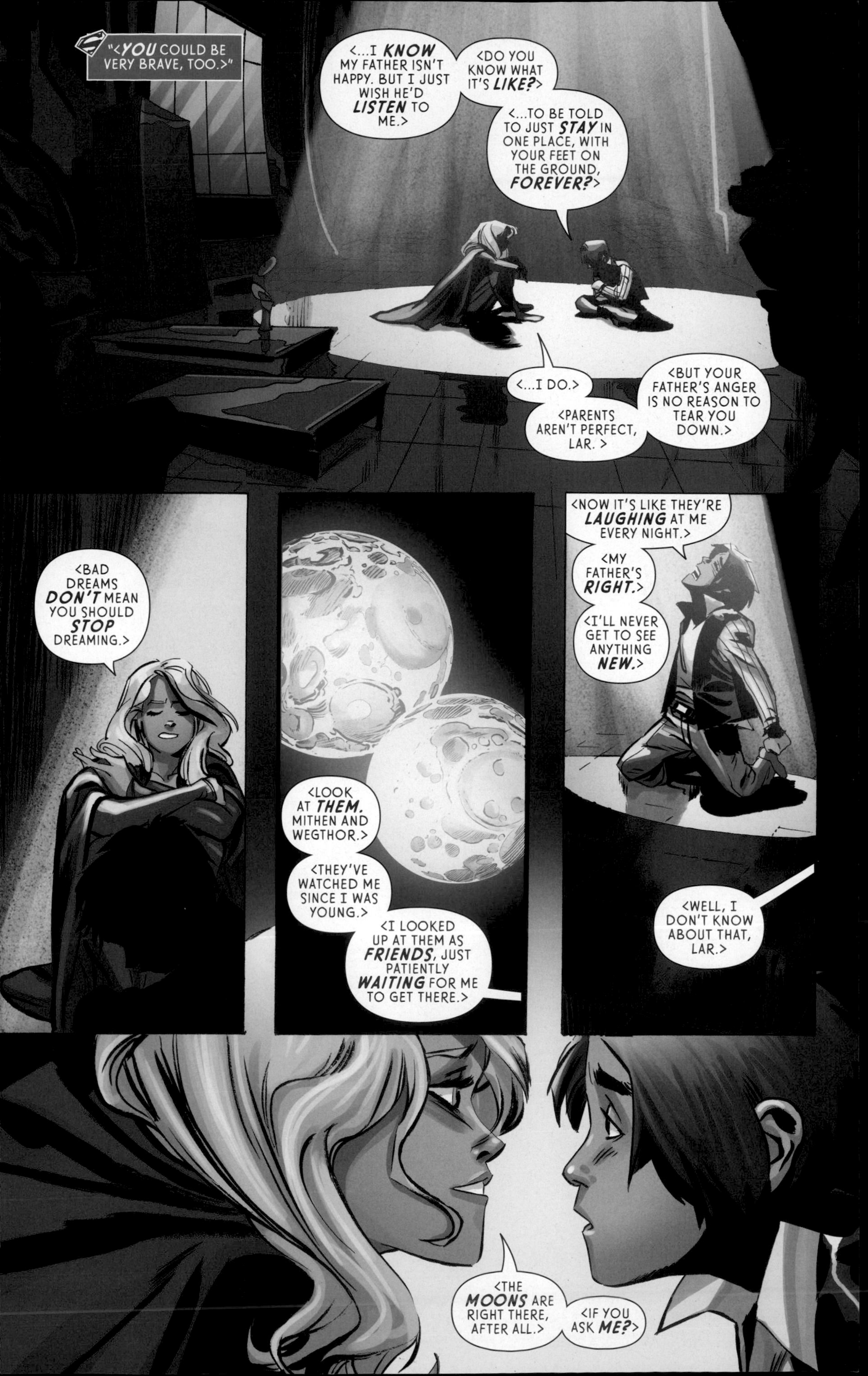
"<YOU COULD BE VERY BRAVE, TOO.>"
<...I KNOW MY FATHER ISN'T HAPPY. BUT I JUST WISH HE'D LISTEN TO ME.>
<DO YOU KNOW WHAT IT'S LIKE?>
<...TO BE TOLD TO JUST STAY IN ONE PLACE, WITH YOUR FEET ON THE GROUND, FOREVER?>
<...I DO.>
<PARENTS AREN'T PERFECT, LAR. >
<BUT YOUR FATHER'S ANGER IS NO REASON TO TEAR YOU DOWN.>
<BAD DREAMS DON'T MEAN YOU SHOULD STOP DREAMING.>
<LOOK AT THEM. MITHEN AND WEGTHOR.>
<THEY'VE WATCHED ME SINCE I WAS YOUNG.>
<I LOOKED UP AT THEM AS FRIENDS, JUST PATIENTLY WAITING FOR ME TO GET THERE.>
<NOW IT'S LIKE THEY'RE LAUGHING AT ME EVERY NIGHT.>
<MY FATHER'S RIGHT.>
<I'LL NEVER GET TO SEE ANYTHING NEW.>
<WELL, I DON'T KNOW ABOUT THAT, LAR.>
<THE MOONS ARE RIGHT THERE, AFTER ALL.>
<IF YOU ASK ME?>

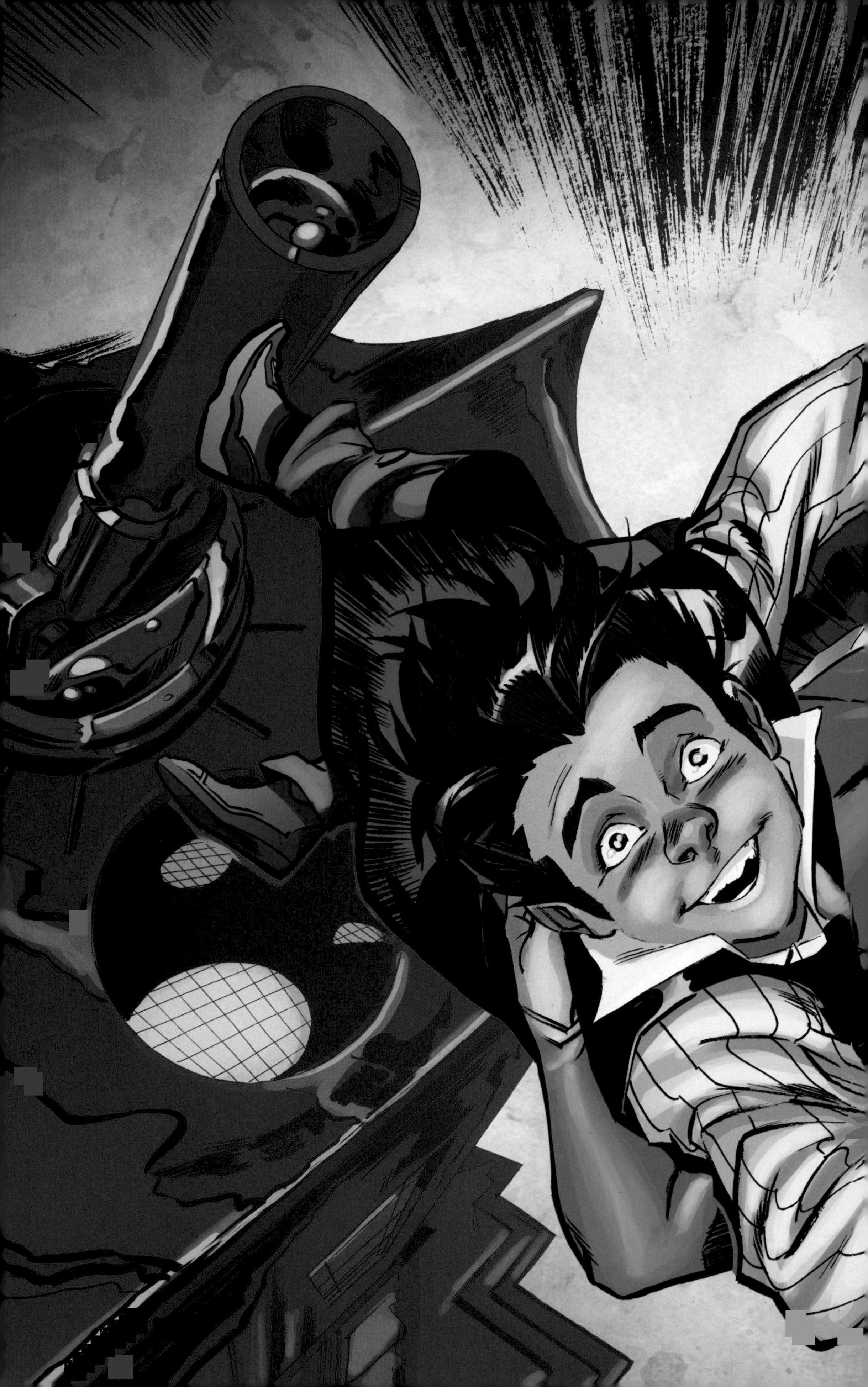

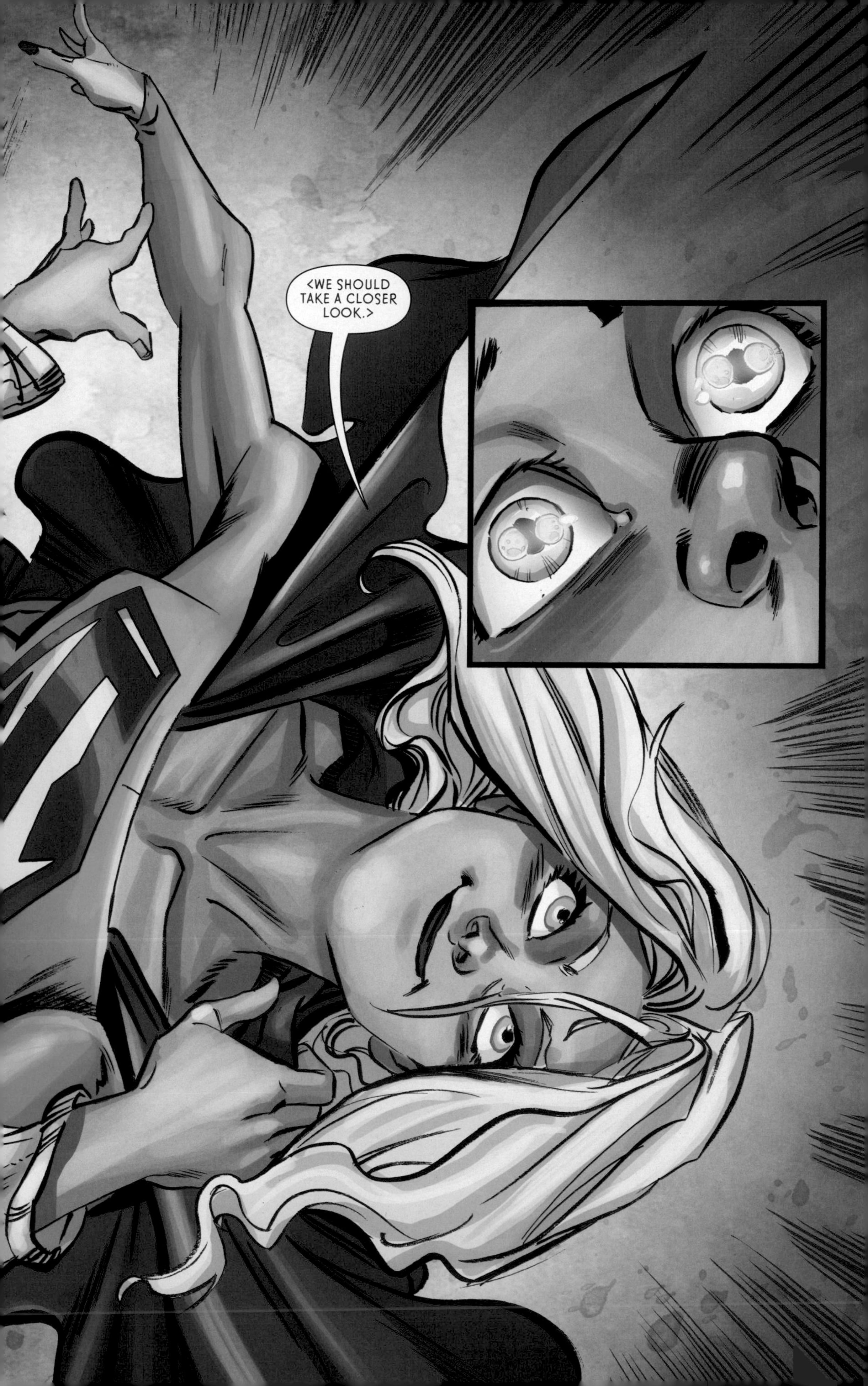
<WE SHOULD TAKE A CLOSER LOOK.>

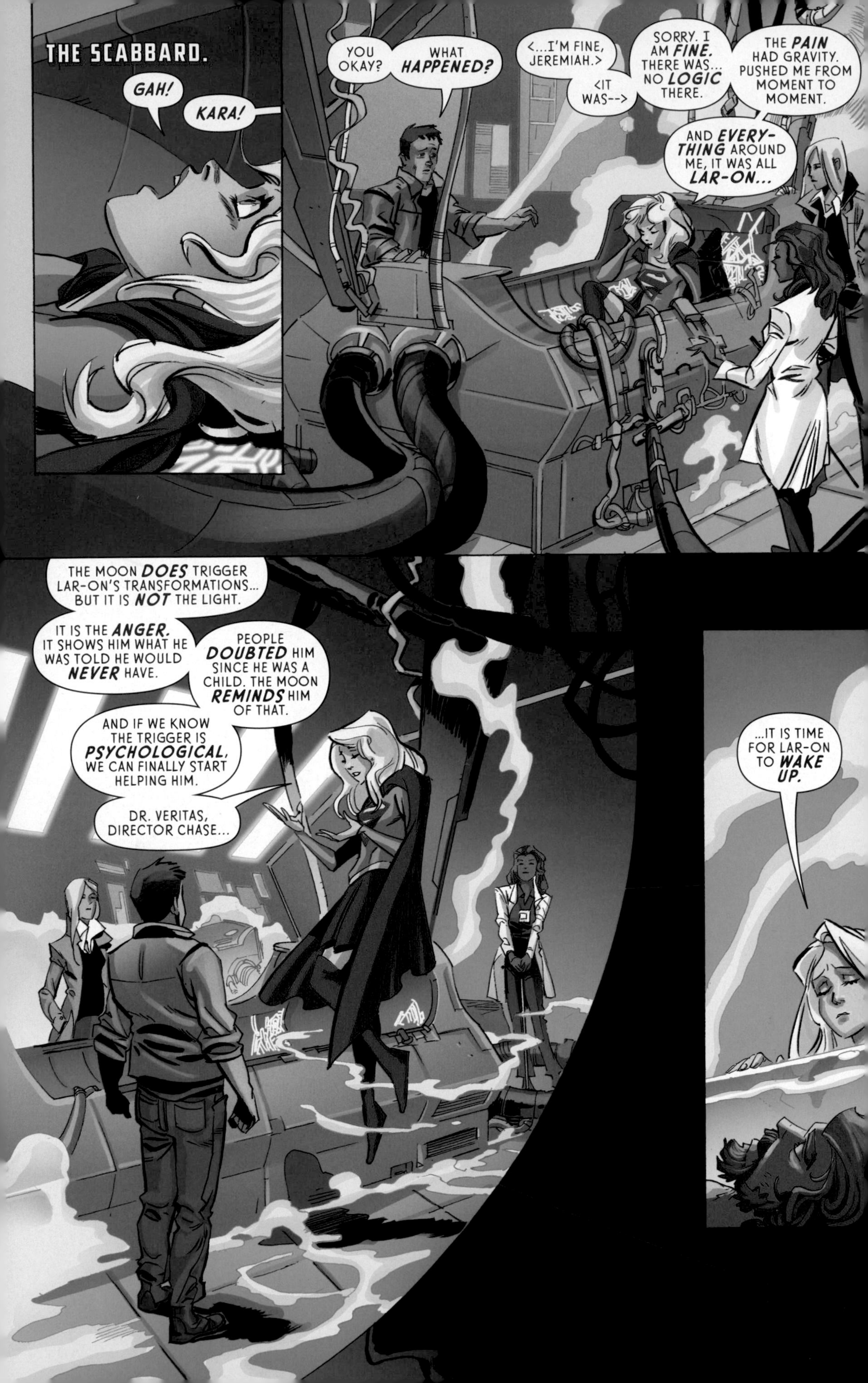
THE SCABBARD.
GAH!
KARA!
YOU OKAY?
WHAT HAPPENED?
<...I'M FINE, JEREMIAH.>
<IT WAS-->
SORRY. I AM FINE. THERE WAS... NO LOGIC THERE.
THE PAIN HAD GRAVITY. PUSHED ME FROM MOMENT TO MOMENT.
AND EVERYTHING AROUND ME, IT WAS ALL LAR-ON...
THE MOON DOES TRIGGER LAR-ON'S TRANSFORMATIONS... BUT IT IS NOT THE LIGHT.
IT IS THE ANGER. IT SHOWS HIM WHAT HE WAS TOLD HE WOULD NEVER HAVE.
PEOPLE DOUBTED HIM SINCE HE WAS A CHILD. THE MOON REMINDS HIM OF THAT.
AND IF WE KNOW THE TRIGGER IS PSYCHOLOGICAL, WE CAN FINALLY START HELPING HIM.
DR. VERITAS, DIRECTOR CHASE...
...IT IS TIME FOR LAR-ON TO WAKE UP.

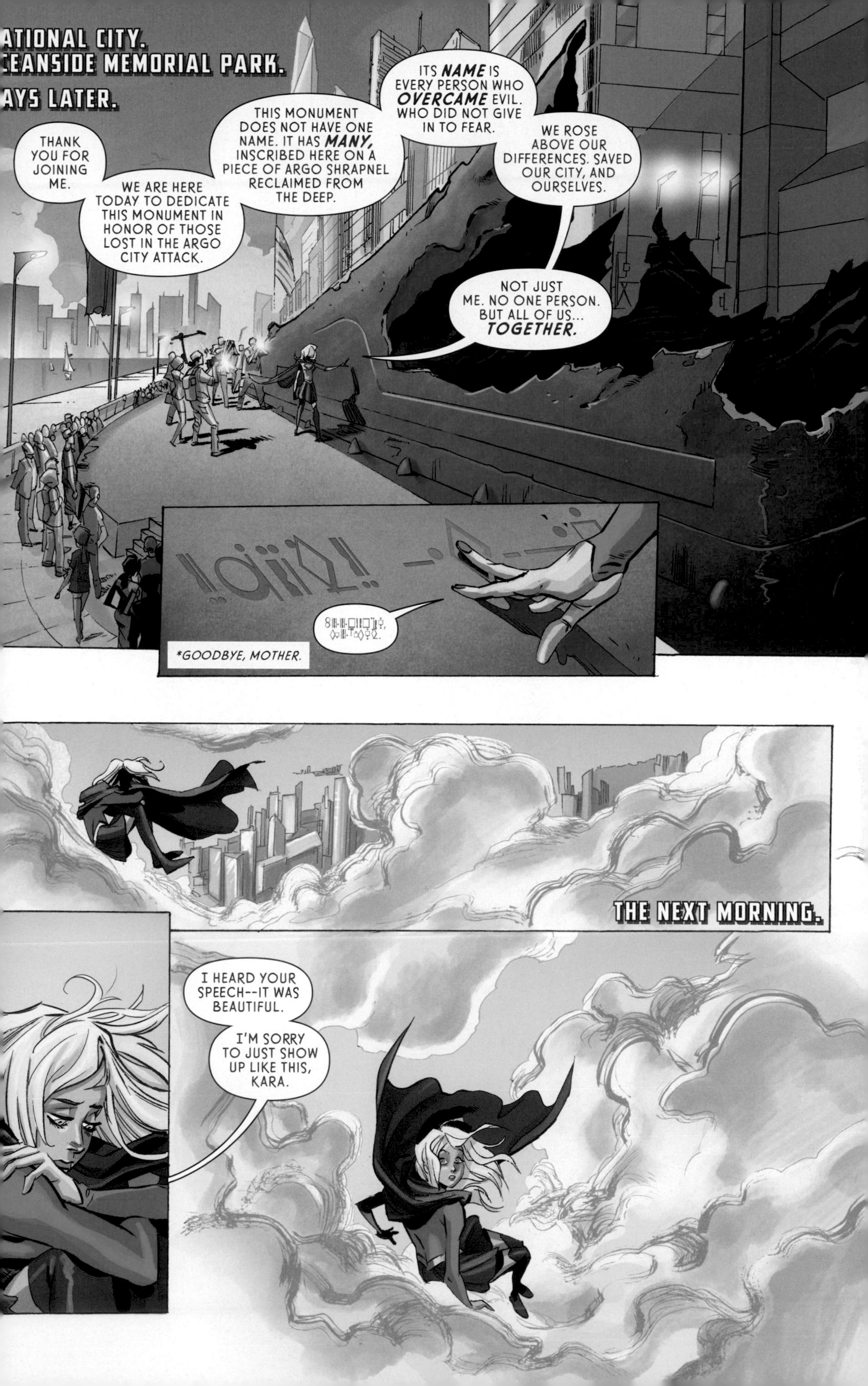
ATIONAL CITY.
CEANSIDE MEMORIAL PARK.
AYS LATER.
THANK YOU FOR JOINING ME.
WE ARE HERE TODAY TO DEDICATE THIS MONUMENT IN HONOR OF THOSE LOST IN THE ARGO CITY ATTACK.
THIS MONUMENT DOES NOT HAVE ONE NAME. IT HAS MANY, INSCRIBED HERE ON A PIECE OF ARGO SHRAPNEL RECLAIMED FROM THE DEEP.
ITS NAME IS EVERY PERSON WHO OVERCAME EVIL. WHO DID NOT GIVE IN TO FEAR.
WE ROSE ABOVE OUR DIFFERENCES. SAVED OUR CITY, AND OURSELVES.
NOT JUST ME. NO ONE PERSON. BUT ALL OF US... TOGETHER.
*GOODBYE, MOTHER.
THE NEXT MORNING.
I HEARD YOUR SPEECH--IT WAS BEAUTIFUL.
I'M SORRY TO JUST SHOW UP LIKE THIS, KARA.

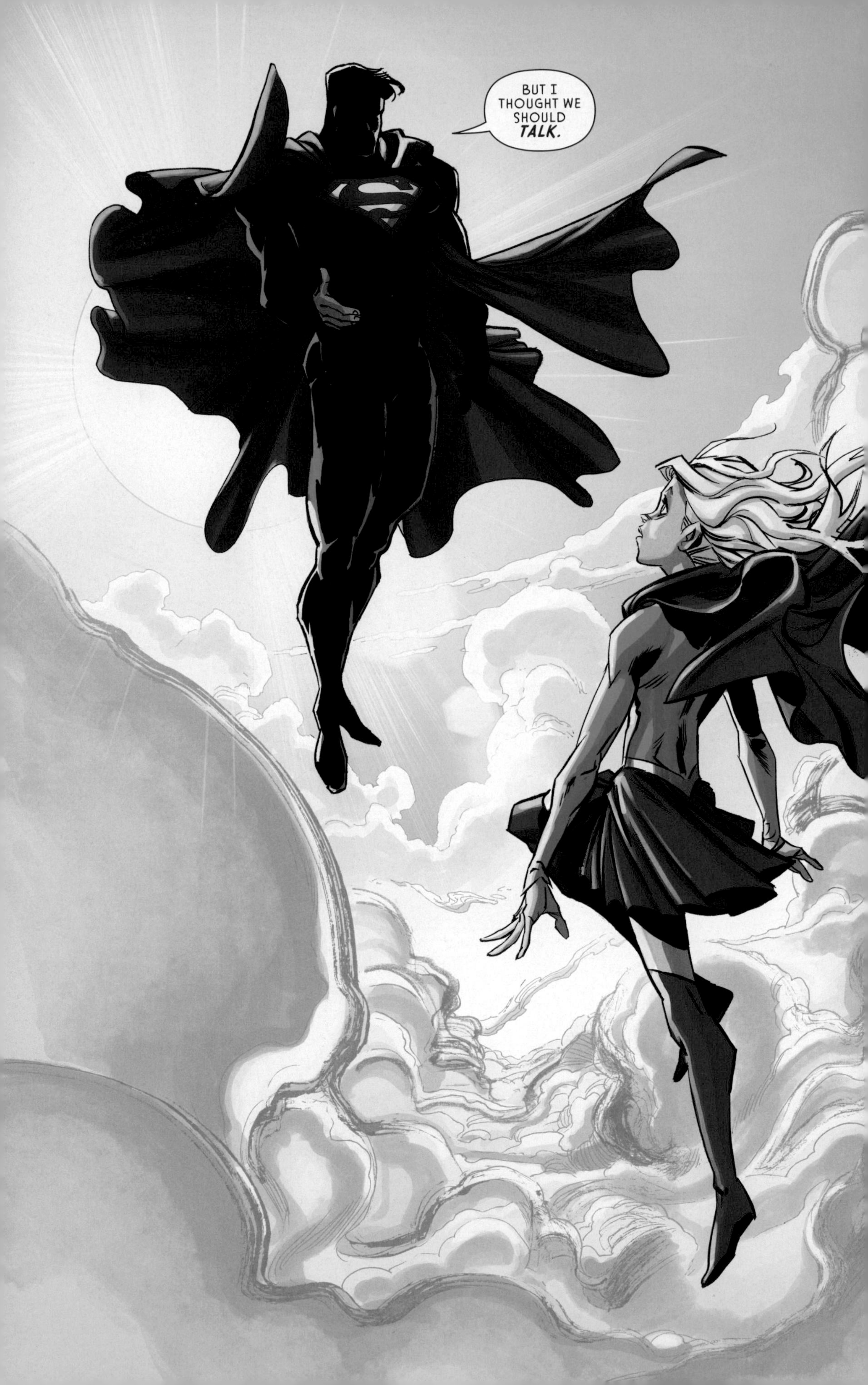
BUT I THOUGHT WE SHOULD *TALK.*

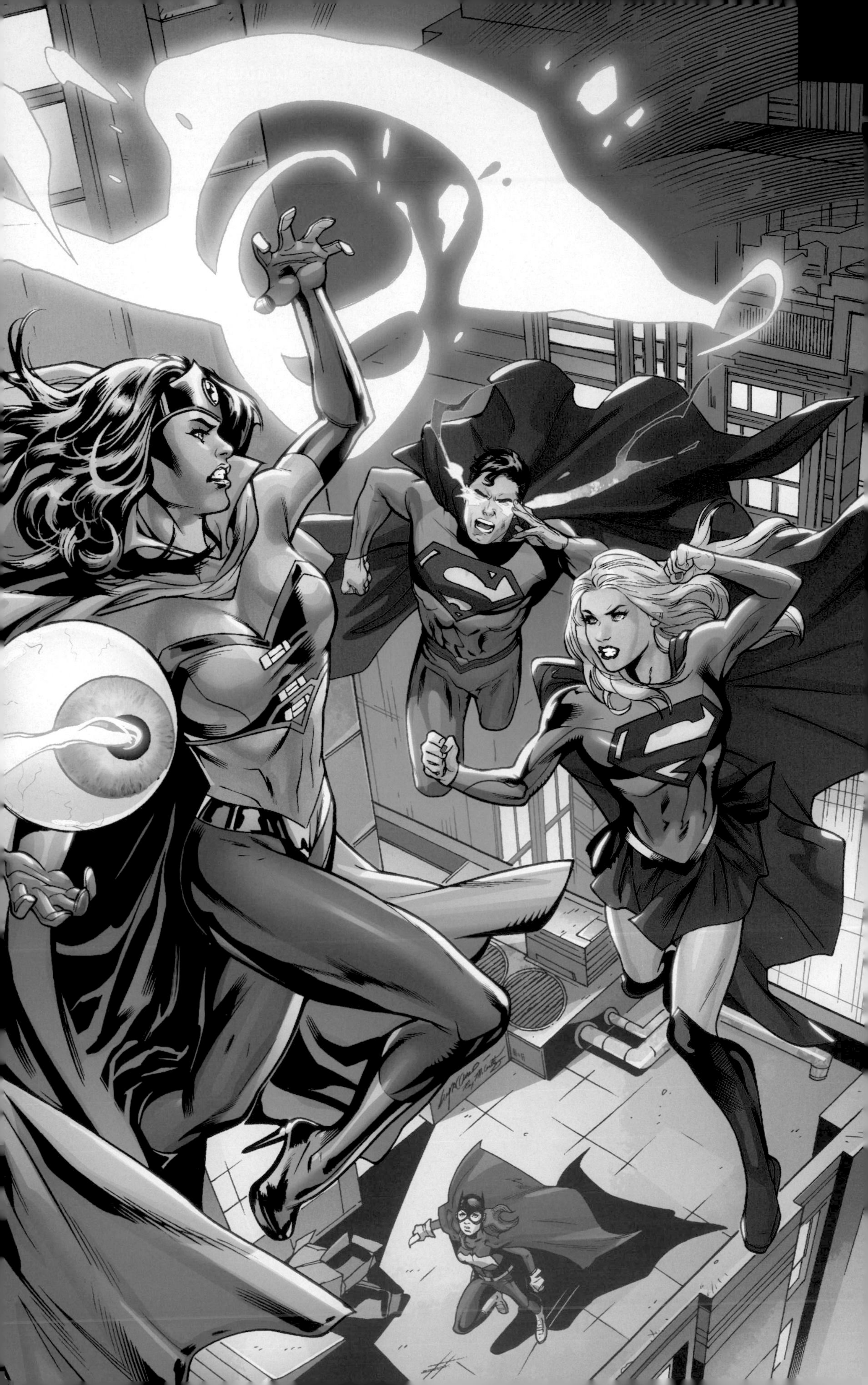

"FAMILY OF TOMORROW"

STEVE ORLANDO writer * MATIAS BERGARA artist * MICHAEL ATIYEH colorist
cover by EMANUELA LUPACCHINO, RAY MCCARTHY and HI-FI

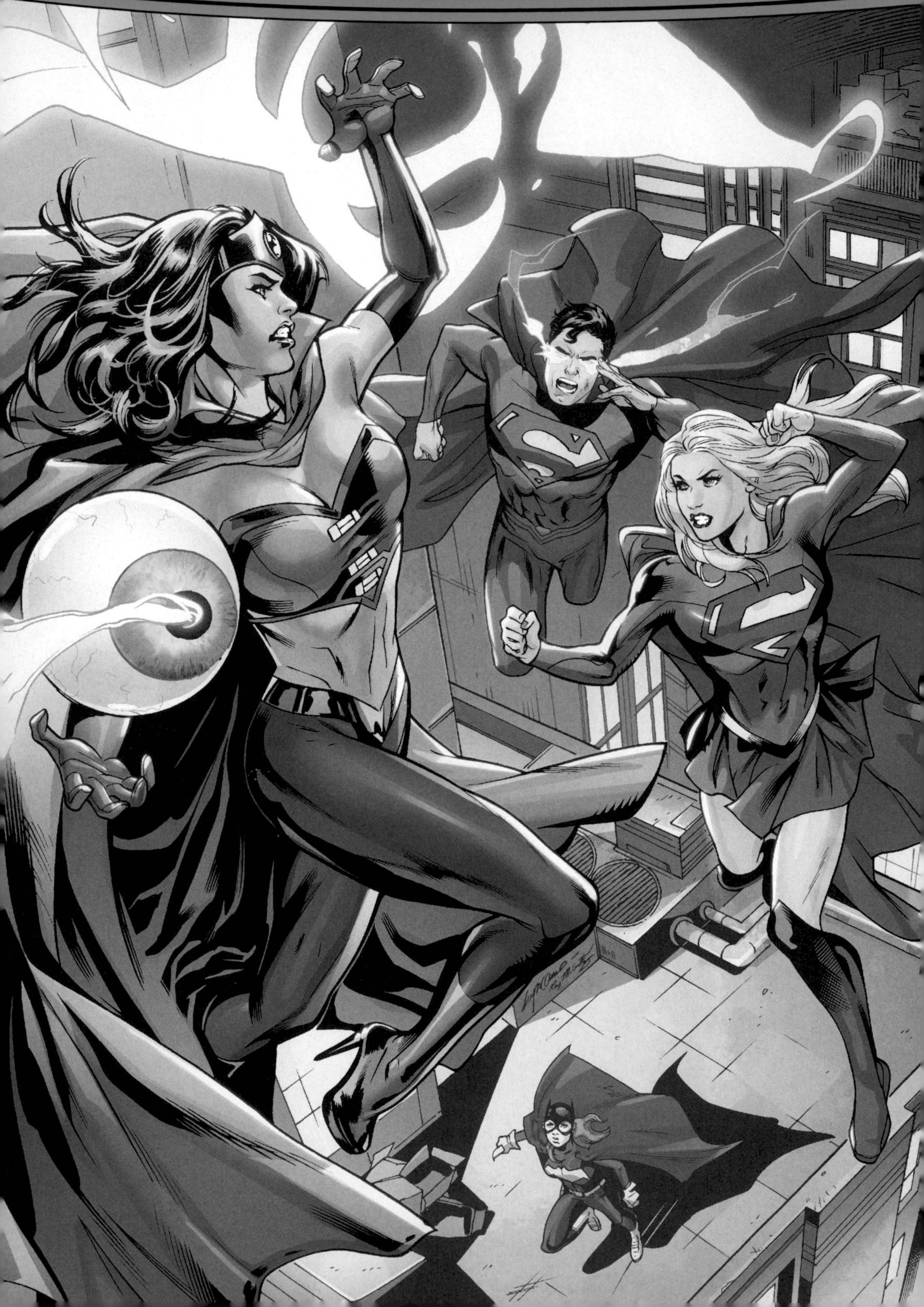

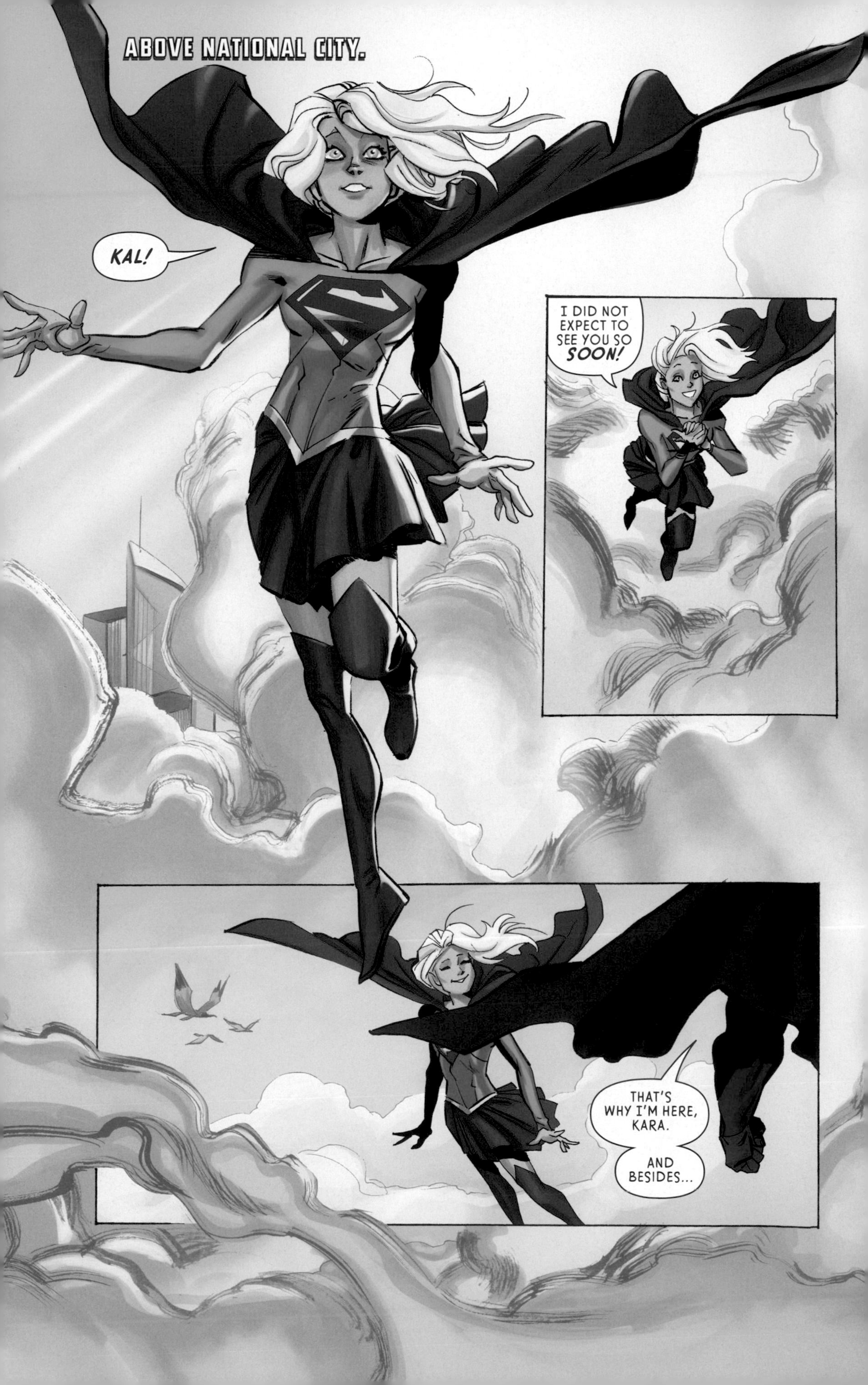
ABOVE NATIONAL CITY.
KAL!
I DID NOT EXPECT TO SEE YOU SO SOON!
THAT'S WHY I'M HERE, KARA.
AND BESIDES...

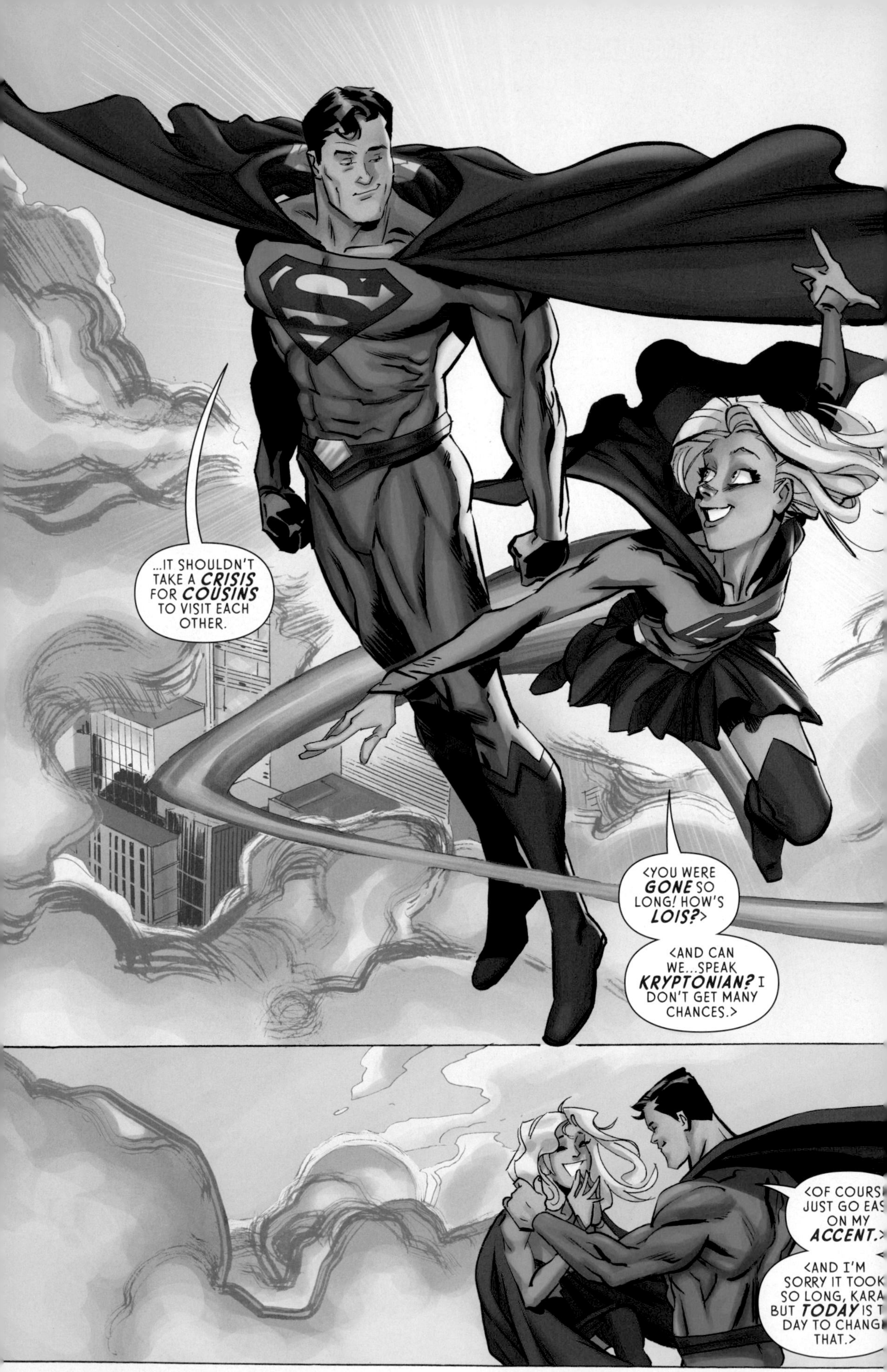
...IT SHOULDN'T TAKE A CRISIS FOR COUSINS TO VISIT EACH OTHER.
<YOU WERE GONE SO LONG! HOW'S LOIS?>
<AND CAN WE...SPEAK KRYPTONIAN? I DON'T GET MANY CHANCES.>
<OF COURS JUST GO EAS ON MY ACCENT.>
<AND I'M SORRY IT TOOK SO LONG, KARA BUT TODAY IS T DAY TO CHANG THAT.>

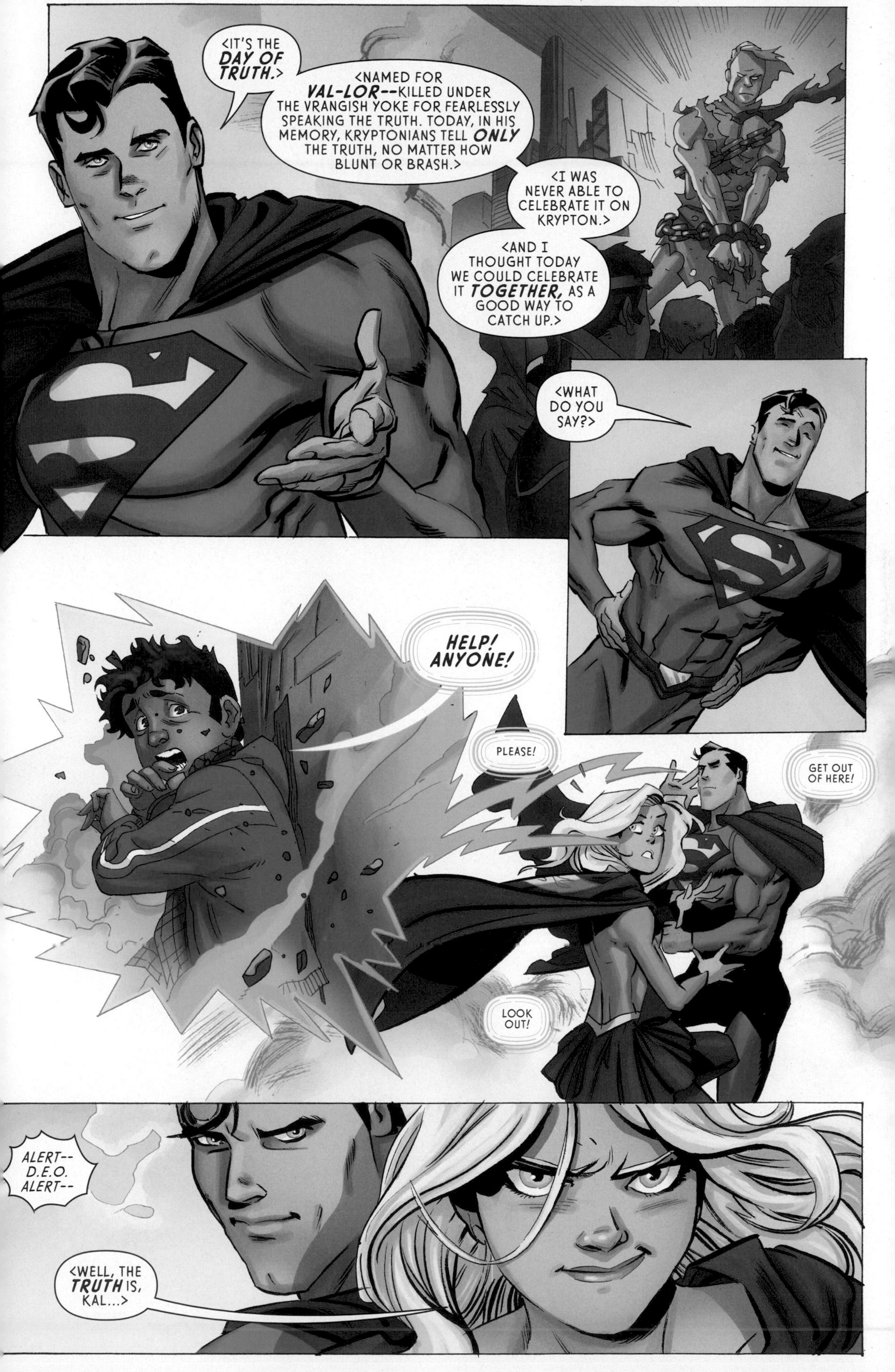
<IT'S THE DAY OF TRUTH.>
<NAMED FOR VAL-LOR--KILLED UNDER THE VRANGISH YOKE FOR FEARLESSLY SPEAKING THE TRUTH. TODAY, IN HIS MEMORY, KRYPTONIANS TELL ONLY THE TRUTH, NO MATTER HOW BLUNT OR BRASH.>
<I WAS NEVER ABLE TO CELEBRATE IT ON KRYPTON.>
<AND I THOUGHT TODAY WE COULD CELEBRATE IT TOGETHER, AS A GOOD WAY TO CATCH UP.>
<WHAT DO YOU SAY?>
HELP! ANYONE!
PLEASE!
GET OUT OF HERE!
LOOK OUT!
ALERT-- D.E.O. ALERT--
<WELL, THE TRUTH IS, KAL...>

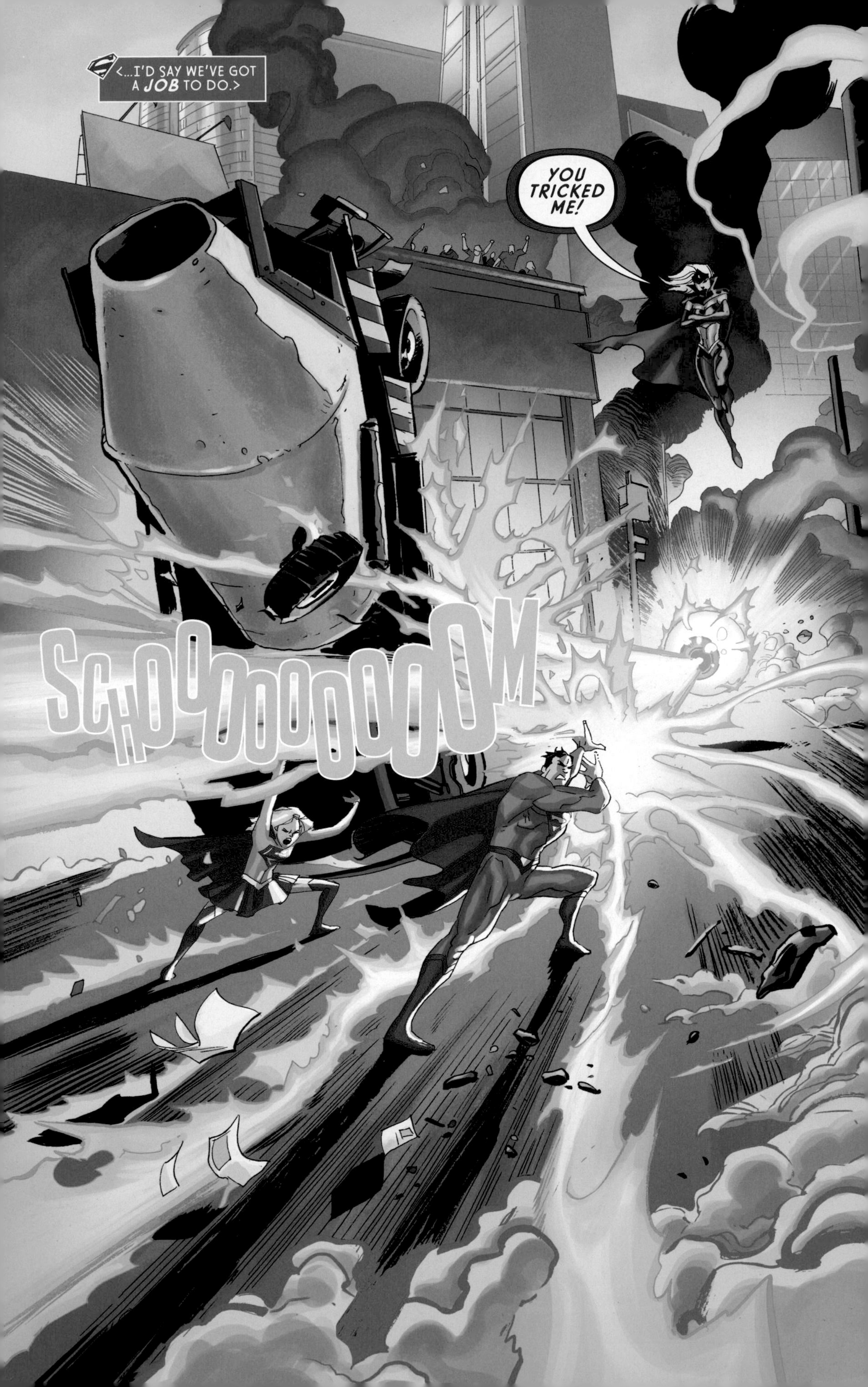
<...I'D SAY WE'VE GOT A JOB TO DO.>
YOU TRICKED ME!
SCHOOOOOOOOOOM

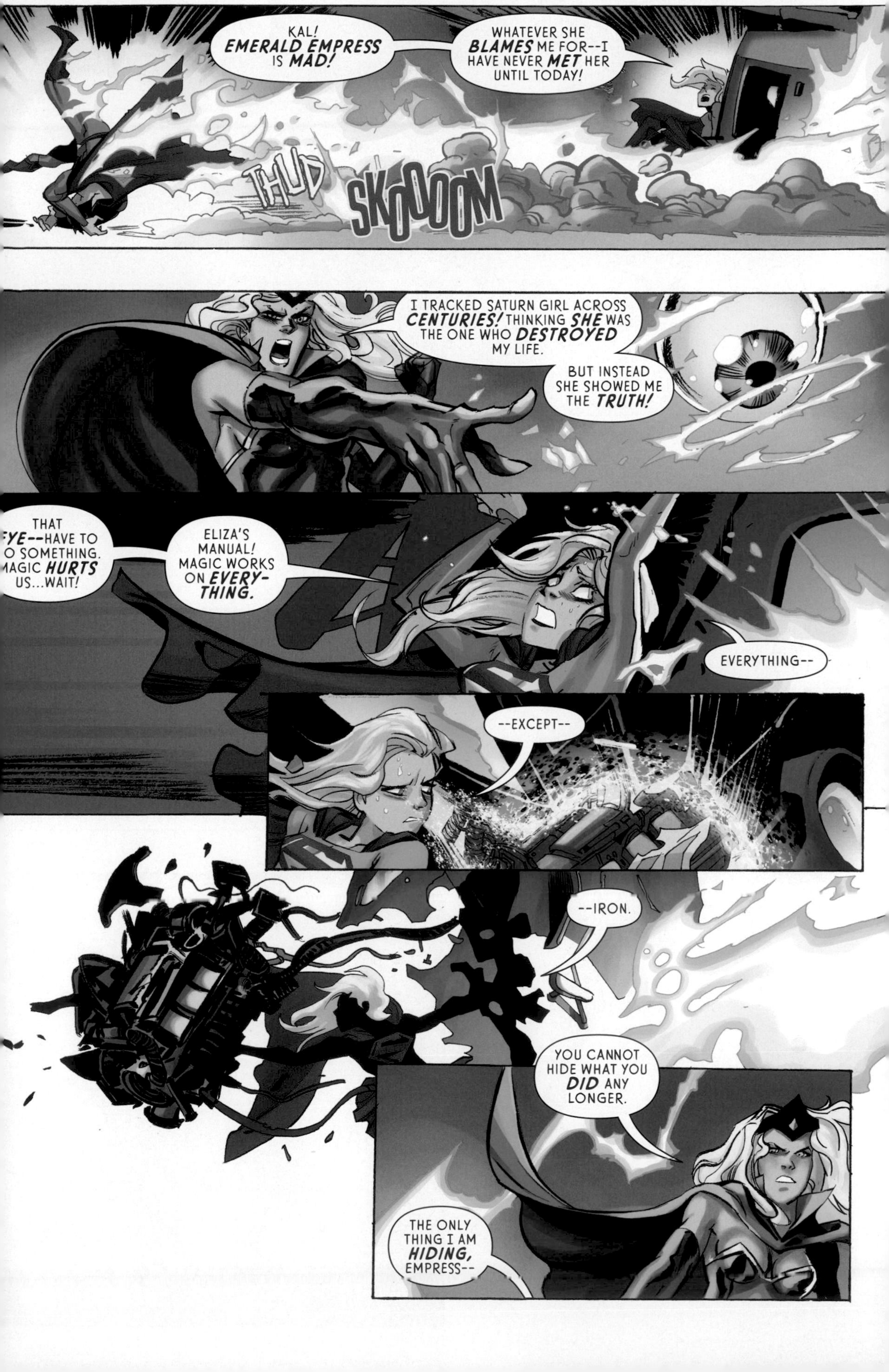
KAL! EMERALD EMPRESS IS MAD!
WHATEVER SHE BLAMES ME FOR--I HAVE NEVER MET HER UNTIL TODAY!
THUD
SKOOOOM
I TRACKED SATURN GIRL ACROSS CENTURIES! THINKING SHE WAS THE ONE WHO DESTROYED MY LIFE.
BUT INSTEAD SHE SHOWED ME THE TRUTH!
THAT EYE--HAVE TO DO SOMETHING. MAGIC HURTS US...WAIT!
ELIZA'S MANUAL! MAGIC WORKS ON EVERYTHING.
EVERYTHING--
--EXCEPT--
--IRON.
YOU CANNOT HIDE WHAT YOU DID ANY LONGER.
THE ONLY THING I AM HIDING, EMPRESS--

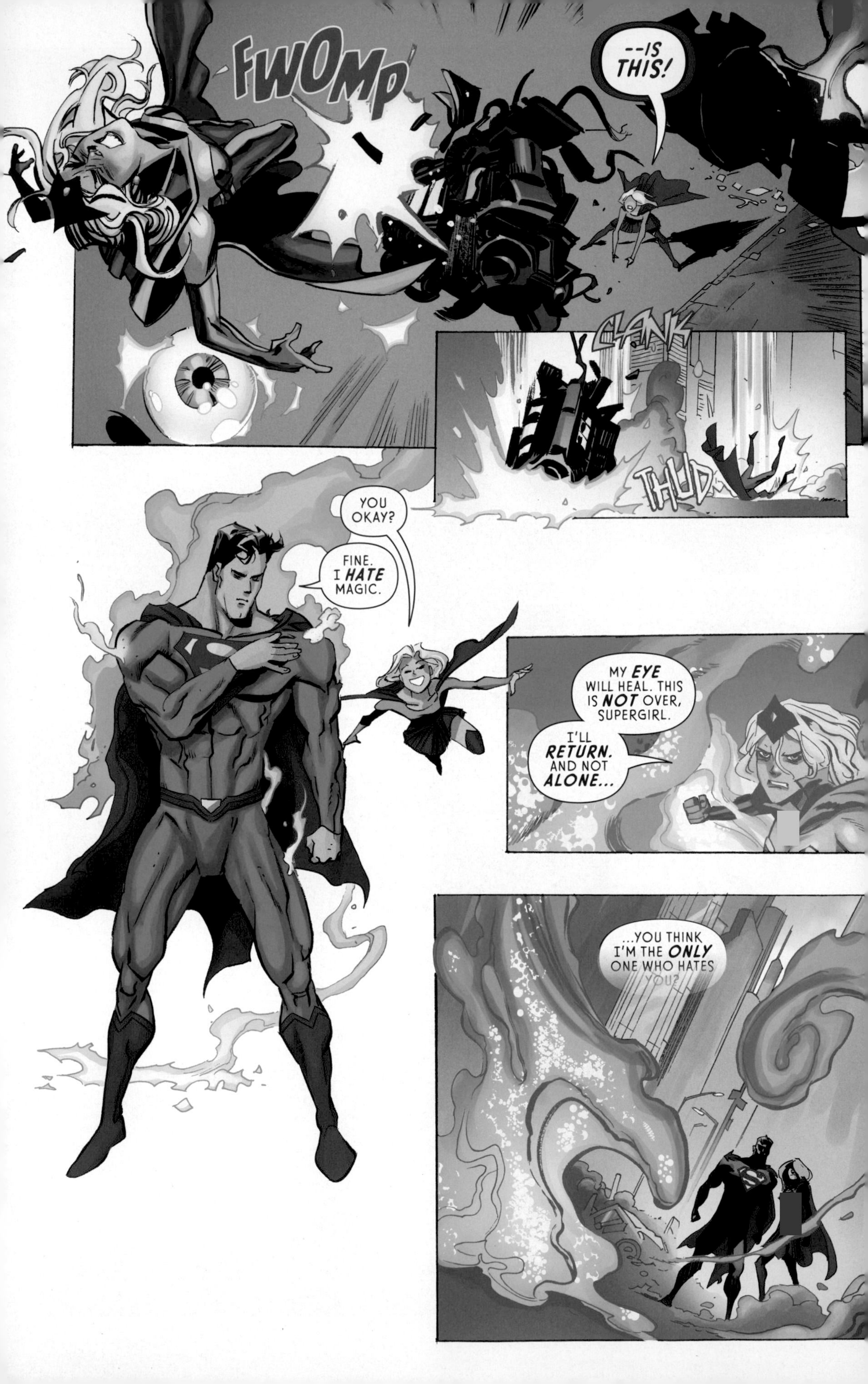
FWOMP
--IS THIS!
CLANK
THUD
YOU OKAY?
FINE. I HATE MAGIC.
MY EYE WILL HEAL. THIS IS NOT OVER, SUPERGIRL.
I'LL RETURN. AND NOT ALONE...
...YOU THINK I'M THE ONLY ONE WHO HATES YOU?

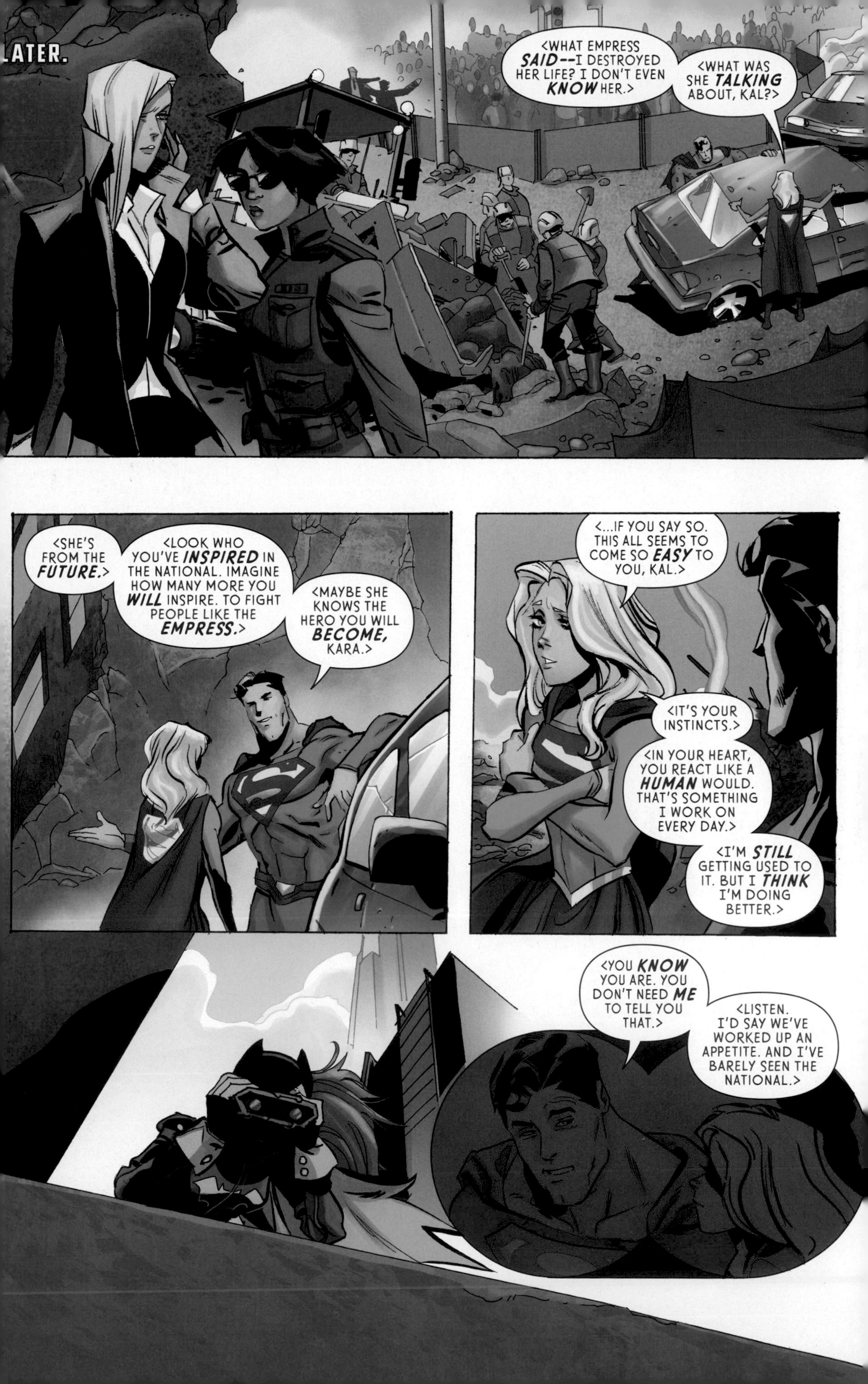
LATER.
<WHAT EMPRESS SAID--I DESTROYED HER LIFE? I DON'T EVEN KNOW HER.>
<WHAT WAS SHE TALKING ABOUT, KAL?>
<SHE'S FROM THE FUTURE.>
<LOOK WHO YOU'VE INSPIRED IN THE NATIONAL. IMAGINE HOW MANY MORE YOU WILL INSPIRE. TO FIGHT PEOPLE LIKE THE EMPRESS.>
<MAYBE SHE KNOWS THE HERO YOU WILL BECOME, KARA.>
<...IF YOU SAY SO. THIS ALL SEEMS TO COME SO EASY TO YOU, KAL.>
<IT'S YOUR INSTINCTS.>
<IN YOUR HEART, YOU REACT LIKE A HUMAN WOULD. THAT'S SOMETHING I WORK ON EVERY DAY.>
<I'M STILL GETTING USED TO IT. BUT I THINK I'M DOING BETTER.>
<YOU KNOW YOU ARE. YOU DON'T NEED ME TO TELL YOU THAT.>
<LISTEN. I'D SAY WE'VE WORKED UP AN APPETITE. AND I'VE BARELY SEEN THE NATIONAL.>

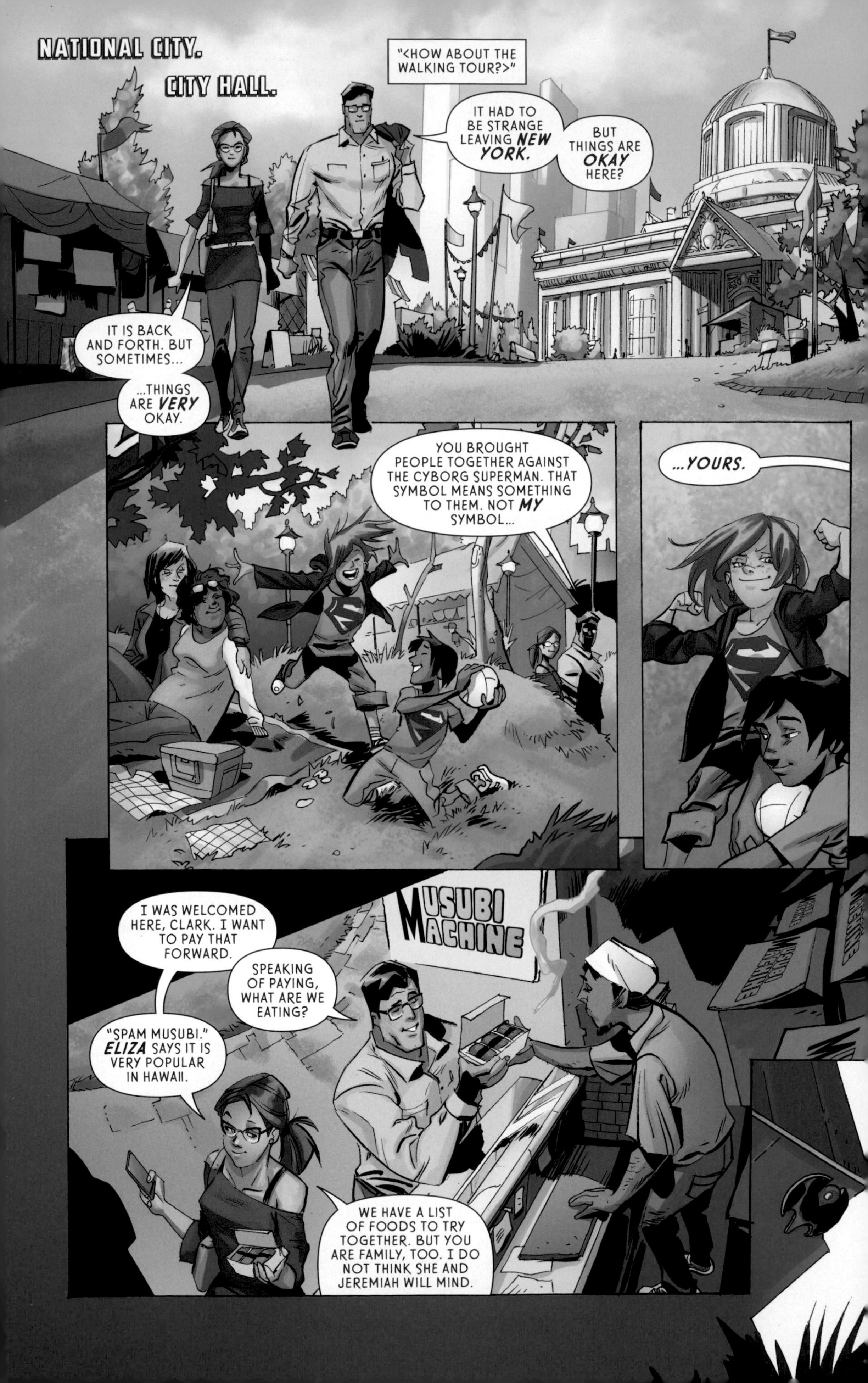
NATIONAL CITY.
CITY HALL.
"<HOW ABOUT THE WALKING TOUR?>"
IT HAD TO BE STRANGE LEAVING NEW YORK.
BUT THINGS ARE OKAY HERE?
IT IS BACK AND FORTH. BUT SOMETIMES...
...THINGS ARE VERY OKAY.
YOU BROUGHT PEOPLE TOGETHER AGAINST THE CYBORG SUPERMAN. THAT SYMBOL MEANS SOMETHING TO THEM. NOT MY SYMBOL...
...YOURS.
MUSUBI MACHINE
I WAS WELCOMED HERE, CLARK. I WANT TO PAY THAT FORWARD.
SPEAKING OF PAYING, WHAT ARE WE EATING?
"SPAM MUSUBI." ELIZA SAYS IT IS VERY POPULAR IN HAWAII.
WE HAVE A LIST OF FOODS TO TRY TOGETHER. BUT YOU ARE FAMILY, TOO. I DO NOT THINK SHE AND JEREMIAH WILL MIND.

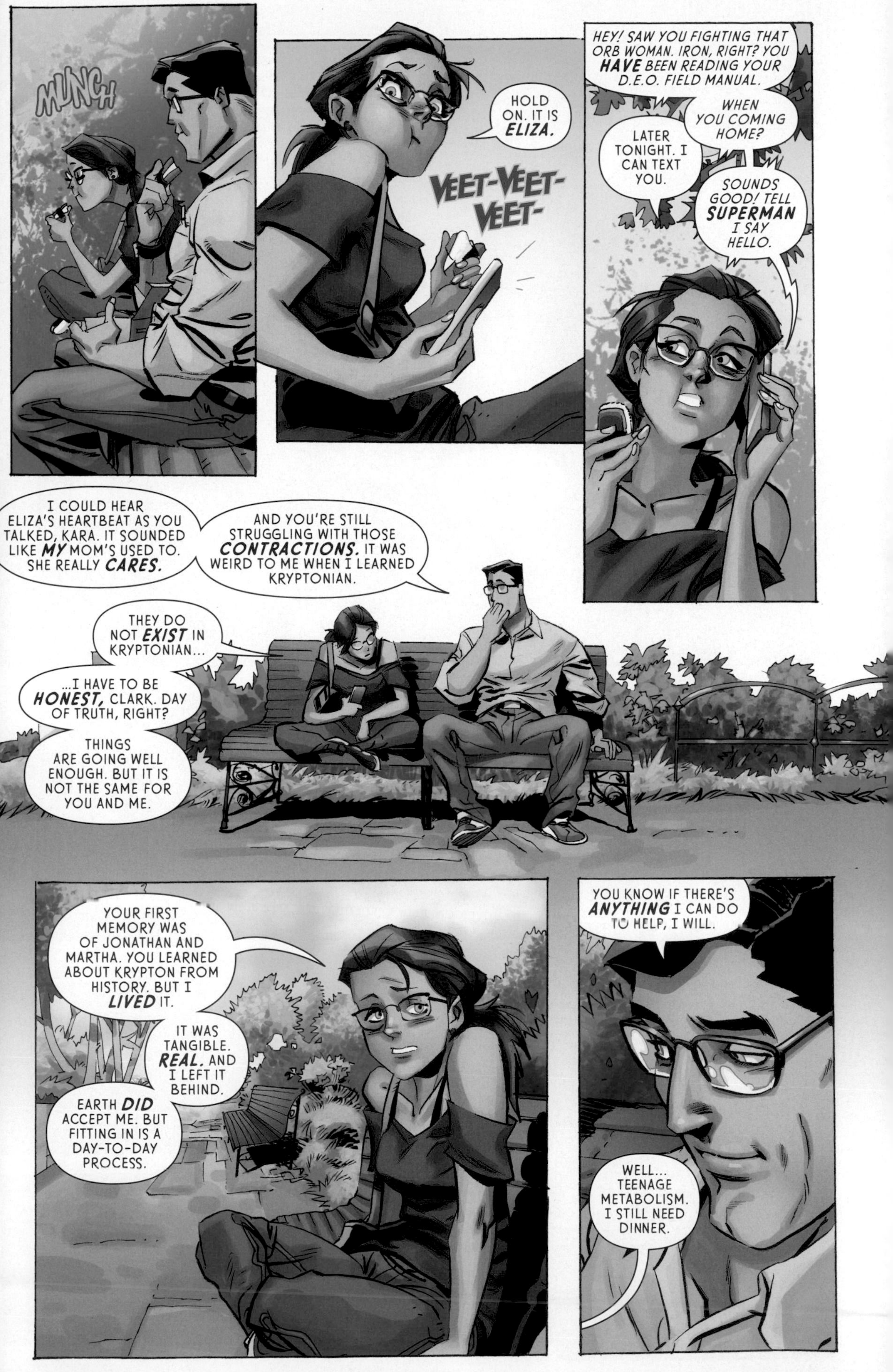
MUNCH
HOLD ON. IT IS ELIZA.
VEET-VEET-VEET-
HEY! SAW YOU FIGHTING THAT ORB WOMAN. IRON, RIGHT? YOU HAVE BEEN READING YOUR D.E.O. FIELD MANUAL.
WHEN YOU COMING HOME?
LATER TONIGHT. I CAN TEXT YOU.
SOUNDS GOOD! TELL SUPERMAN I SAY HELLO.
I COULD HEAR ELIZA'S HEARTBEAT AS YOU TALKED, KARA. IT SOUNDED LIKE MY MOM'S USED TO. SHE REALLY CARES.
AND YOU'RE STILL STRUGGLING WITH THOSE CONTRACTIONS. IT WAS WEIRD TO ME WHEN I LEARNED KRYPTONIAN.
THEY DO NOT EXIST IN KRYPTONIAN...
...I HAVE TO BE HONEST, CLARK. DAY OF TRUTH, RIGHT?
THINGS ARE GOING WELL ENOUGH. BUT IT IS NOT THE SAME FOR YOU AND ME.
YOUR FIRST MEMORY WAS OF JONATHAN AND MARTHA. YOU LEARNED ABOUT KRYPTON FROM HISTORY. BUT I LIVED IT.
IT WAS TANGIBLE. REAL. AND I LEFT IT BEHIND.
EARTH DID ACCEPT ME. BUT FITTING IN IS A DAY-TO-DAY PROCESS.
YOU KNOW IF THERE'S ANYTHING I CAN DO TO HELP, I WILL.
WELL... TEENAGE METABOLISM. I STILL NEED DINNER.

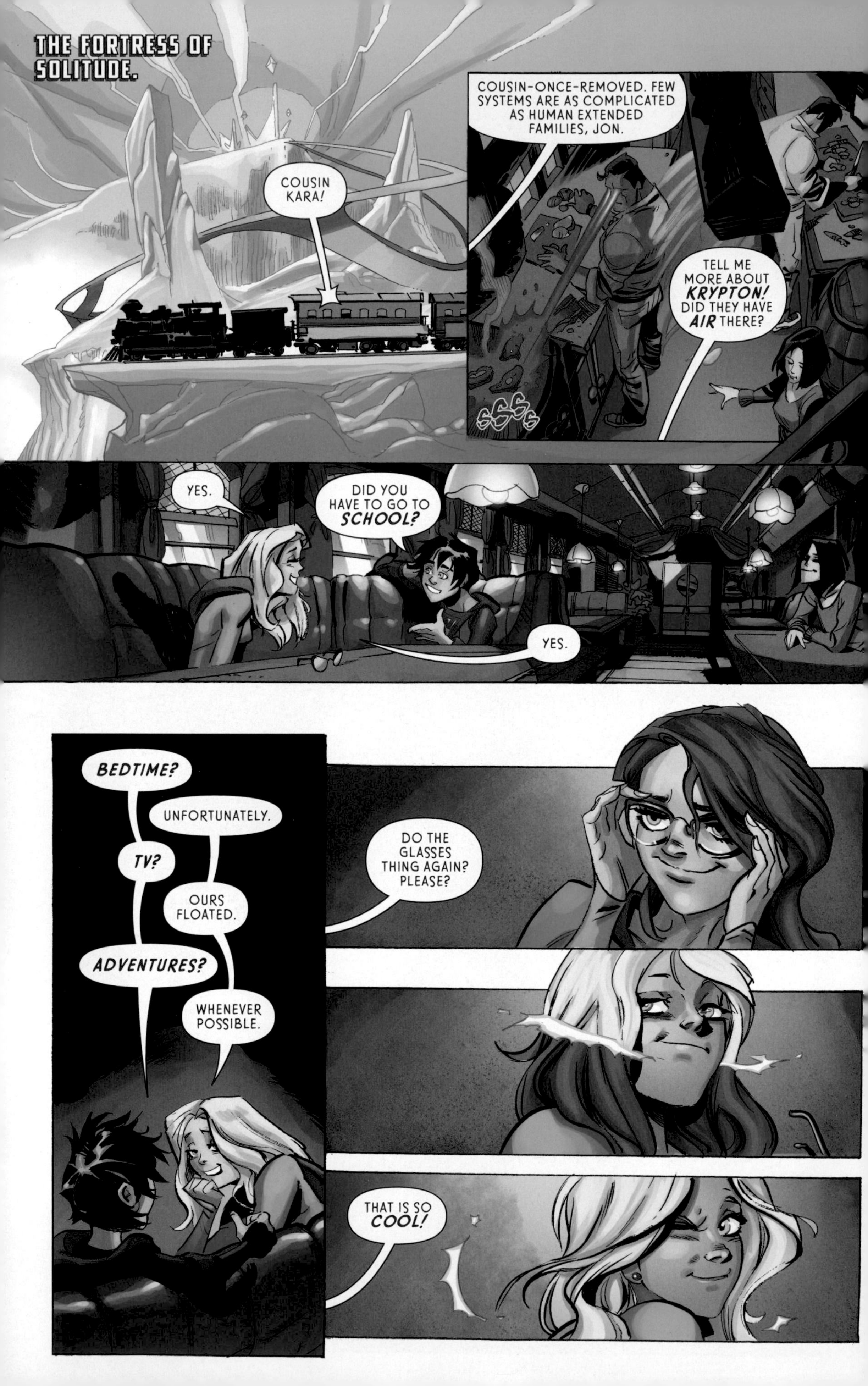
THE FORTRESS OF SOLITUDE.
COUSIN KARA!
COUSIN-ONCE-REMOVED. FEW SYSTEMS ARE AS COMPLICATED AS HUMAN EXTENDED FAMILIES, JON.
TELL ME MORE ABOUT KRYPTON! DID THEY HAVE AIR THERE?
YES.
DID YOU HAVE TO GO TO SCHOOL?
YES.
BEDTIME?
UNFORTUNATELY.
TV?
OURS FLOATED.
ADVENTURES?
WHENEVER POSSIBLE.
DO THE GLASSES THING AGAIN? PLEASE?
THAT IS SO COOL!

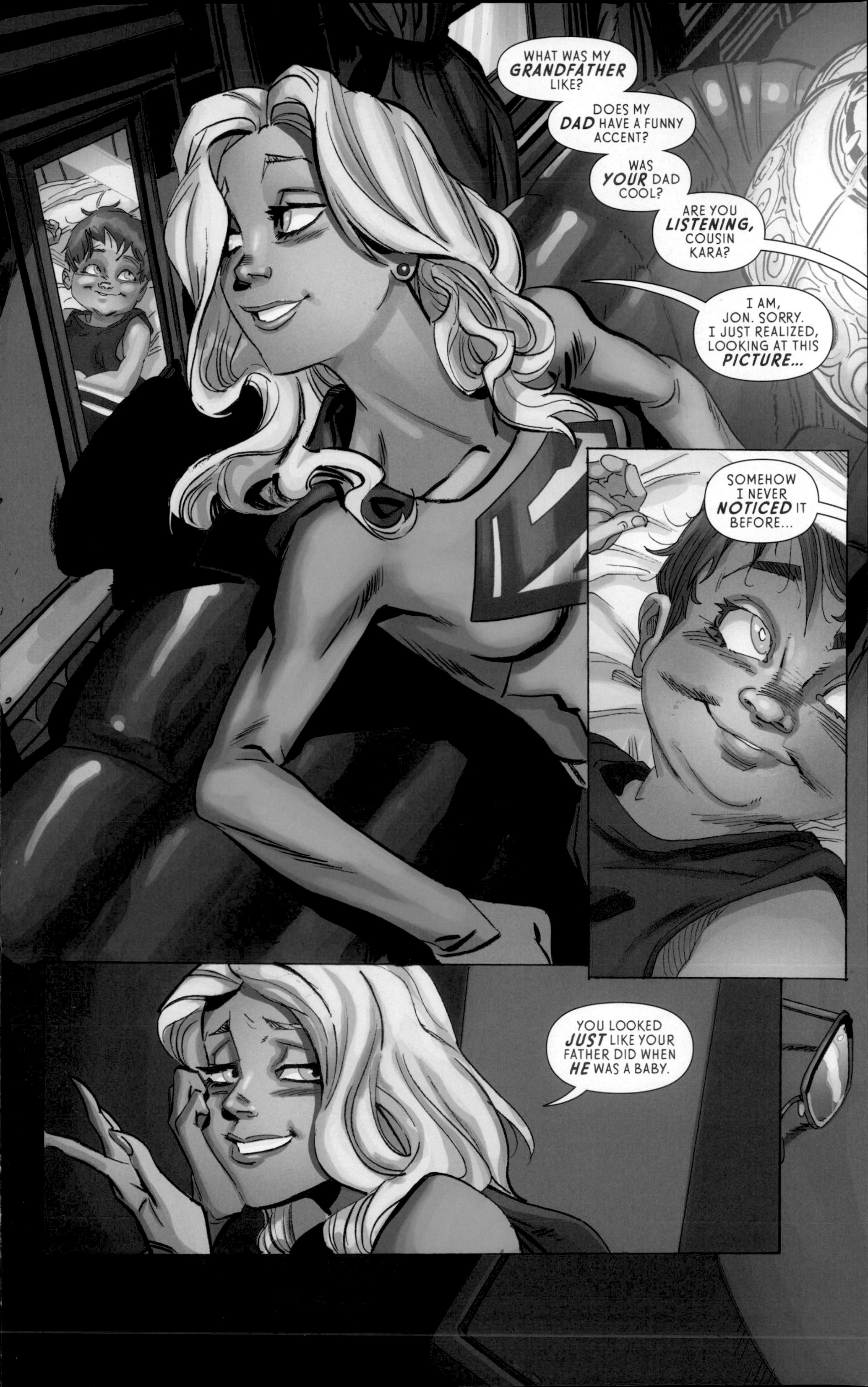
WHAT WAS MY GRANDFATHER LIKE?
DOES MY DAD HAVE A FUNNY ACCENT?
WAS YOUR DAD COOL?
ARE YOU LISTENING, COUSIN KARA?
I AM, JON. SORRY. I JUST REALIZED, LOOKING AT THIS PICTURE...
SOMEHOW I NEVER NOTICED IT BEFORE...
YOU LOOKED JUST LIKE YOUR FATHER DID WHEN HE WAS A BABY.

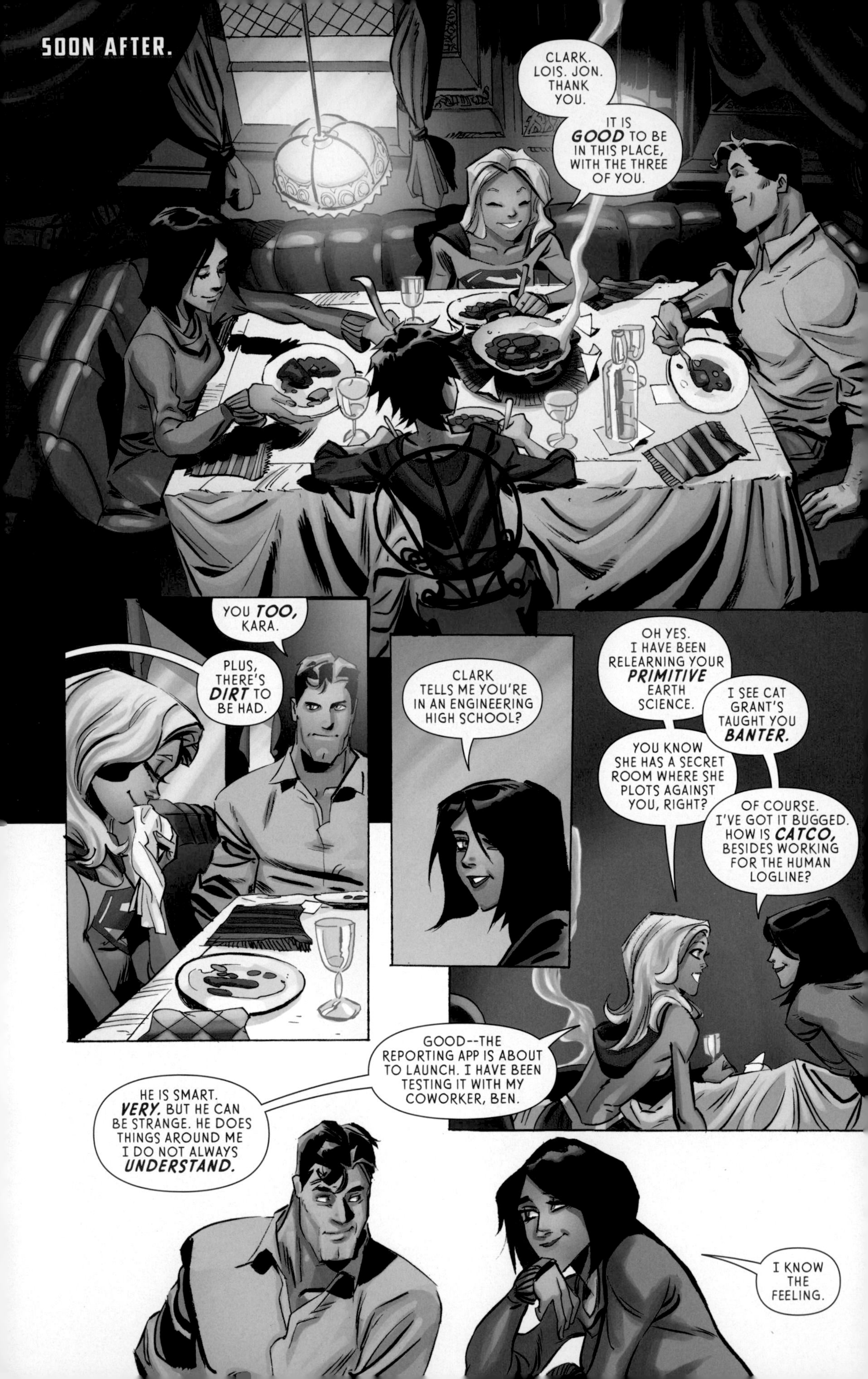

SOON AFTER.
CLARK. LOIS. JON. THANK YOU.
IT IS GOOD TO BE IN THIS PLACE, WITH THE THREE OF YOU.
YOU TOO, KARA.
PLUS, THERE'S DIRT TO BE HAD.
CLARK TELLS ME YOU'RE IN AN ENGINEERING HIGH SCHOOL?
OH YES. I HAVE BEEN RELEARNING YOUR PRIMITIVE EARTH SCIENCE.
I SEE CAT GRANT'S TAUGHT YOU BANTER.
YOU KNOW SHE HAS A SECRET ROOM WHERE SHE PLOTS AGAINST YOU, RIGHT?
OF COURSE. I'VE GOT IT BUGGED. HOW IS CATCO, BESIDES WORKING FOR THE HUMAN LOGLINE?
GOOD--THE REPORTING APP IS ABOUT TO LAUNCH. I HAVE BEEN TESTING IT WITH MY COWORKER, BEN.
HE IS SMART. VERY. BUT HE CAN BE STRANGE. HE DOES THINGS AROUND ME I DO NOT ALWAYS UNDERSTAND.
I KNOW THE FEELING.

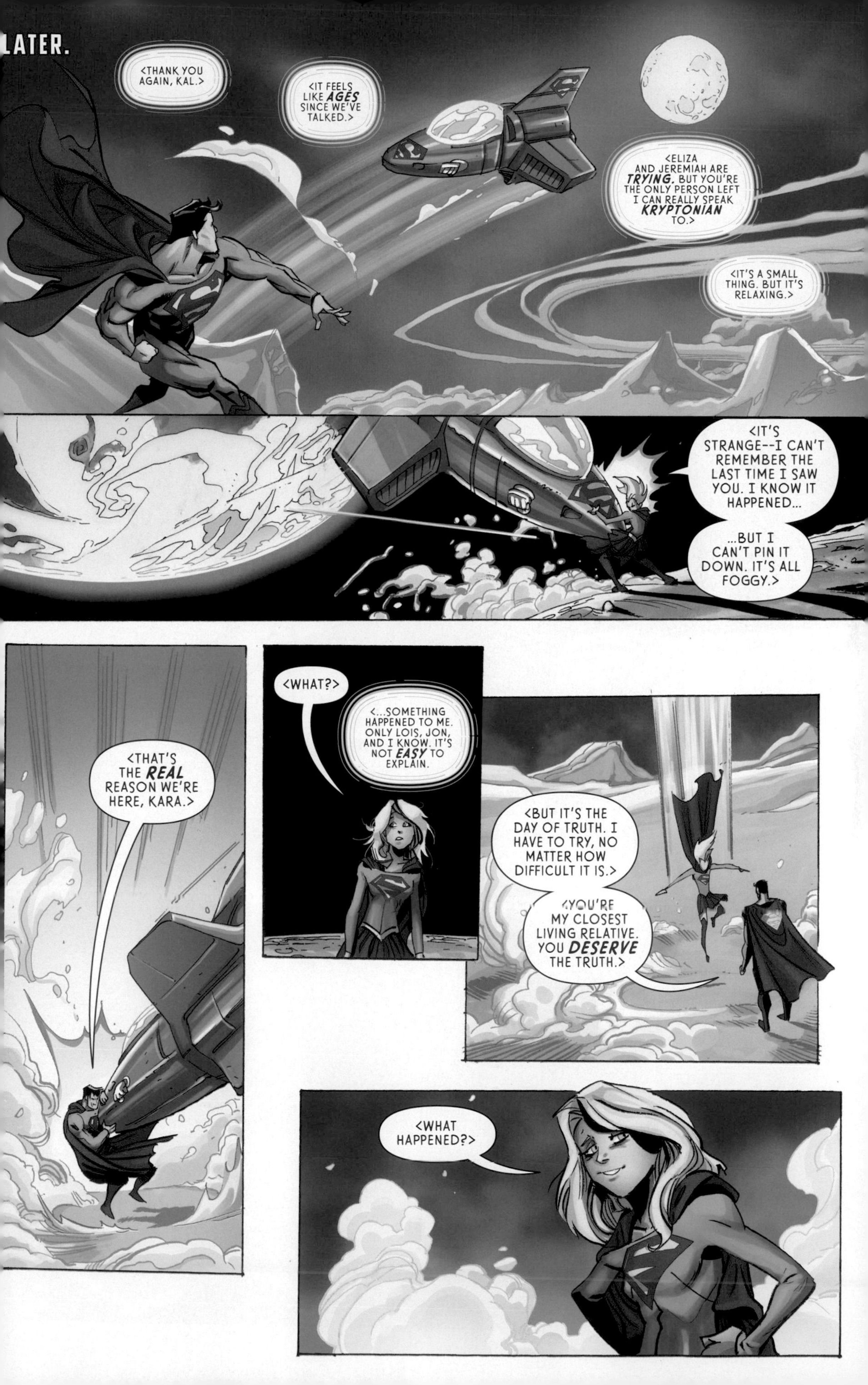
LATER.
<THANK YOU AGAIN, KAL.>
<IT FEELS LIKE AGES SINCE WE'VE TALKED.>
<ELIZA AND JEREMIAH ARE TRYING. BUT YOU'RE THE ONLY PERSON LEFT I CAN REALLY SPEAK KRYPTONIAN TO.>
<IT'S A SMALL THING. BUT IT'S RELAXING.>
<IT'S STRANGE--I CAN'T REMEMBER THE LAST TIME I SAW YOU. I KNOW IT HAPPENED...
...BUT I CAN'T PIN IT DOWN. IT'S ALL FOGGY.>
<THAT'S THE REAL REASON WE'RE HERE, KARA.>
<WHAT?>
<...SOMETHING HAPPENED TO ME. ONLY LOIS, JON, AND I KNOW. IT'S NOT EASY TO EXPLAIN.
<BUT IT'S THE DAY OF TRUTH. I HAVE TO TRY, NO MATTER HOW DIFFICULT IT IS.>
<YOU'RE MY CLOSEST LIVING RELATIVE. YOU DESERVE THE TRUTH.>
<WHAT HAPPENED?>

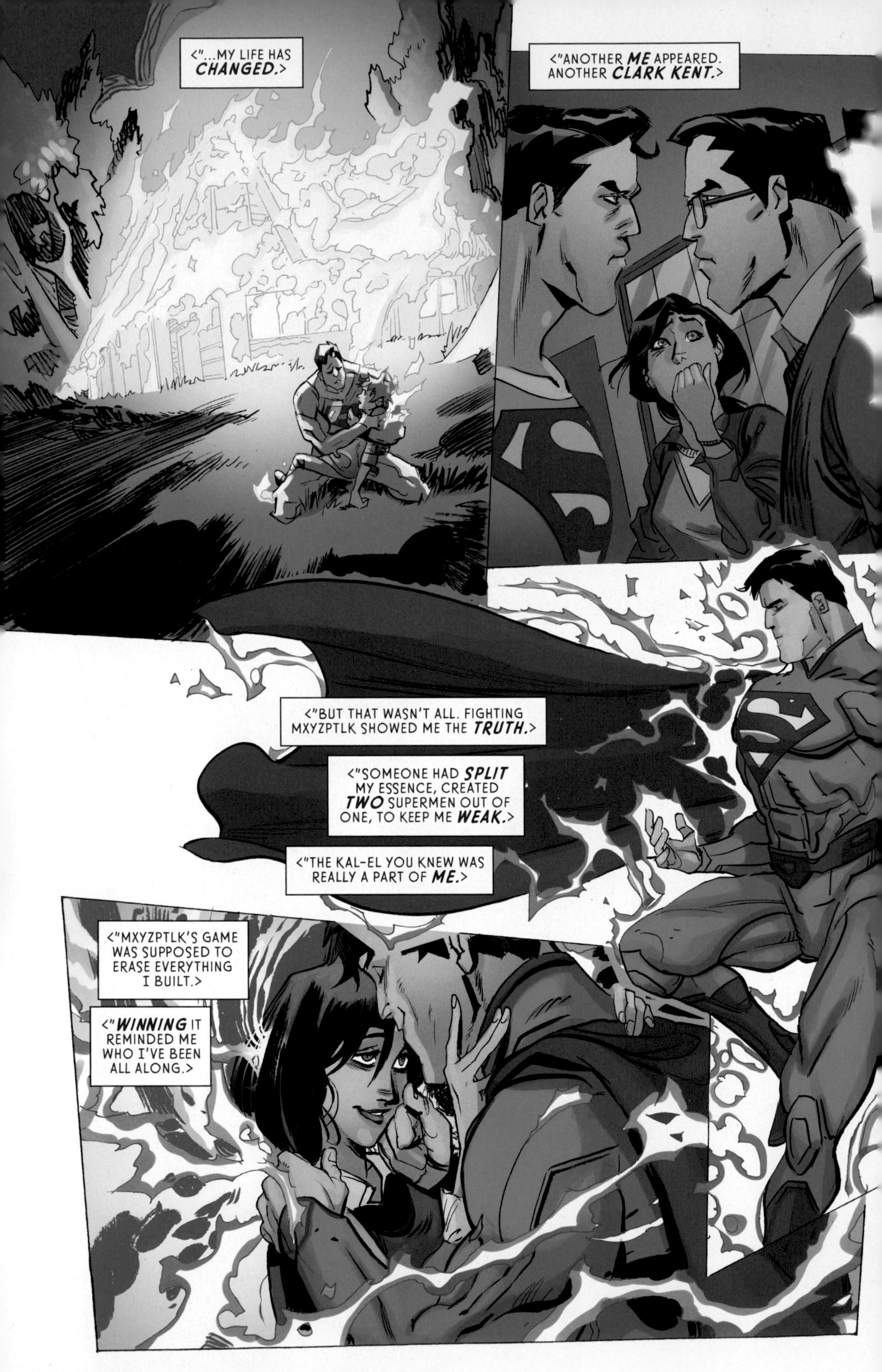

<"...MY LIFE HAS CHANGED.>
<"ANOTHER ME APPEARED. ANOTHER CLARK KENT.>
<"BUT THAT WASN'T ALL. FIGHTING MXYZPTLK SHOWED ME THE TRUTH.>
<"SOMEONE HAD SPLIT MY ESSENCE, CREATED TWO SUPERMEN OUT OF ONE, TO KEEP ME WEAK.>
<"THE KAL-EL YOU KNEW WAS REALLY A PART OF ME.>
<"MXYZPTLK'S GAME WAS SUPPOSED TO ERASE EVERYTHING I BUILT.>
<"WINNING IT REMINDED ME WHO I'VE BEEN ALL ALONG.>

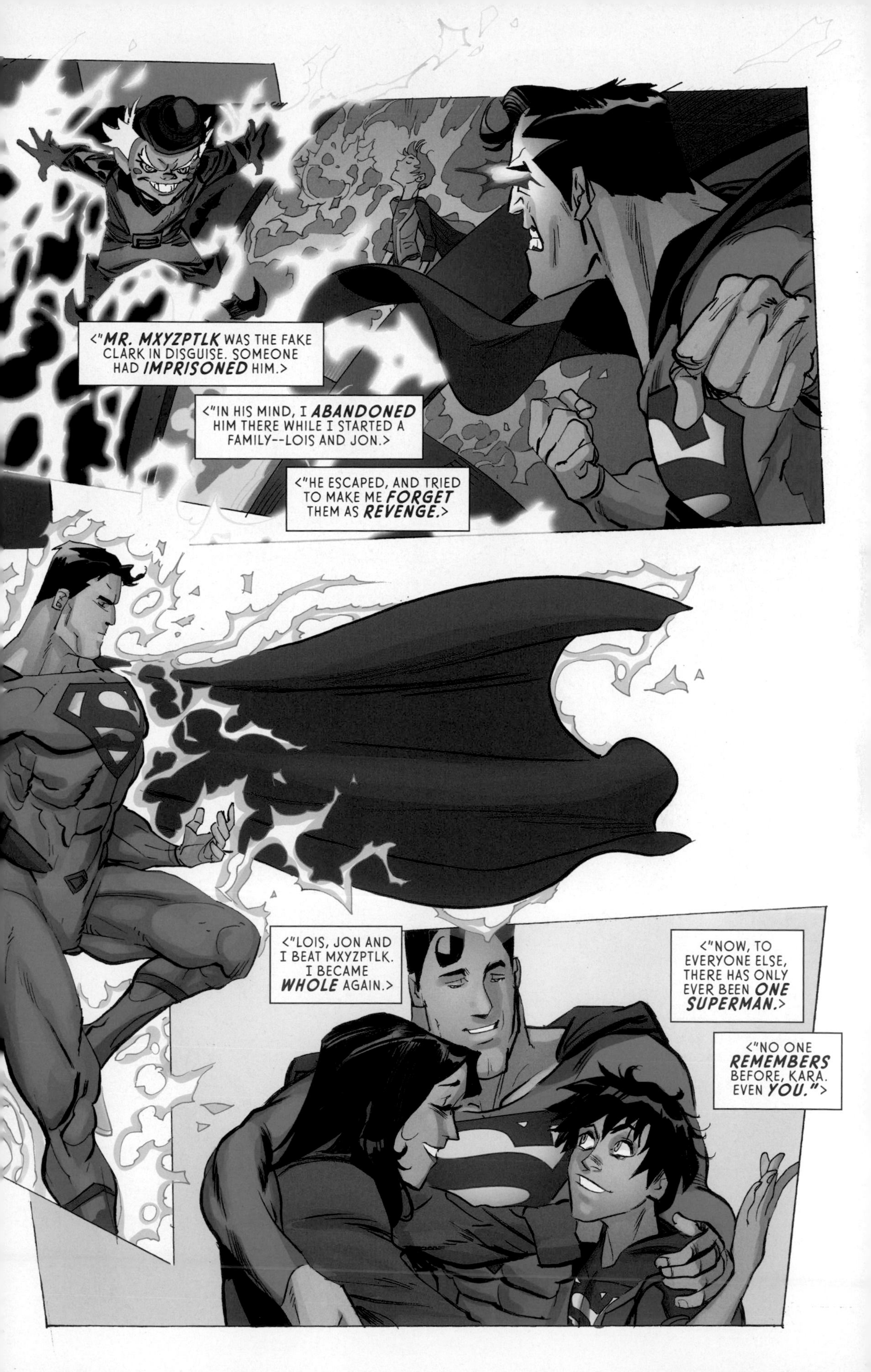
<"MR. MXYZPTLK WAS THE FAKE CLARK IN DISGUISE. SOMEONE HAD IMPRISONED HIM.>
<"IN HIS MIND, I ABANDONED HIM THERE WHILE I STARTED A FAMILY--LOIS AND JON.>
<"HE ESCAPED, AND TRIED TO MAKE ME FORGET THEM AS REVENGE.>
<"LOIS, JON AND I BEAT MXYZPTLK. I BECAME WHOLE AGAIN.>
<"NOW, TO EVERYONE ELSE, THERE HAS ONLY EVER BEEN ONE SUPERMAN.>
<"NO ONE REMEMBERS BEFORE, KARA. EVEN YOU.">

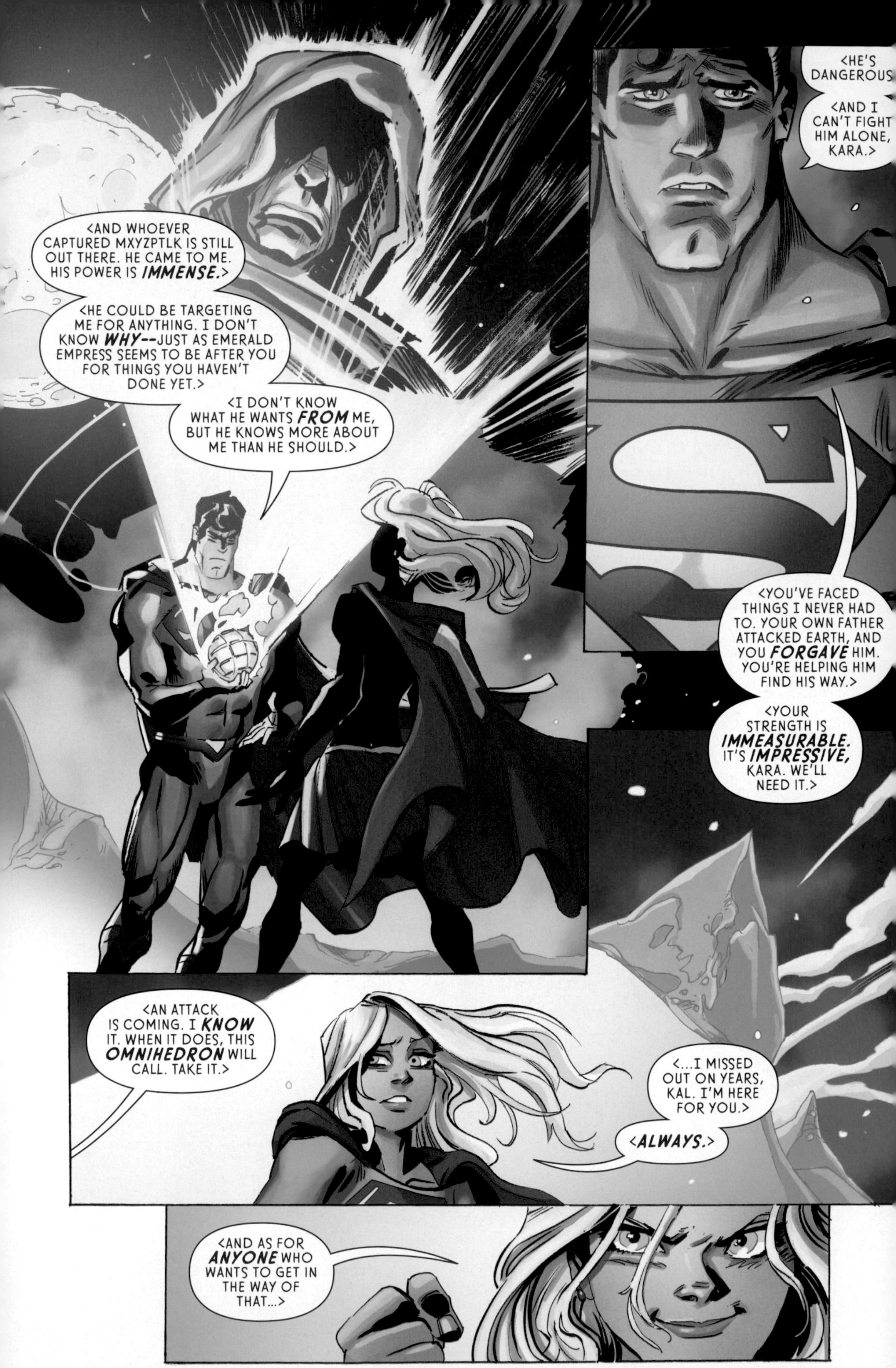
<HE'S DANGEROUS
<AND I CAN'T FIGHT HIM ALONE, KARA.>
<AND WHOEVER CAPTURED MXYZPTLK IS STILL OUT THERE. HE CAME TO ME. HIS POWER IS *IMMENSE.*>
<HE COULD BE TARGETING ME FOR ANYTHING. I DON'T KNOW *WHY*--JUST AS EMERALD EMPRESS SEEMS TO BE AFTER YOU FOR THINGS YOU HAVEN'T DONE YET.>
<I DON'T KNOW WHAT HE WANTS *FROM* ME, BUT HE KNOWS MORE ABOUT ME THAN HE SHOULD.>
<YOU'VE FACED THINGS I NEVER HAD TO. YOUR OWN FATHER ATTACKED EARTH, AND YOU *FORGAVE* HIM. YOU'RE HELPING HIM FIND HIS WAY.>
<YOUR STRENGTH IS *IMMEASURABLE.* IT'S *IMPRESSIVE,* KARA. WE'LL NEED IT.>
<AN ATTACK IS COMING. I *KNOW* IT. WHEN IT DOES, THIS *OMNIHEDRON* WILL CALL. TAKE IT.>
<...I MISSED OUT ON YEARS, KAL. I'M HERE FOR YOU.>
<*ALWAYS.*>
<AND AS FOR *ANYONE* WHO WANTS TO GET IN THE WAY OF THAT...>

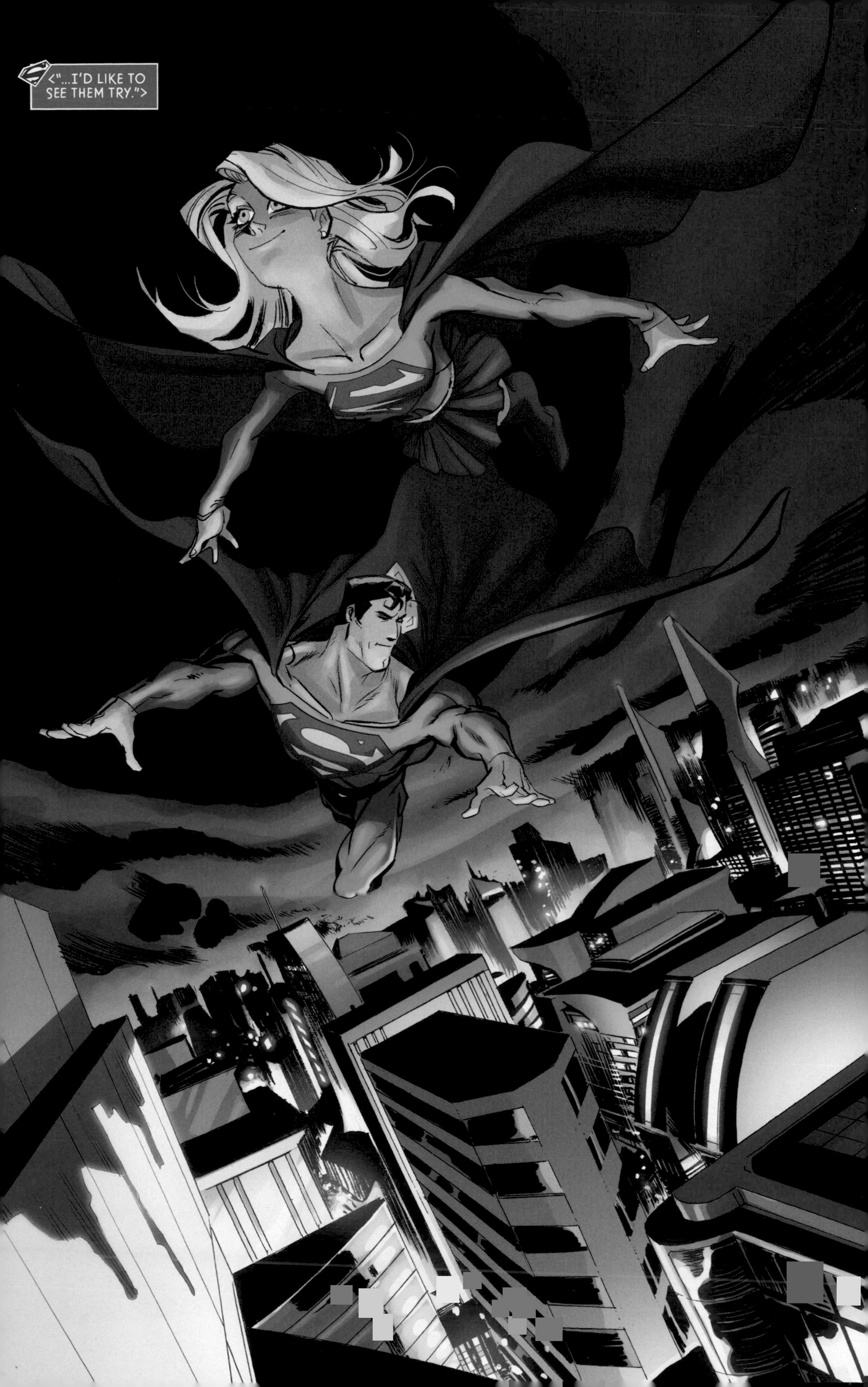
<"...I'D LIKE TO SEE THEM TRY.">

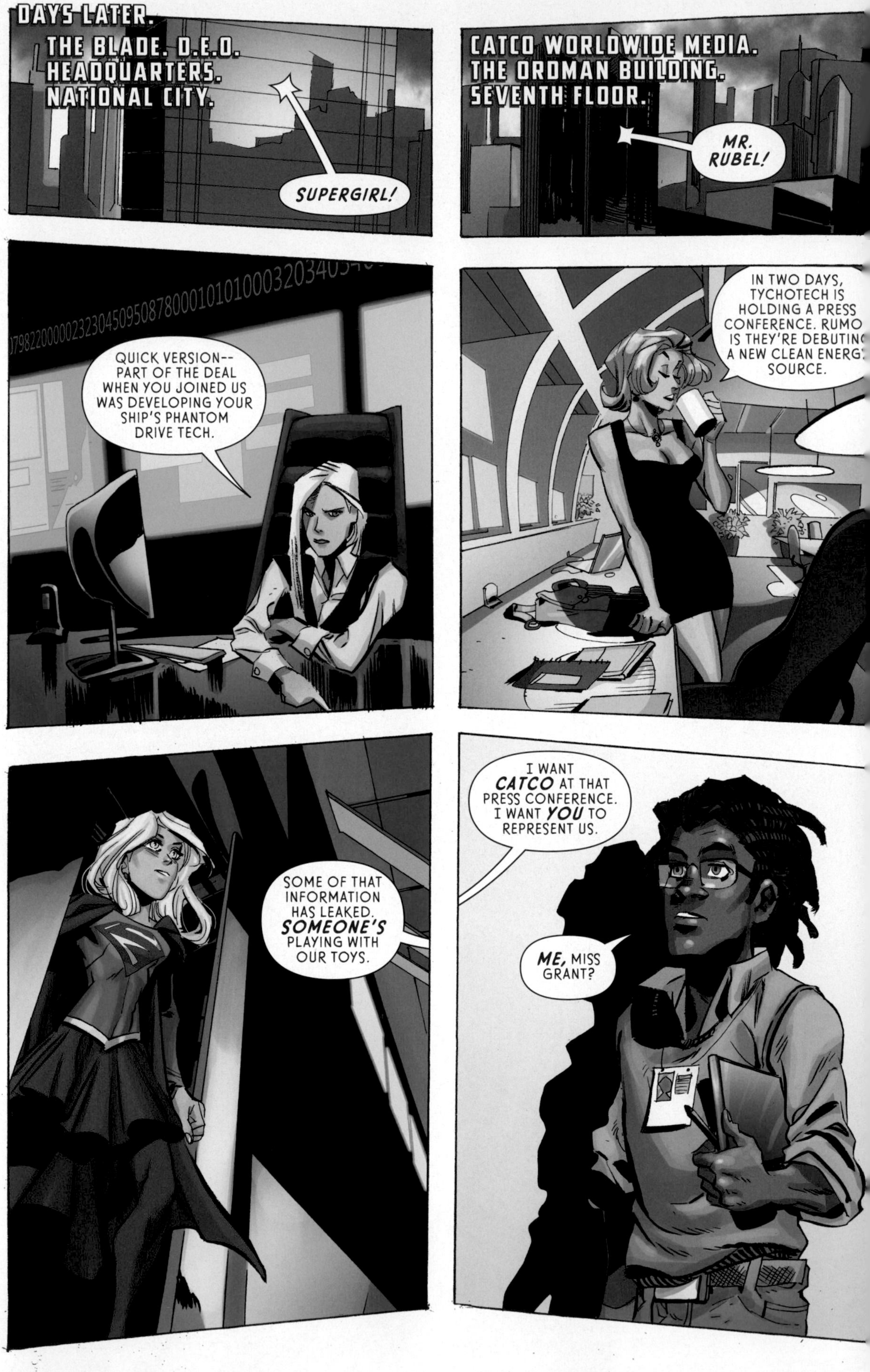
DAYS LATER.
THE BLADE. D.E.O. HEADQUARTERS. NATIONAL CITY.
SUPERGIRL!
CATCO WORLDWIDE MEDIA. THE ORDMAN BUILDING. SEVENTH FLOOR.
MR. RUBEL!
QUICK VERSION-- PART OF THE DEAL WHEN YOU JOINED US WAS DEVELOPING YOUR SHIP'S PHANTOM DRIVE TECH.
IN TWO DAYS, TYCHOTECH IS HOLDING A PRESS CONFERENCE. RUMO IS THEY'RE DEBUTIN A NEW CLEAN ENERG SOURCE.
SOME OF THAT INFORMATION HAS LEAKED. SOMEONE'S PLAYING WITH OUR TOYS.
I WANT CATCO AT THAT PRESS CONFERENCE. I WANT YOU TO REPRESENT US.
ME, MISS GRANT?

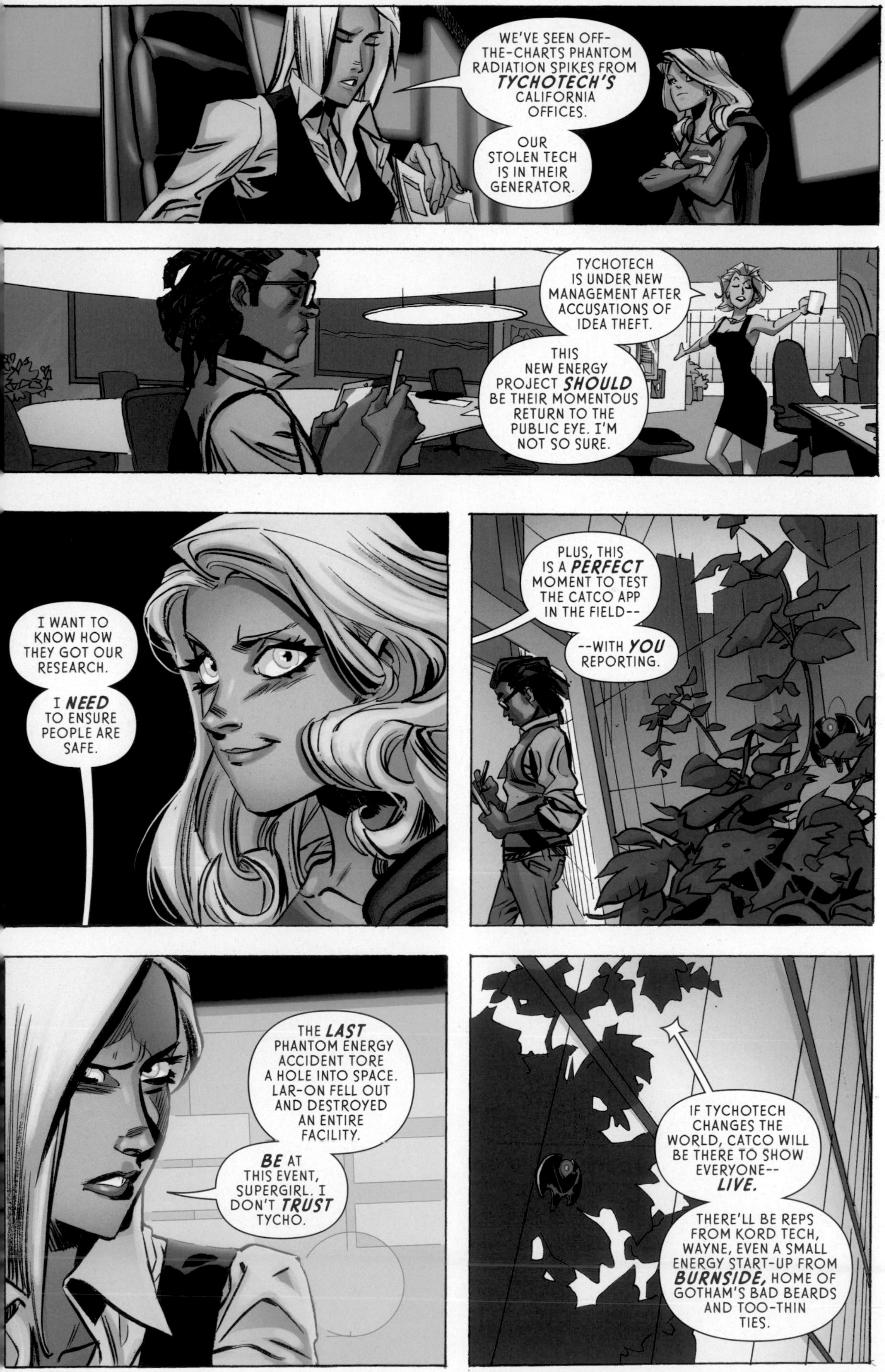
WE'VE SEEN OFF-THE-CHARTS PHANTOM RADIATION SPIKES FROM TYCHOTECH'S CALIFORNIA OFFICES.
OUR STOLEN TECH IS IN THEIR GENERATOR.
TYCHOTECH IS UNDER NEW MANAGEMENT AFTER ACCUSATIONS OF IDEA THEFT.
THIS NEW ENERGY PROJECT SHOULD BE THEIR MOMENTOUS RETURN TO THE PUBLIC EYE. I'M NOT SO SURE.
I WANT TO KNOW HOW THEY GOT OUR RESEARCH.
I NEED TO ENSURE PEOPLE ARE SAFE.
PLUS, THIS IS A PERFECT MOMENT TO TEST THE CATCO APP IN THE FIELD--
--WITH YOU REPORTING.
THE LAST PHANTOM ENERGY ACCIDENT TORE A HOLE INTO SPACE. LAR-ON FELL OUT AND DESTROYED AN ENTIRE FACILITY.
BE AT THIS EVENT, SUPERGIRL. I DON'T TRUST TYCHO.
IF TYCHOTECH CHANGES THE WORLD, CATCO WILL BE THERE TO SHOW EVERYONE-- LIVE.
THERE'LL BE REPS FROM KORD TECH, WAYNE, EVEN A SMALL ENERGY START-UP FROM BURNSIDE, HOME OF GOTHAM'S BAD BEARDS AND TOO-THIN TIES.

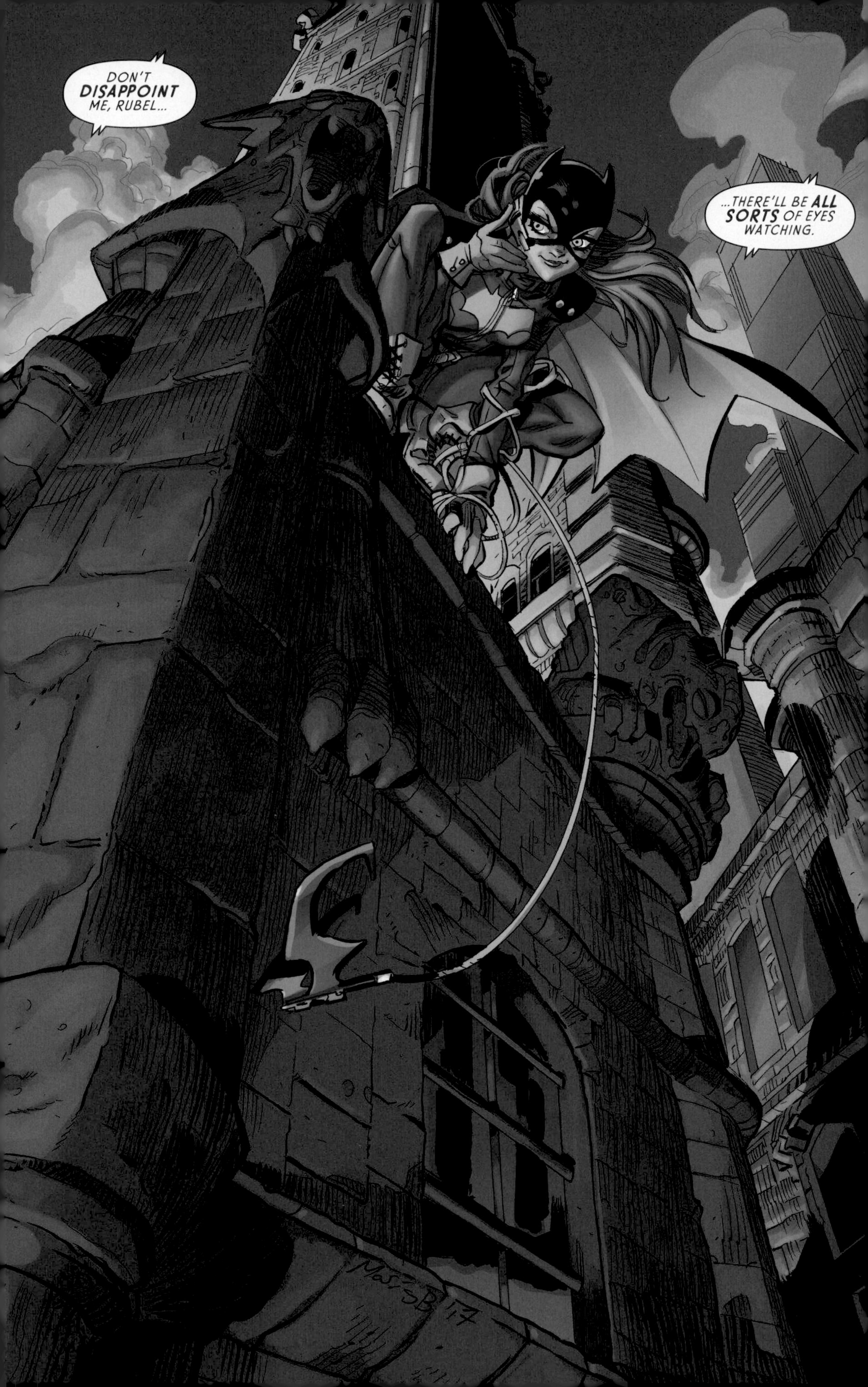
DON'T DISAPPOINT ME, RUBEL...
...THERE'LL BE ALL SORTS OF EYES WATCHING.

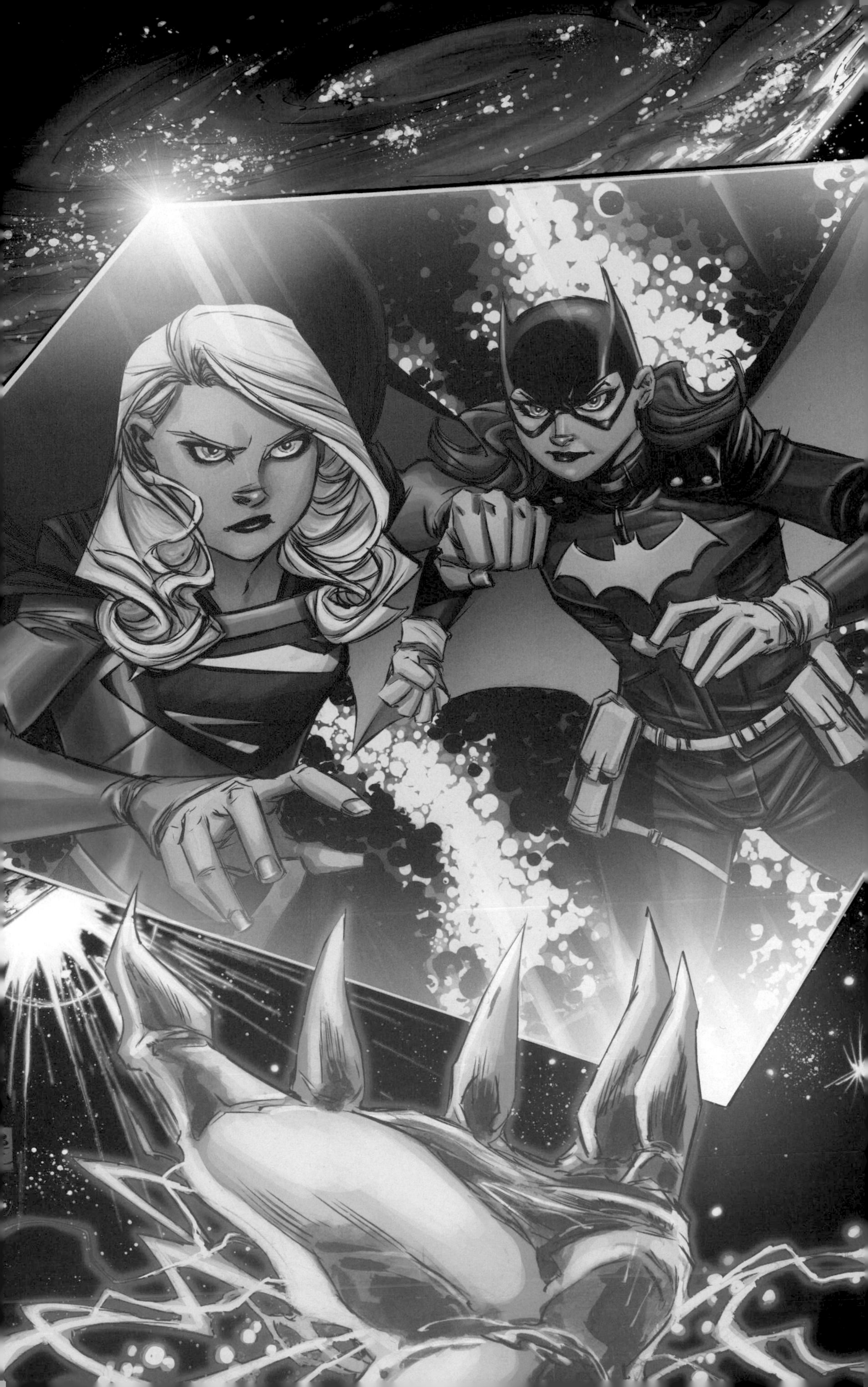

"ESCAPE FROM THE PHANTOM ZONE PART ONE"

STEVE ORLANDO writer * BRIAN CHING artist * MICHAEL ATIYEH colorist
cover by BRIAN CHING and MICHAEL ATIYEH

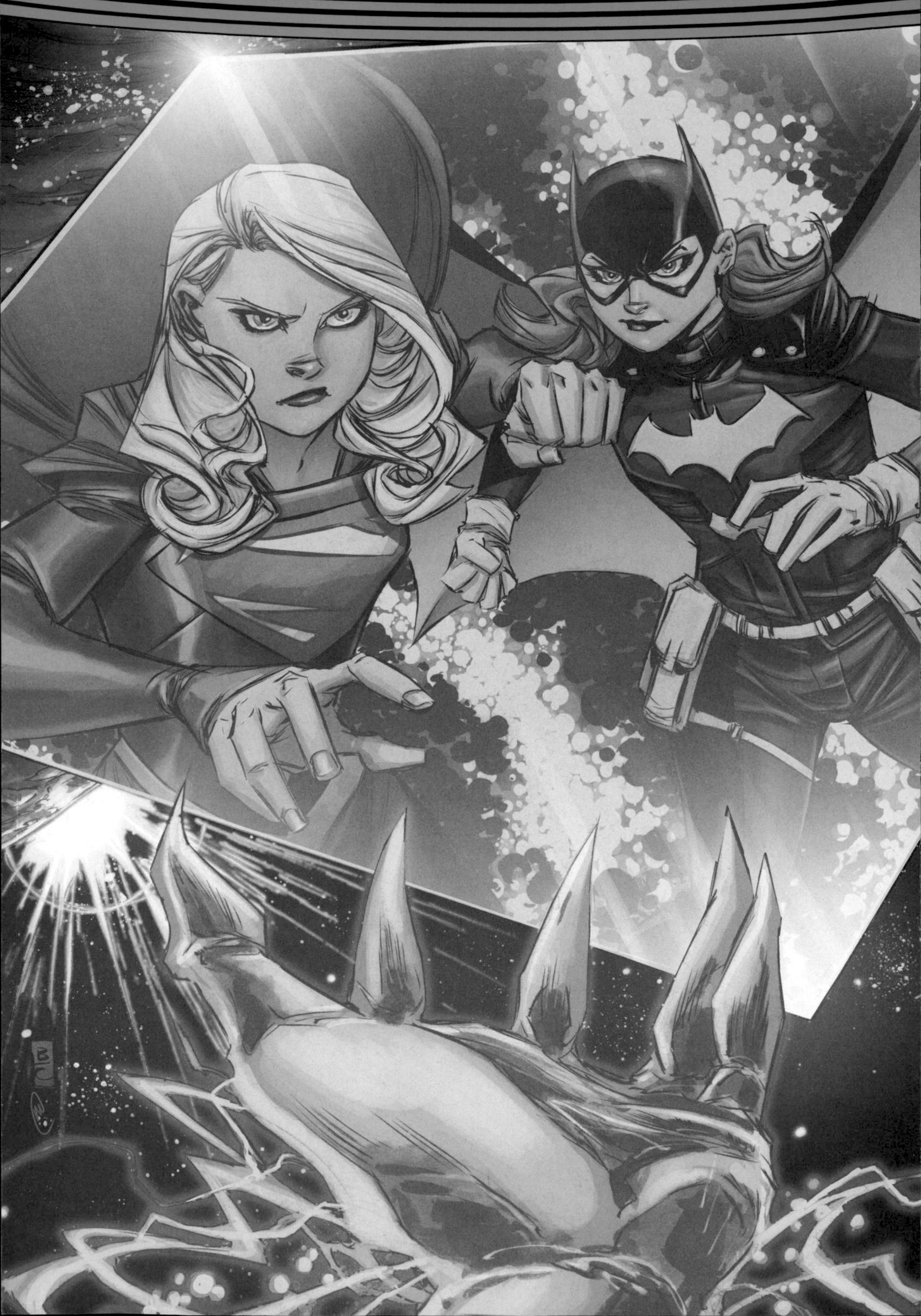

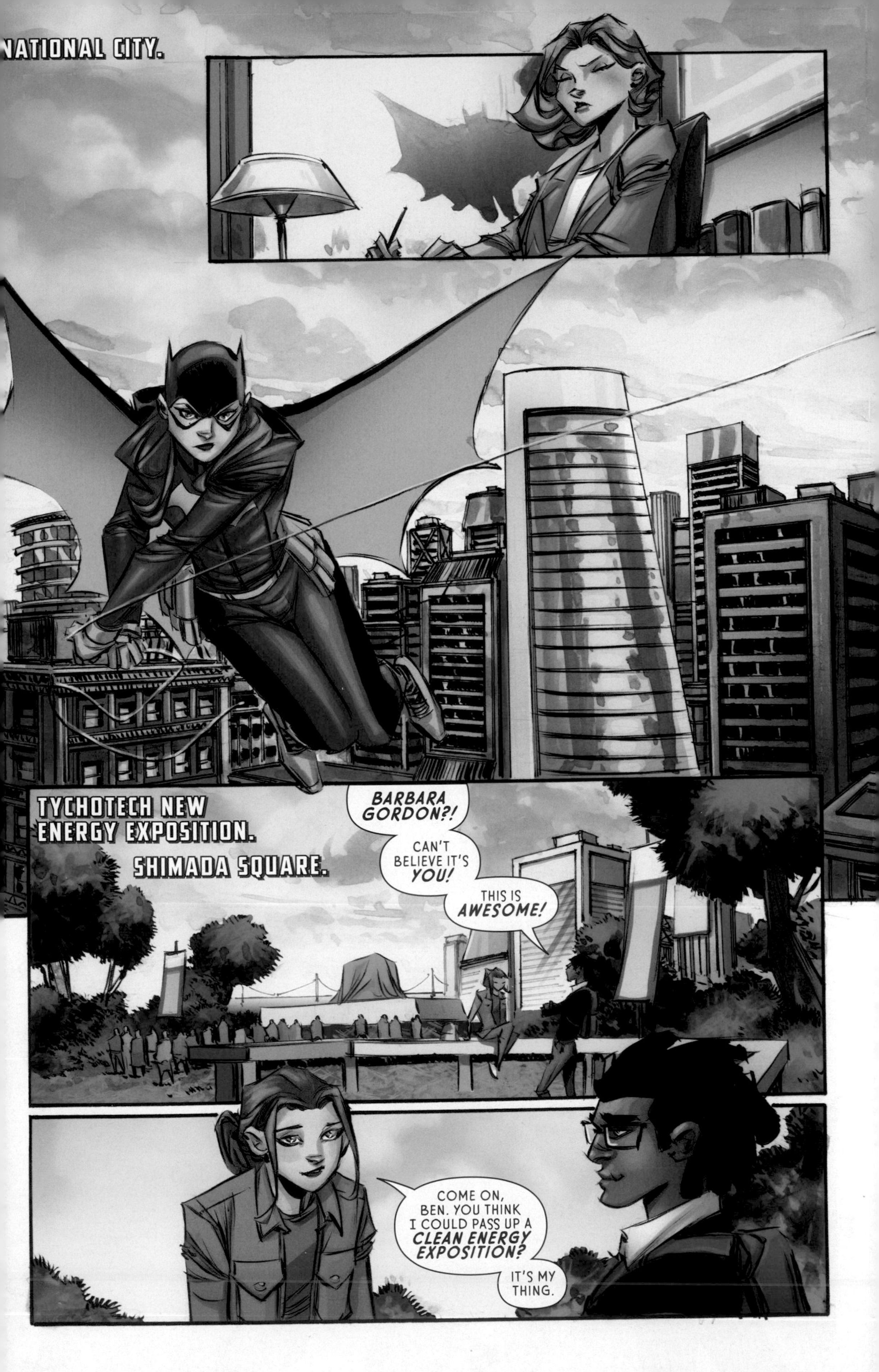
NATIONAL CITY.
TYCHOTECH NEW ENERGY EXPOSITION.
SHIMADA SQUARE.
BARBARA GORDON?!
CAN'T BELIEVE IT'S YOU!
THIS IS AWESOME!
COME ON, BEN. YOU THINK I COULD PASS UP A CLEAN ENERGY EXPOSITION?
IT'S MY THING.

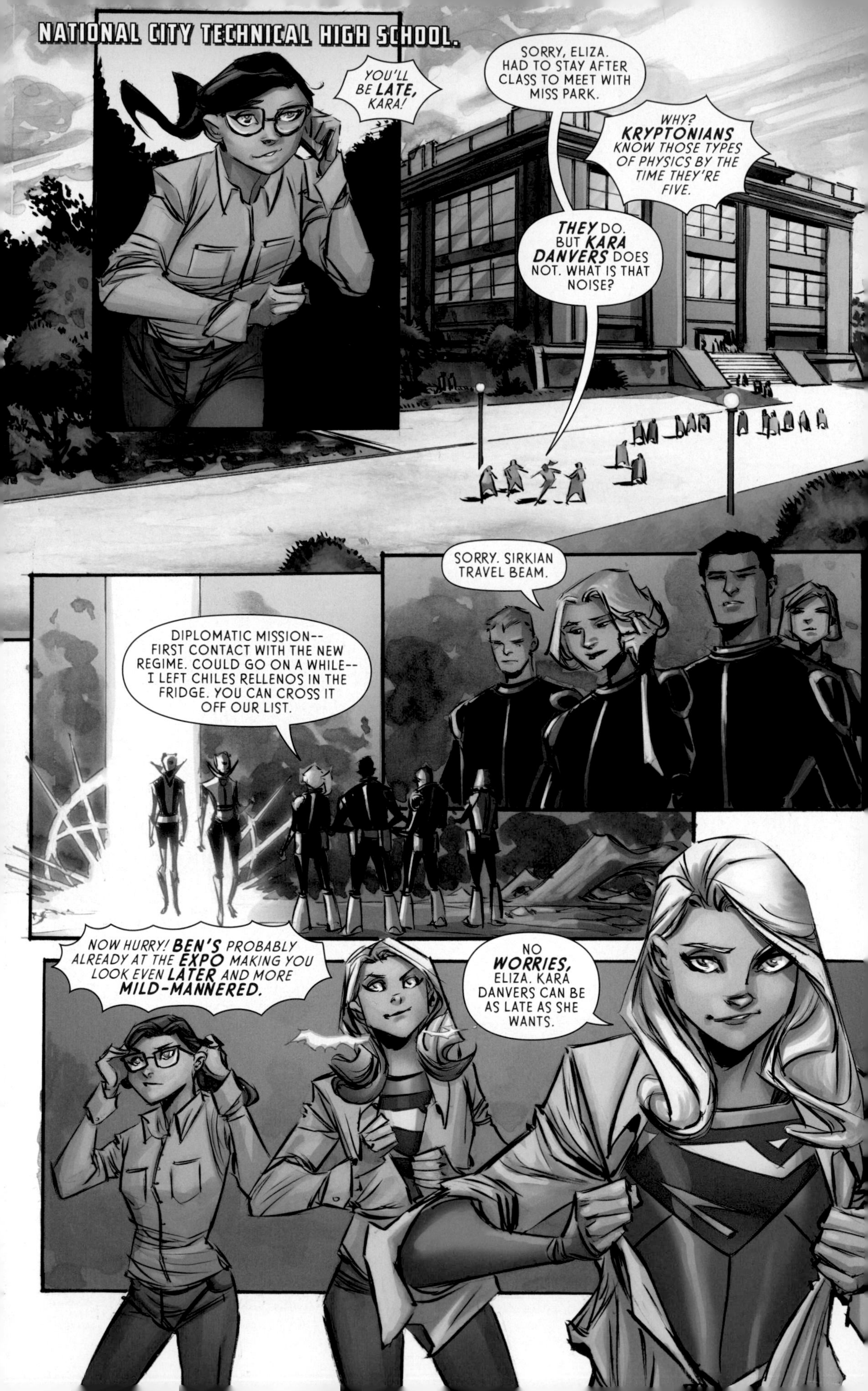
NATIONAL CITY TECHNICAL HIGH SCHOOL.
YOU'LL BE LATE, KARA!
SORRY, ELIZA. HAD TO STAY AFTER CLASS TO MEET WITH MISS PARK.
WHY? KRYPTONIANS KNOW THOSE TYPES OF PHYSICS BY THE TIME THEY'RE FIVE.
THEY DO. BUT KARA DANVERS DOES NOT. WHAT IS THAT NOISE?
SORRY. SIRKIAN TRAVEL BEAM.
DIPLOMATIC MISSION-- FIRST CONTACT WITH THE NEW REGIME. COULD GO ON A WHILE-- I LEFT CHILES RELLENOS IN THE FRIDGE. YOU CAN CROSS IT OFF OUR LIST.
NOW HURRY! BEN'S PROBABLY ALREADY AT THE EXPO MAKING YOU LOOK EVEN LATER AND MORE MILD-MANNERED.
NO WORRIES, ELIZA. KARA DANVERS CAN BE AS LATE AS SHE WANTS.

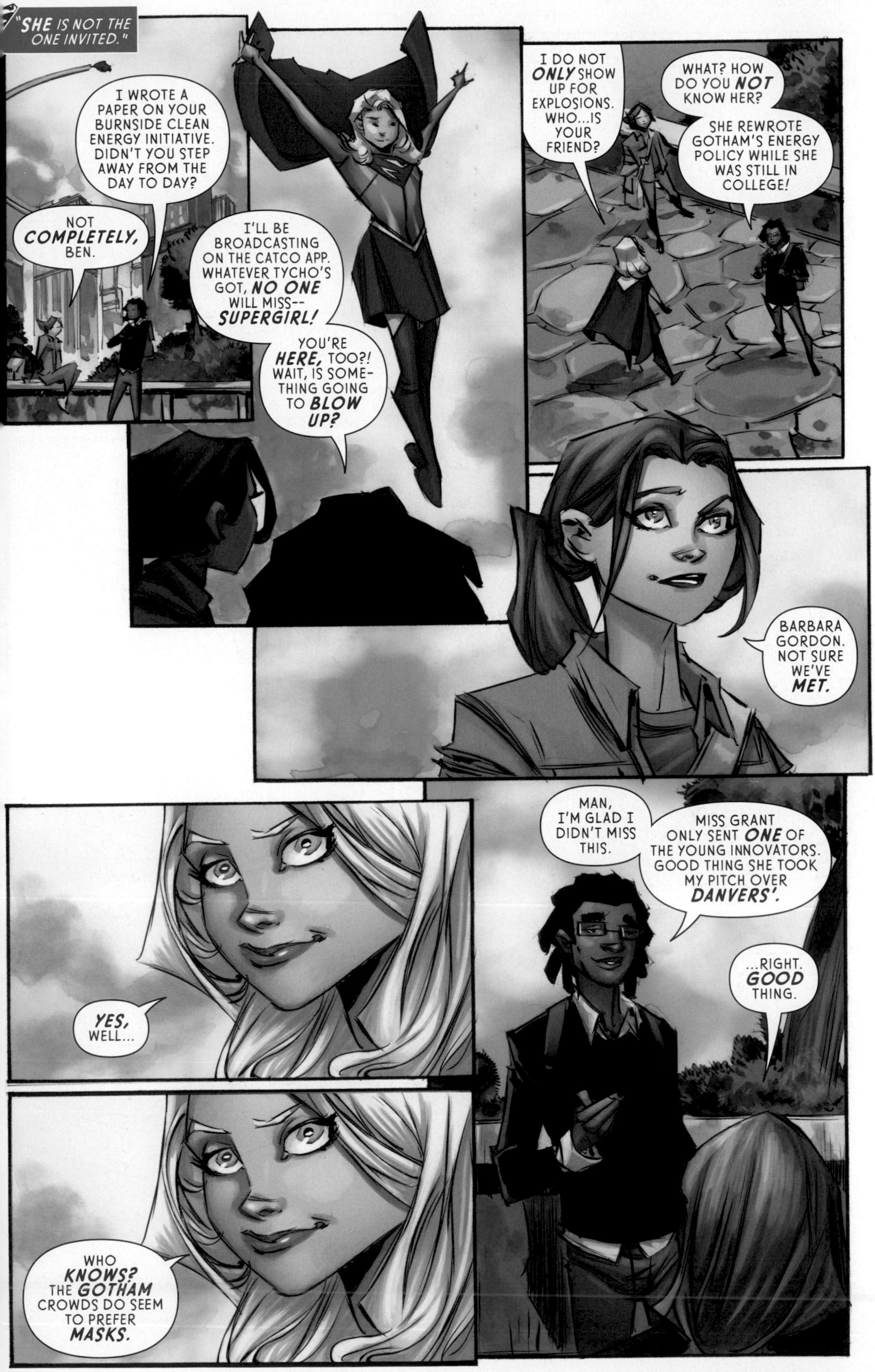
"SHE IS NOT THE ONE INVITED."
I WROTE A PAPER ON YOUR BURNSIDE CLEAN ENERGY INITIATIVE. DIDN'T YOU STEP AWAY FROM THE DAY TO DAY?
NOT COMPLETELY, BEN.
I'LL BE BROADCASTING ON THE CATCO APP. WHATEVER TYCHO'S GOT, NO ONE WILL MISS-- SUPERGIRL!
YOU'RE HERE, TOO?! WAIT, IS SOME-THING GOING TO BLOW UP?
I DO NOT ONLY SHOW UP FOR EXPLOSIONS. WHO...IS YOUR FRIEND?
WHAT? HOW DO YOU NOT KNOW HER?
SHE REWROTE GOTHAM'S ENERGY POLICY WHILE SHE WAS STILL IN COLLEGE!
BARBARA GORDON. NOT SURE WE'VE MET.
YES, WELL...
WHO KNOWS? THE GOTHAM CROWDS DO SEEM TO PREFER MASKS.
MAN, I'M GLAD I DIDN'T MISS THIS.
MISS GRANT ONLY SENT ONE OF THE YOUNG INNOVATORS. GOOD THING SHE TOOK MY PITCH OVER DANVERS'.
...RIGHT. GOOD THING.

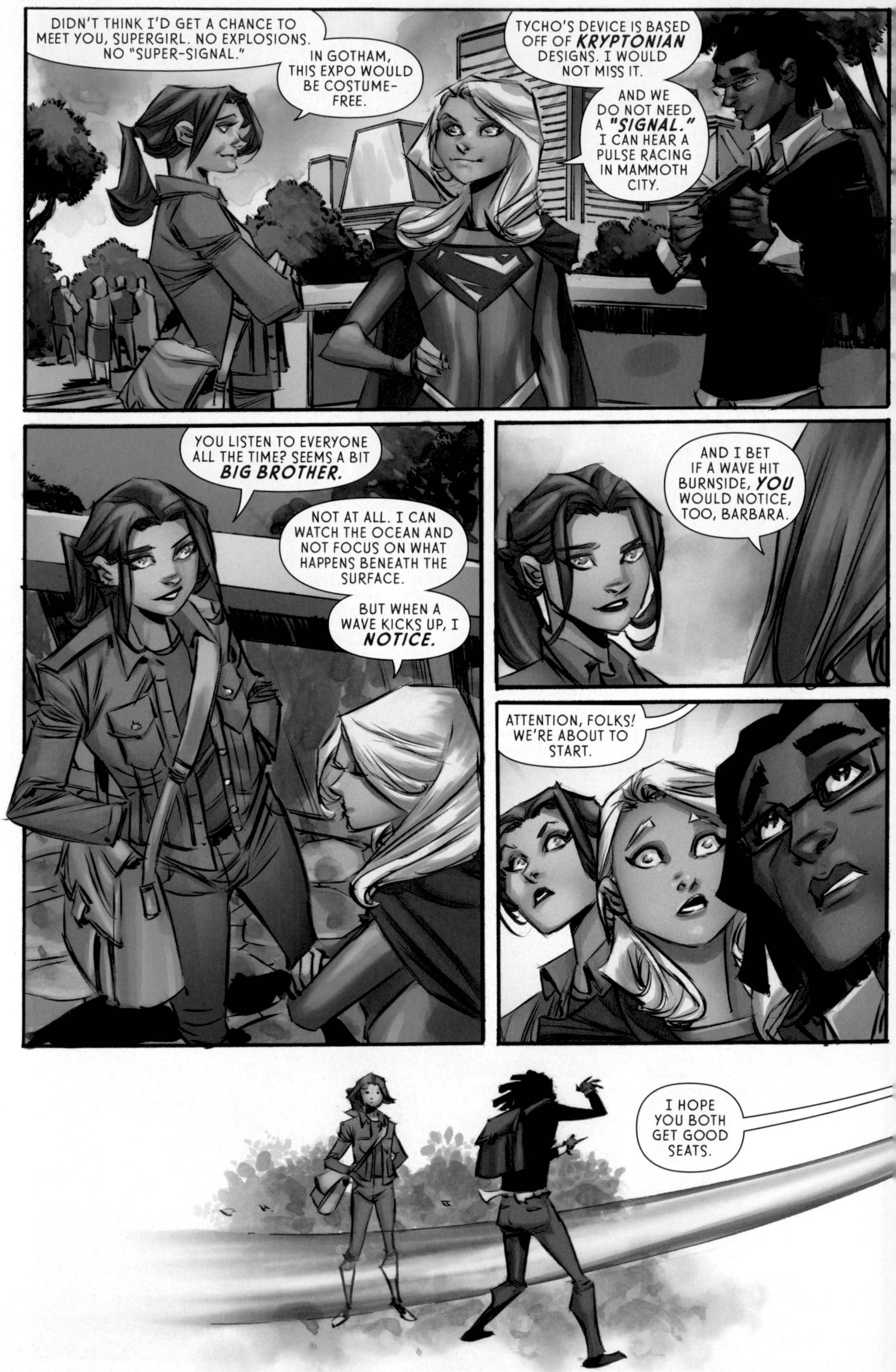
DIDN'T THINK I'D GET A CHANCE TO MEET YOU, SUPERGIRL. NO EXPLOSIONS. NO "SUPER-SIGNAL."
IN GOTHAM, THIS EXPO WOULD BE COSTUME-FREE.
TYCHO'S DEVICE IS BASED OFF OF KRYPTONIAN DESIGNS. I WOULD NOT MISS IT.
AND WE DO NOT NEED A "SIGNAL." I CAN HEAR A PULSE RACING IN MAMMOTH CITY.
YOU LISTEN TO EVERYONE ALL THE TIME? SEEMS A BIT BIG BROTHER.
NOT AT ALL. I CAN WATCH THE OCEAN AND NOT FOCUS ON WHAT HAPPENS BENEATH THE SURFACE.
BUT WHEN A WAVE KICKS UP, I NOTICE.
AND I BET IF A WAVE HIT BURNSIDE, YOU WOULD NOTICE, TOO, BARBARA.
ATTENTION, FOLKS! WE'RE ABOUT TO START.
I HOPE YOU BOTH GET GOOD SEATS.

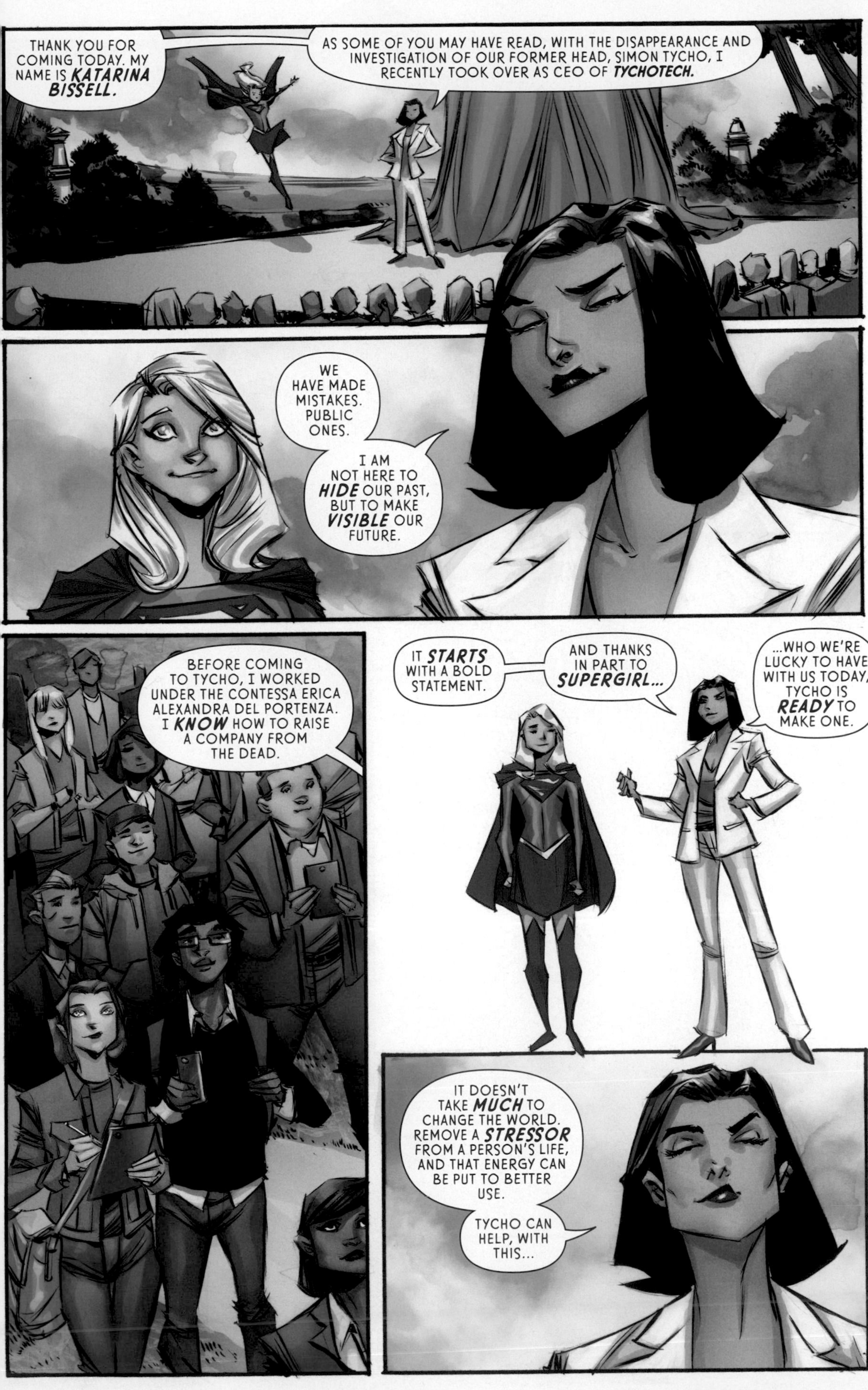
THANK YOU FOR COMING TODAY. MY NAME IS KATARINA BISSELL.
AS SOME OF YOU MAY HAVE READ, WITH THE DISAPPEARANCE AND INVESTIGATION OF OUR FORMER HEAD, SIMON TYCHO, I RECENTLY TOOK OVER AS CEO OF TYCHOTECH.
WE HAVE MADE MISTAKES. PUBLIC ONES.
I AM NOT HERE TO HIDE OUR PAST, BUT TO MAKE VISIBLE OUR FUTURE.
BEFORE COMING TO TYCHO, I WORKED UNDER THE CONTESSA ERICA ALEXANDRA DEL PORTENZA. I KNOW HOW TO RAISE A COMPANY FROM THE DEAD.
IT STARTS WITH A BOLD STATEMENT.
AND THANKS IN PART TO SUPERGIRL...
...WHO WE'RE LUCKY TO HAVE WITH US TODAY, TYCHO IS READY TO MAKE ONE.
IT DOESN'T TAKE MUCH TO CHANGE THE WORLD. REMOVE A STRESSOR FROM A PERSON'S LIFE, AND THAT ENERGY CAN BE PUT TO BETTER USE.
TYCHO CAN HELP, WITH THIS...

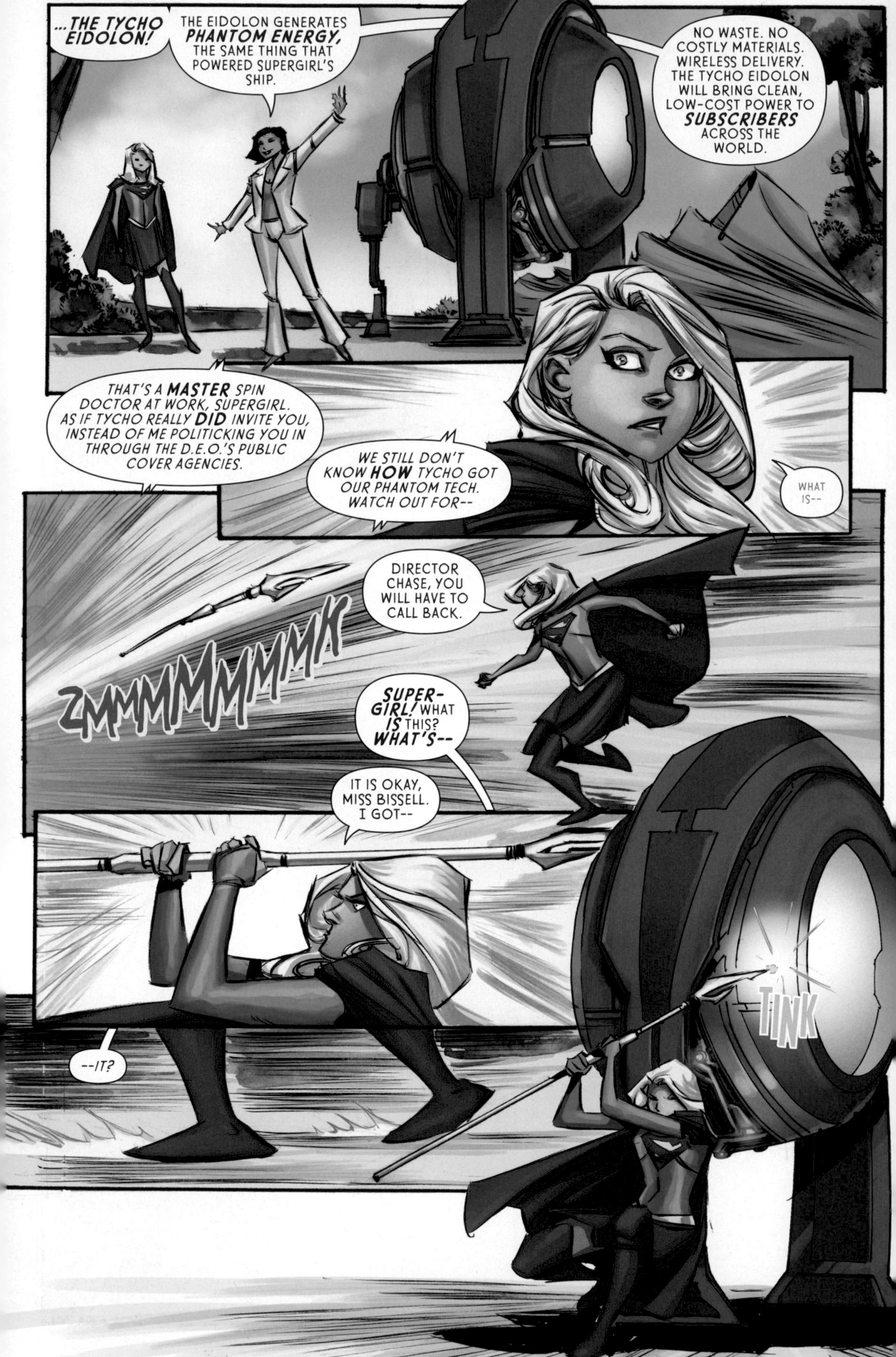
...THE TYCHO EIDOLON!
THE EIDOLON GENERATES PHANTOM ENERGY, THE SAME THING THAT POWERED SUPERGIRL'S SHIP.
NO WASTE. NO COSTLY MATERIALS. WIRELESS DELIVERY. THE TYCHO EIDOLON WILL BRING CLEAN, LOW-COST POWER TO SUBSCRIBERS ACROSS THE WORLD.
THAT'S A MASTER SPIN DOCTOR AT WORK, SUPERGIRL. AS IF TYCHO REALLY DID INVITE YOU, INSTEAD OF ME POLITICKING YOU IN THROUGH THE D.E.O.'S PUBLIC COVER AGENCIES.
WE STILL DON'T KNOW HOW TYCHO GOT OUR PHANTOM TECH. WATCH OUT FOR--
WHAT IS--
DIRECTOR CHASE, YOU WILL HAVE TO CALL BACK.
ZMMMMMMMMK
SUPER-GIRL! WHAT IS THIS? WHAT'S--
IT IS OKAY, MISS BISSELL. I GOT--
--IT?
TINK

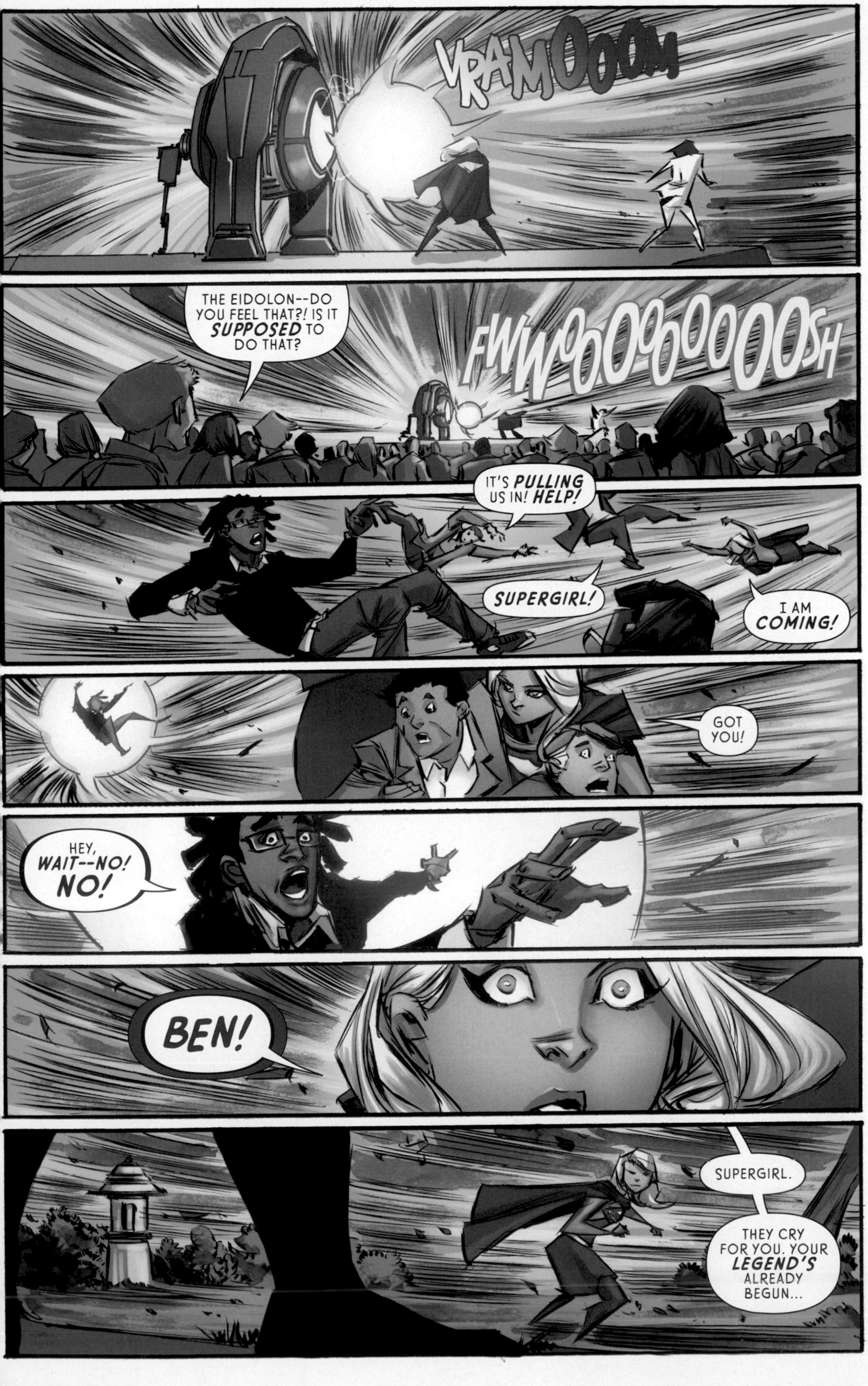
VRAMOOOOM
THE EIDOLON--DO YOU FEEL THAT?! IS IT SUPPOSED TO DO THAT?
FWWOOOOOOOOOSH
IT'S PULLING US IN! HELP!
SUPERGIRL!
I AM COMING!
GOT YOU!
HEY, WAIT--NO! NO!
BEN!
SUPERGIRL.
THEY CRY FOR YOU. YOUR LEGEND'S ALREADY BEGUN...

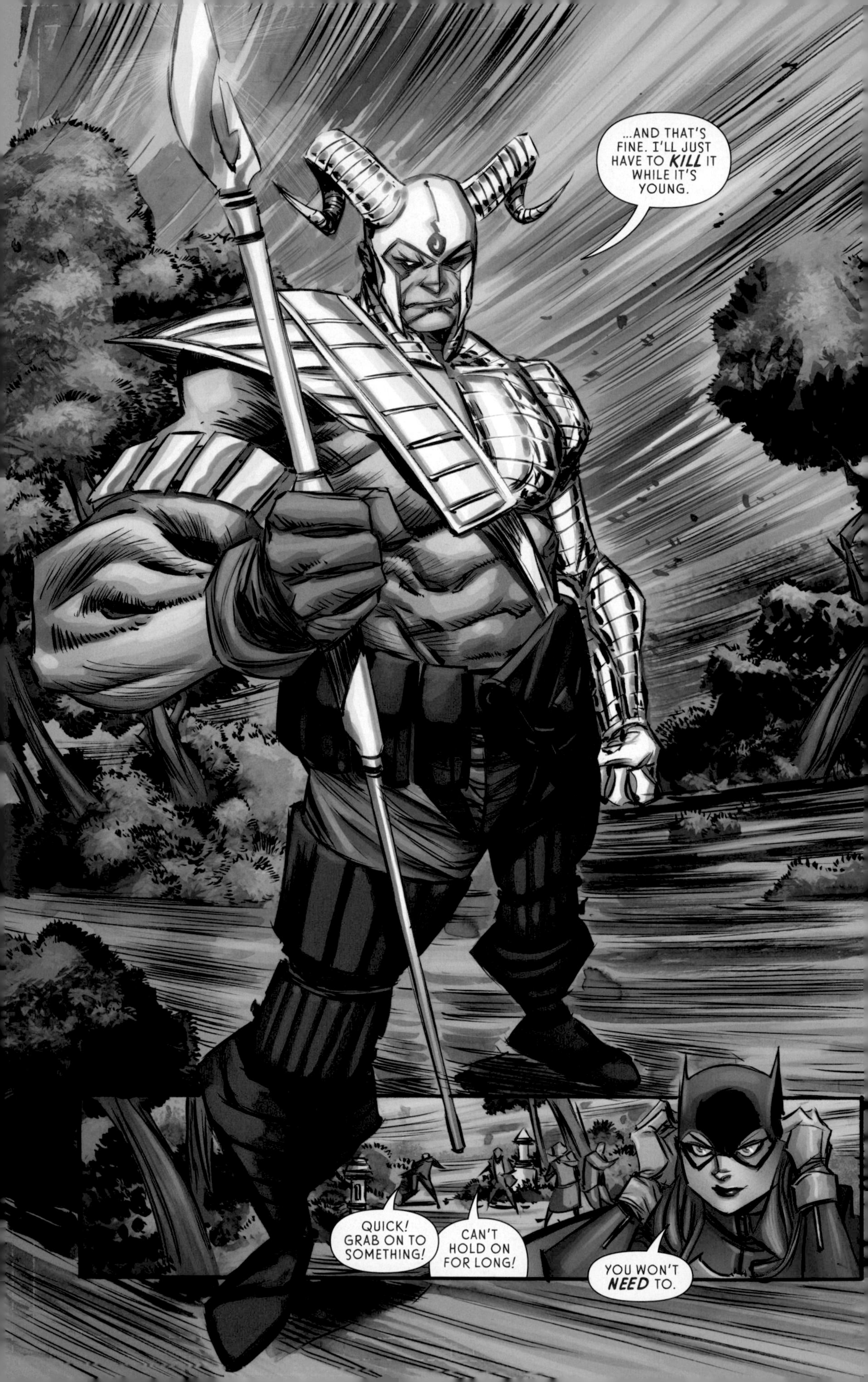
...AND THAT'S FINE. I'LL JUST HAVE TO KILL IT WHILE IT'S YOUNG.
QUICK! GRAB ON TO SOMETHING!
CAN'T HOLD ON FOR LONG!
YOU WON'T NEED TO.

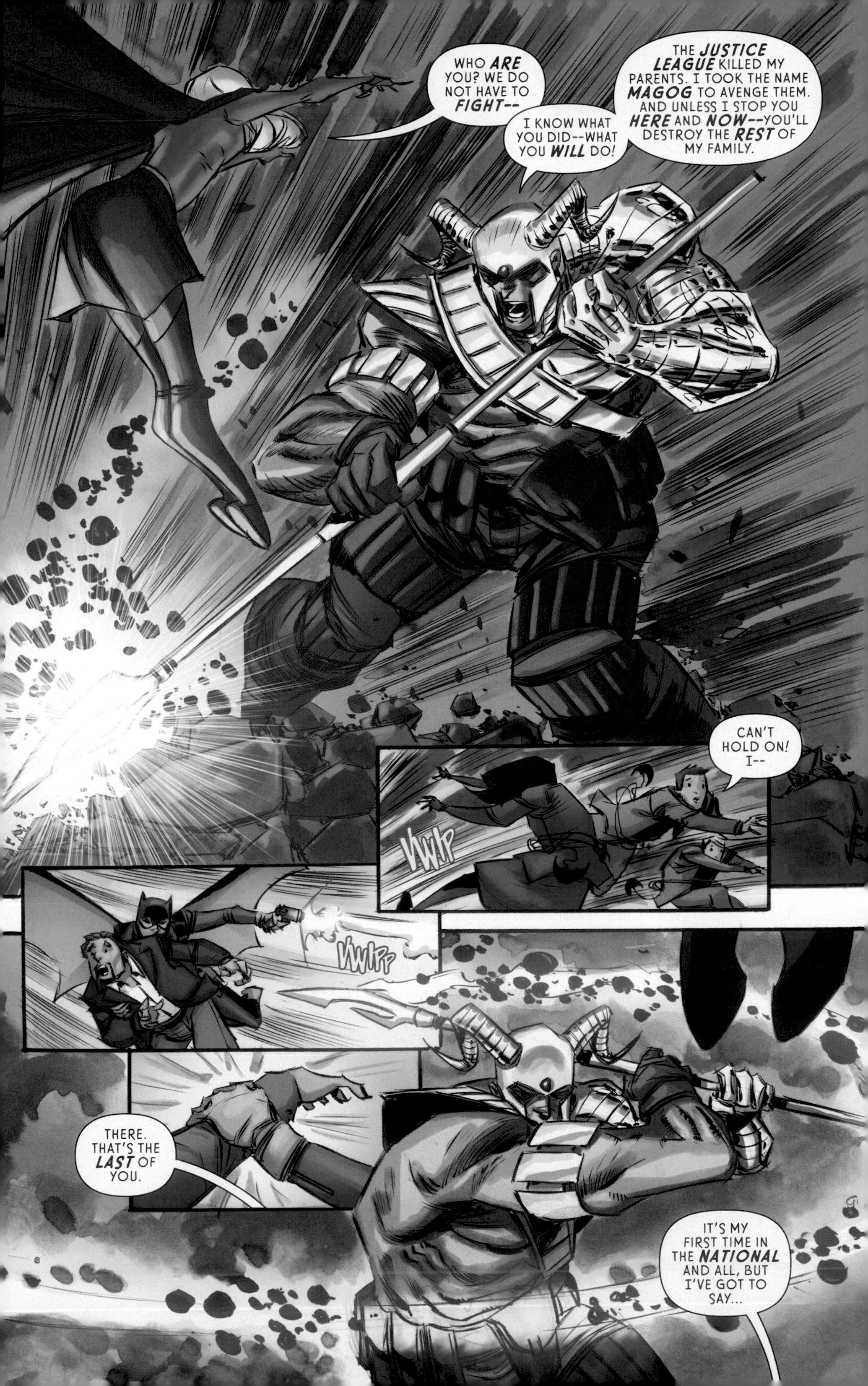
WHO ARE YOU? WE DO NOT HAVE TO FIGHT--
THE JUSTICE LEAGUE KILLED MY PARENTS. I TOOK THE NAME MAGOG TO AVENGE THEM. AND UNLESS I STOP YOU HERE AND NOW--YOU'LL DESTROY THE REST OF MY FAMILY.
I KNOW WHAT YOU DID--WHAT YOU WILL DO!
CAN'T HOLD ON! I--
VWIP
VWIPP
THERE. THAT'S THE LAST OF YOU.
IT'S MY FIRST TIME IN THE NATIONAL AND ALL, BUT I'VE GOT TO SAY...

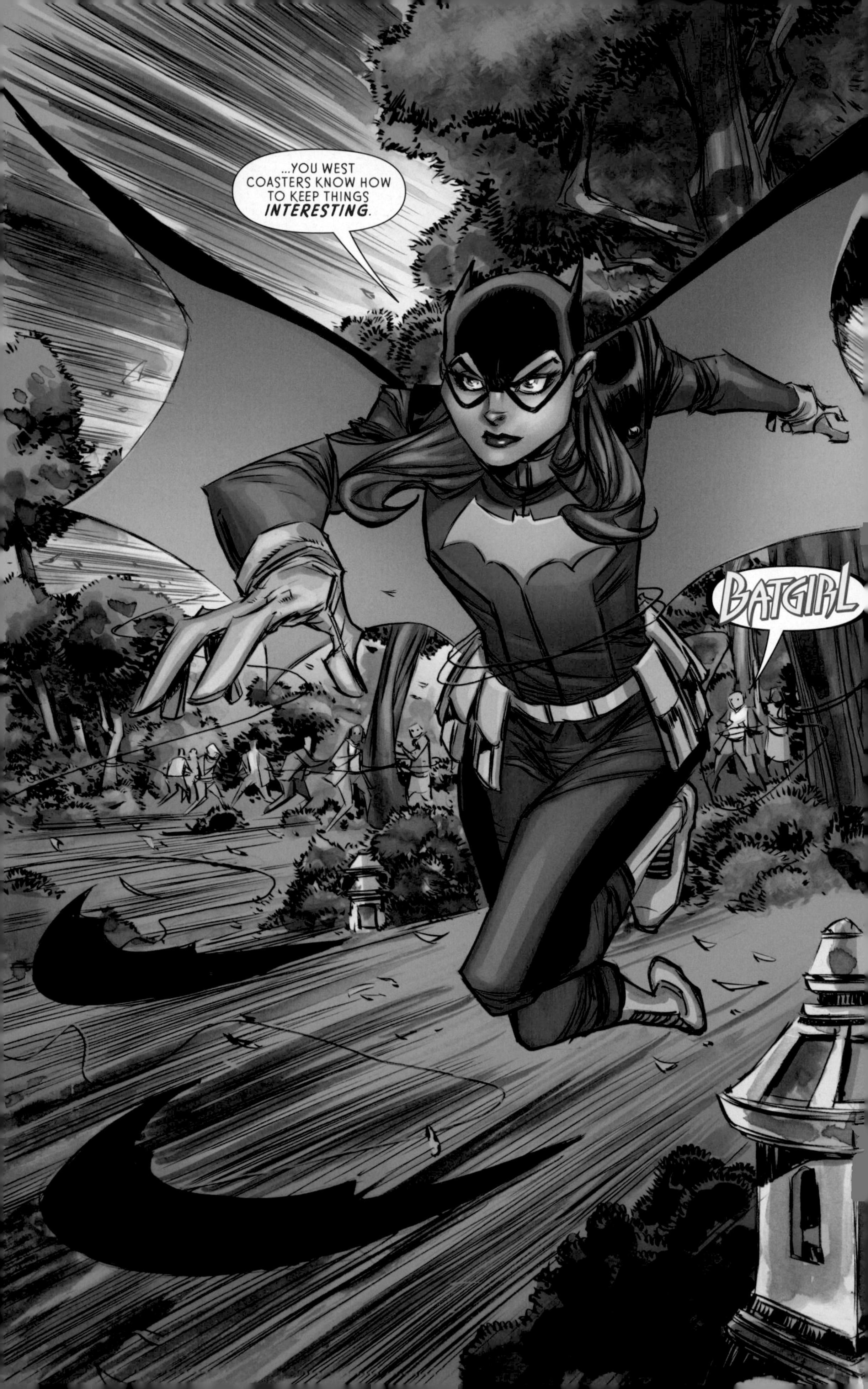
...YOU WEST COASTERS KNOW HOW TO KEEP THINGS *INTERESTING*.
BATGIRL

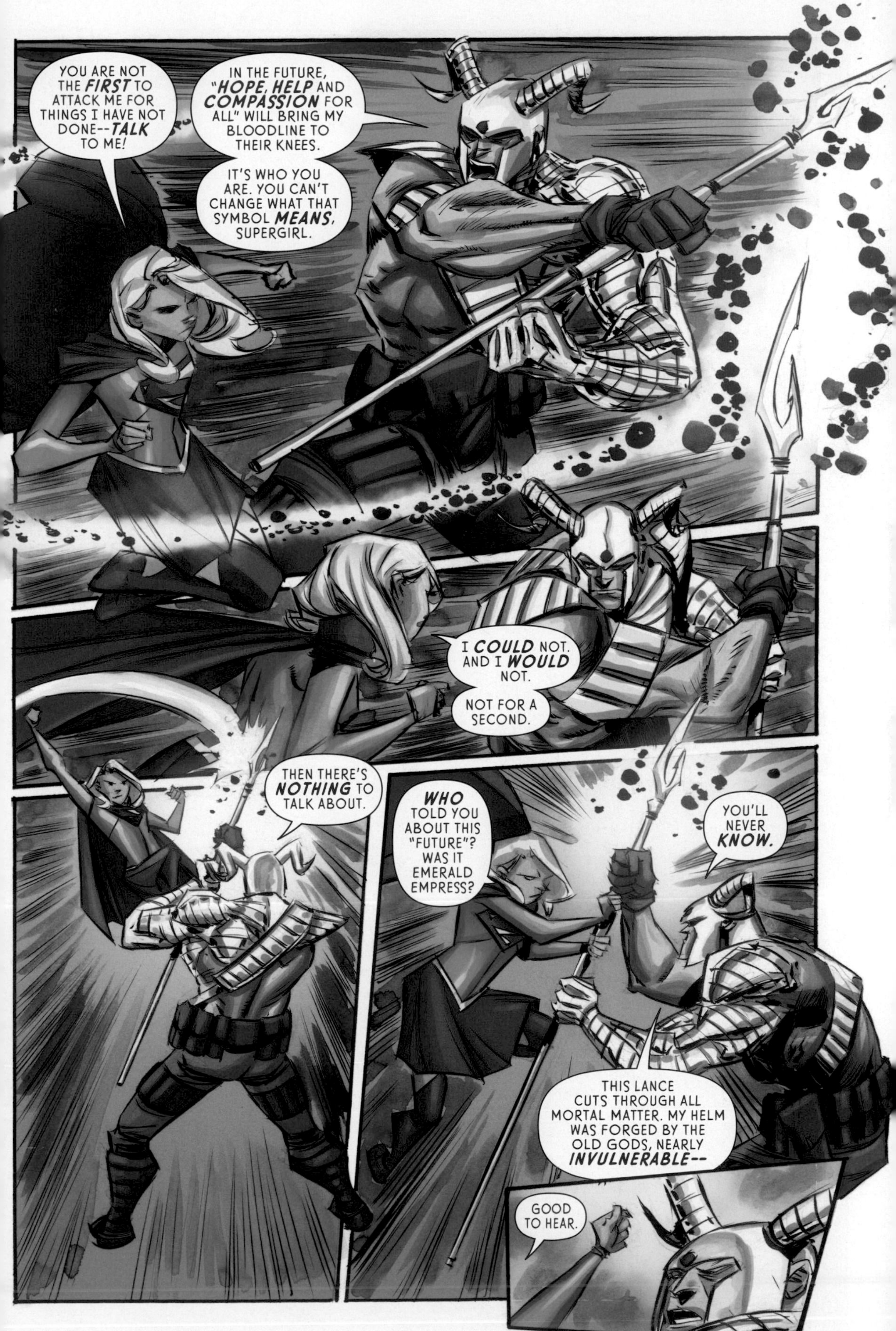
YOU ARE NOT THE FIRST TO ATTACK ME FOR THINGS I HAVE NOT DONE--TALK TO ME!
IN THE FUTURE, "HOPE, HELP AND COMPASSION FOR ALL" WILL BRING MY BLOODLINE TO THEIR KNEES.
IT'S WHO YOU ARE. YOU CAN'T CHANGE WHAT THAT SYMBOL MEANS, SUPERGIRL.
I COULD NOT. AND I WOULD NOT.
NOT FOR A SECOND.
THEN THERE'S NOTHING TO TALK ABOUT.
WHO TOLD YOU ABOUT THIS "FUTURE"? WAS IT EMERALD EMPRESS?
YOU'LL NEVER KNOW.
THIS LANCE CUTS THROUGH ALL MORTAL MATTER. MY HELM WAS FORGED BY THE OLD GODS, NEARLY INVULNERABLE--
GOOD TO HEAR.

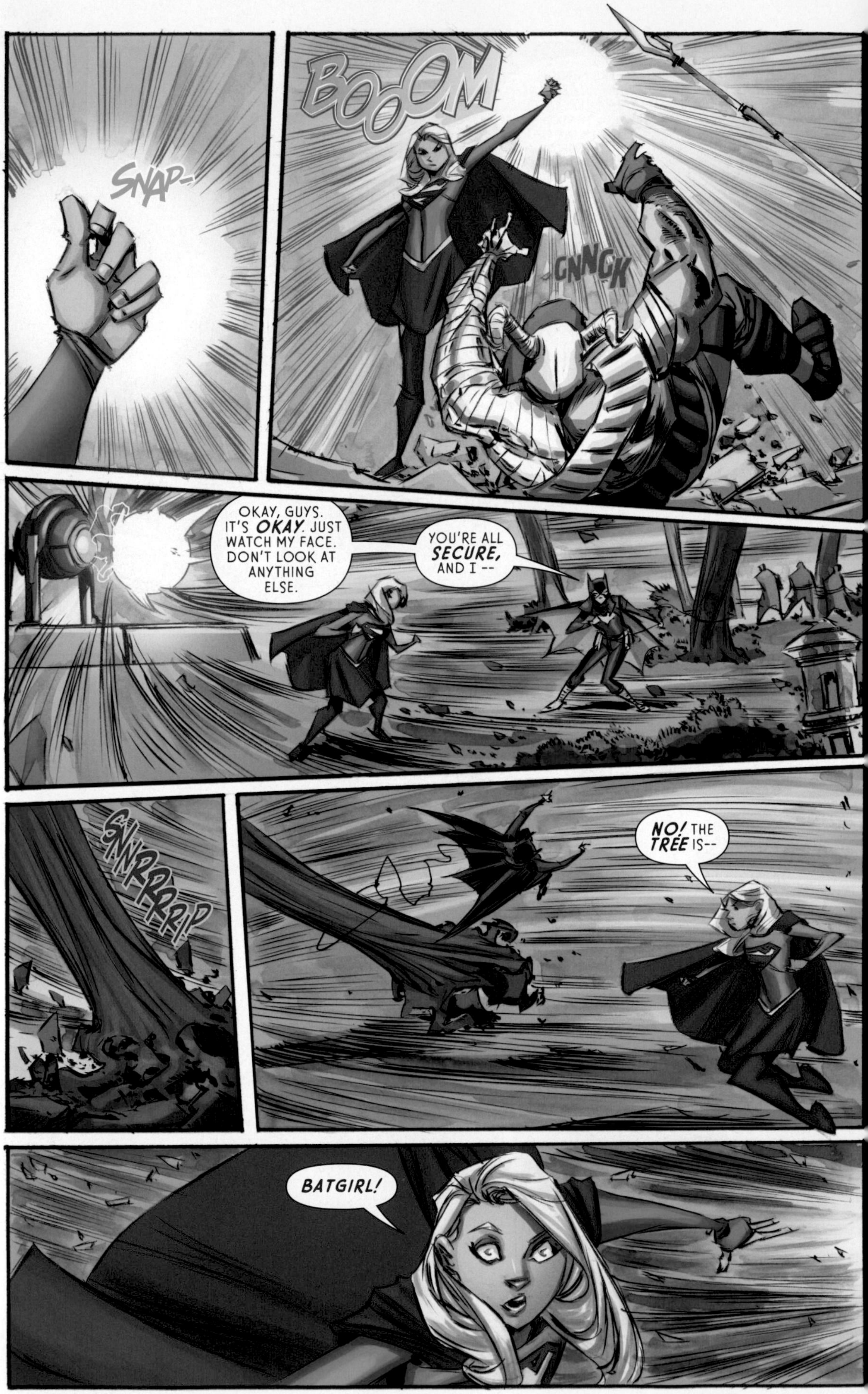
SNAP-
BOOOM
GNNGK
OKAY, GUYS. IT'S OKAY. JUST WATCH MY FACE. DON'T LOOK AT ANYTHING ELSE.
YOU'RE ALL SECURE, AND I --
SNNRRRRIP
NO! THE TREE IS--
BATGIRL!

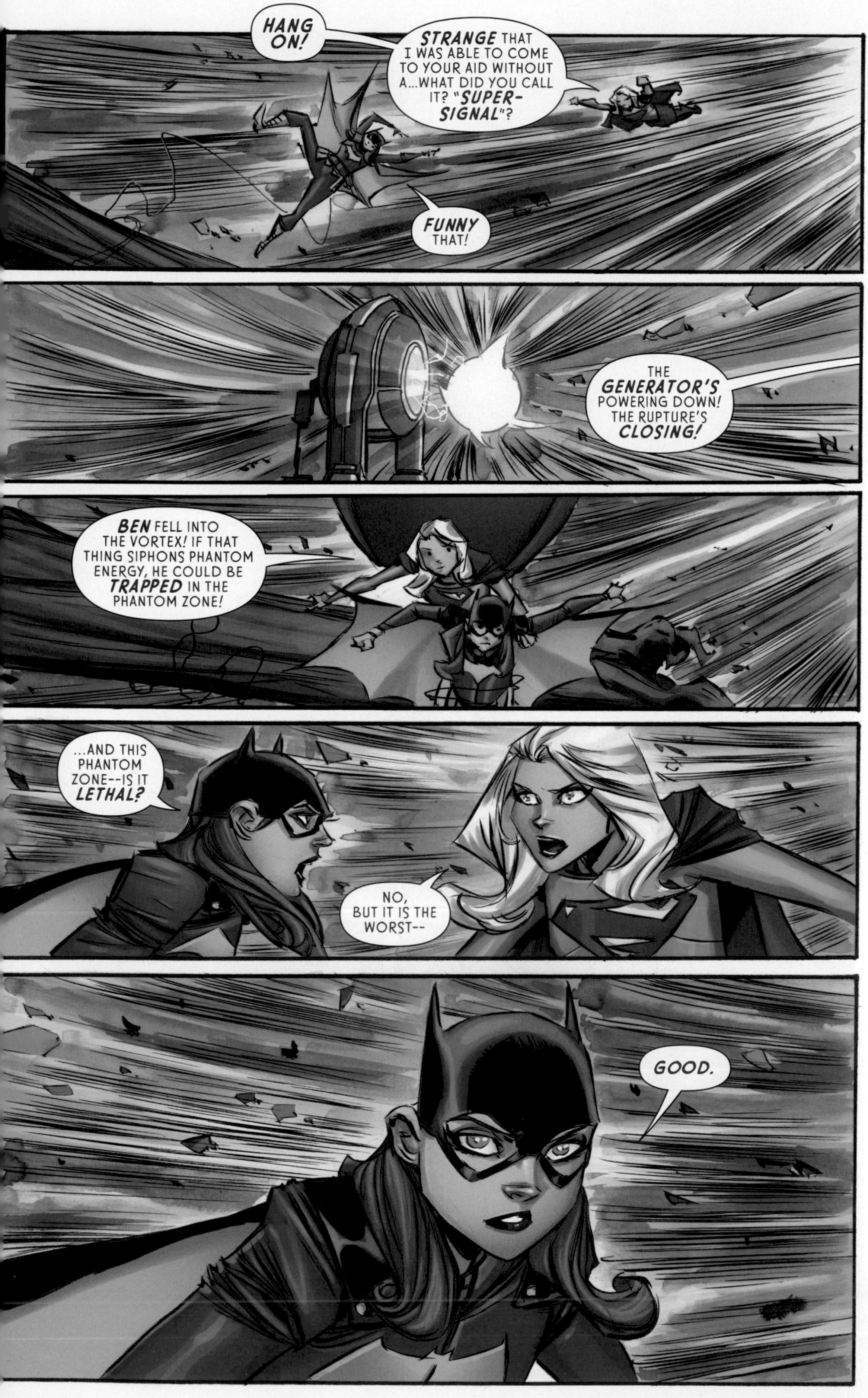
HANG ON!
STRANGE THAT I WAS ABLE TO COME TO YOUR AID WITHOUT A...WHAT DID YOU CALL IT? "SUPER-SIGNAL"?
FUNNY THAT!
THE GENERATOR'S POWERING DOWN! THE RUPTURE'S CLOSING!
BEN FELL INTO THE VORTEX! IF THAT THING SIPHONS PHANTOM ENERGY, HE COULD BE TRAPPED IN THE PHANTOM ZONE!
...AND THIS PHANTOM ZONE--IS IT LETHAL?
NO, BUT IT IS THE WORST--
GOOD.

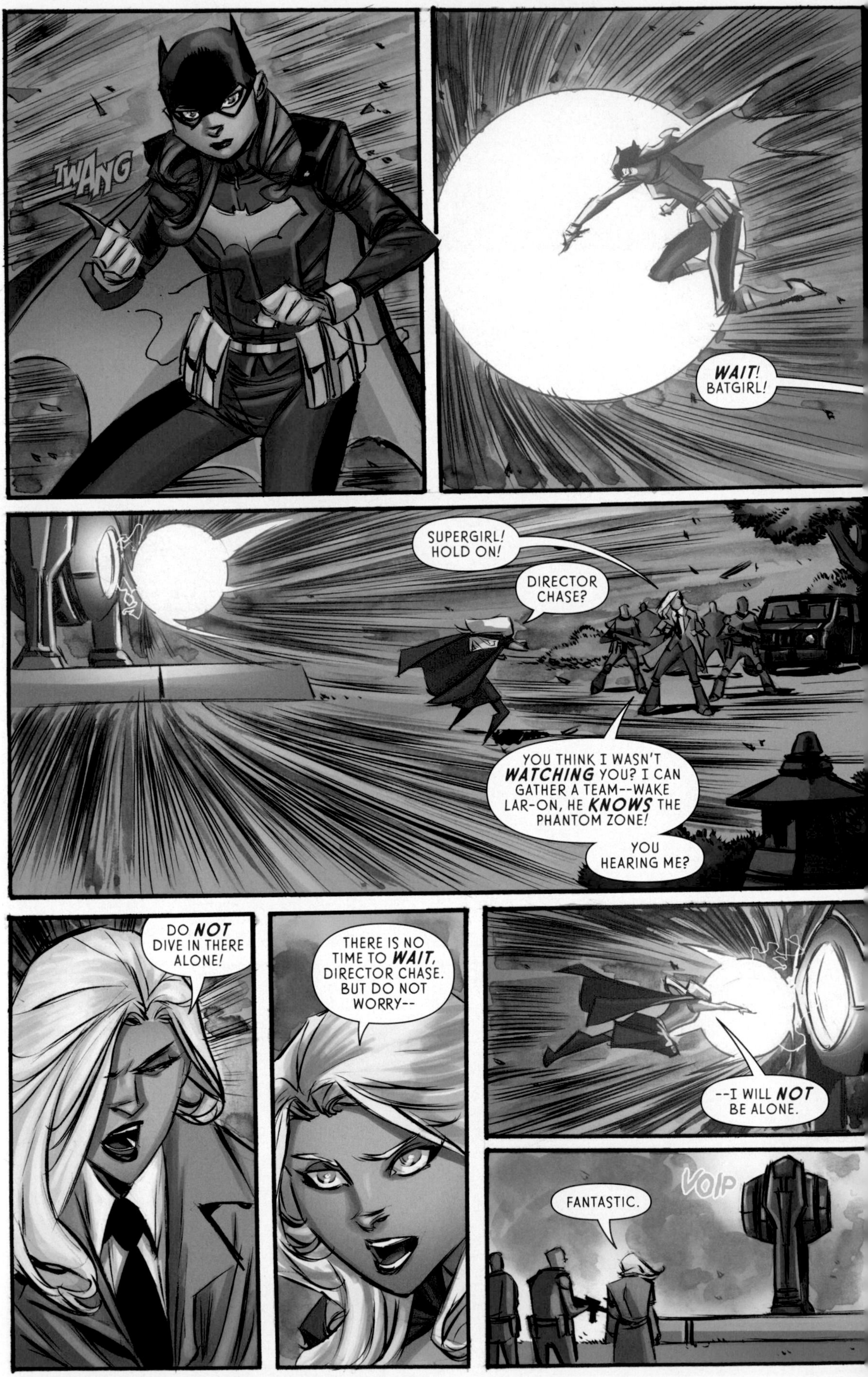
TWANG
WAIT! BATGIRL!
SUPERGIRL! HOLD ON!
DIRECTOR CHASE?
YOU THINK I WASN'T WATCHING YOU? I CAN GATHER A TEAM--WAKE LAR-ON, HE KNOWS THE PHANTOM ZONE!
YOU HEARING ME?
DO NOT DIVE IN THERE ALONE!
THERE IS NO TIME TO WAIT, DIRECTOR CHASE. BUT DO NOT WORRY--
--I WILL NOT BE ALONE.
VOIP
FANTASTIC.

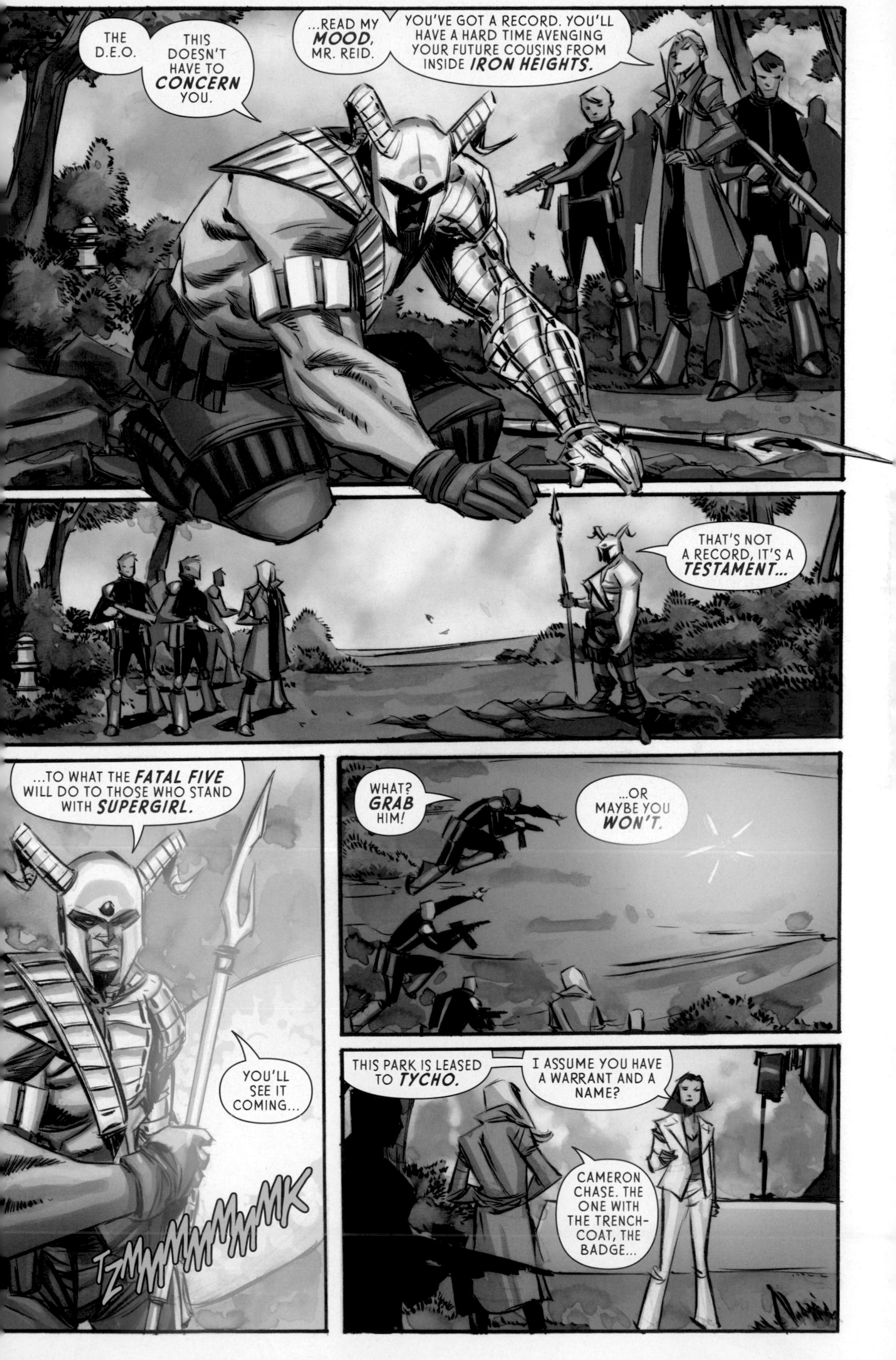
THE D.E.O.
THIS DOESN'T HAVE TO CONCERN YOU.
...READ MY MOOD, MR. REID.
YOU'VE GOT A RECORD. YOU'LL HAVE A HARD TIME AVENGING YOUR FUTURE COUSINS FROM INSIDE IRON HEIGHTS.
THAT'S NOT A RECORD, IT'S A TESTAMENT...
...TO WHAT THE FATAL FIVE WILL DO TO THOSE WHO STAND WITH SUPERGIRL.
YOU'LL SEE IT COMING...
TZMMMMMMMMK
WHAT? GRAB HIM!
...OR MAYBE YOU WON'T.
THIS PARK IS LEASED TO TYCHO.
I ASSUME YOU HAVE A WARRANT AND A NAME?
CAMERON CHASE. THE ONE WITH THE TRENCH-COAT, THE BADGE...

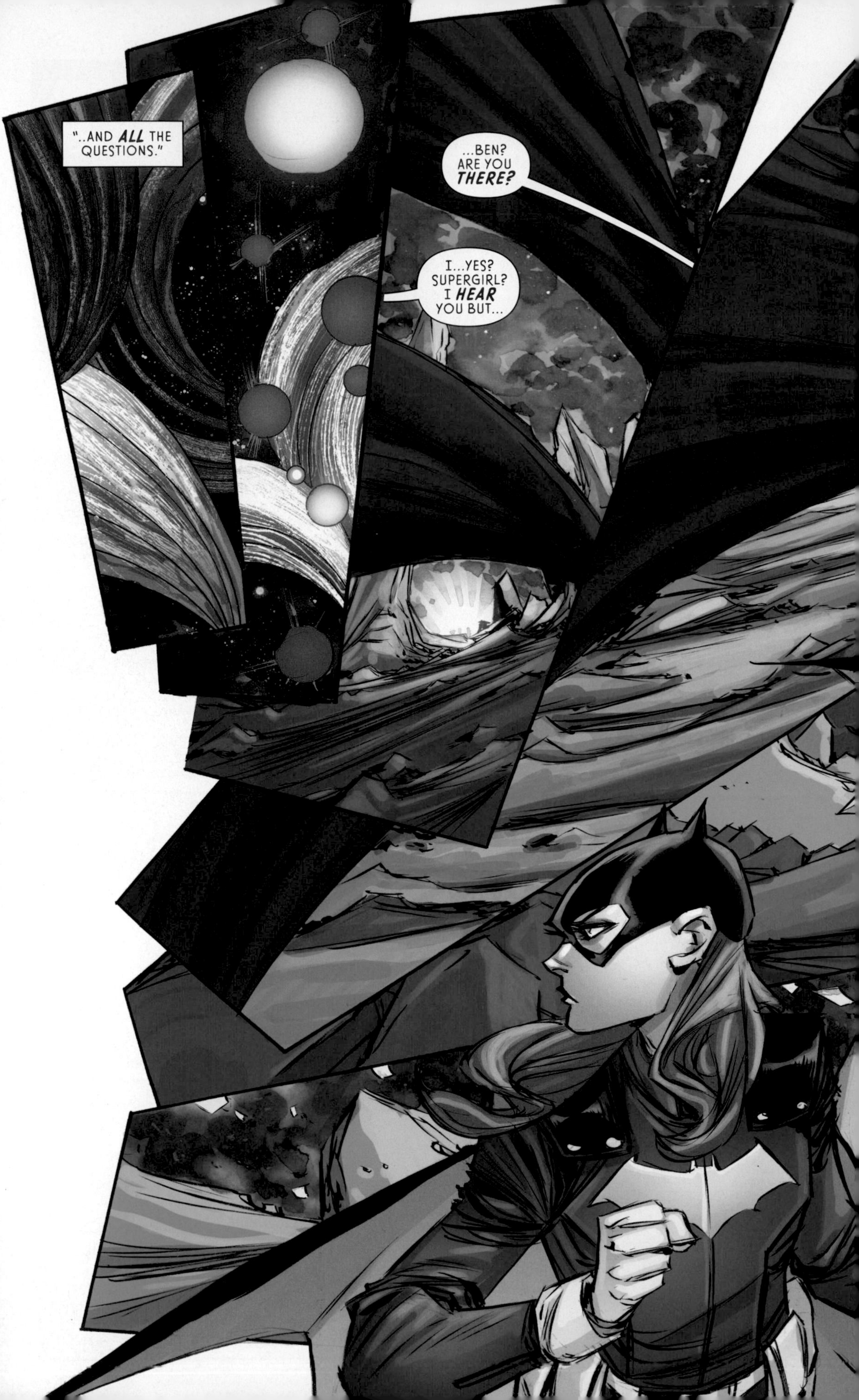
"..AND ALL THE QUESTIONS."
...BEN? ARE YOU THERE?
I...YES? SUPERGIRL? I HEAR YOU BUT...

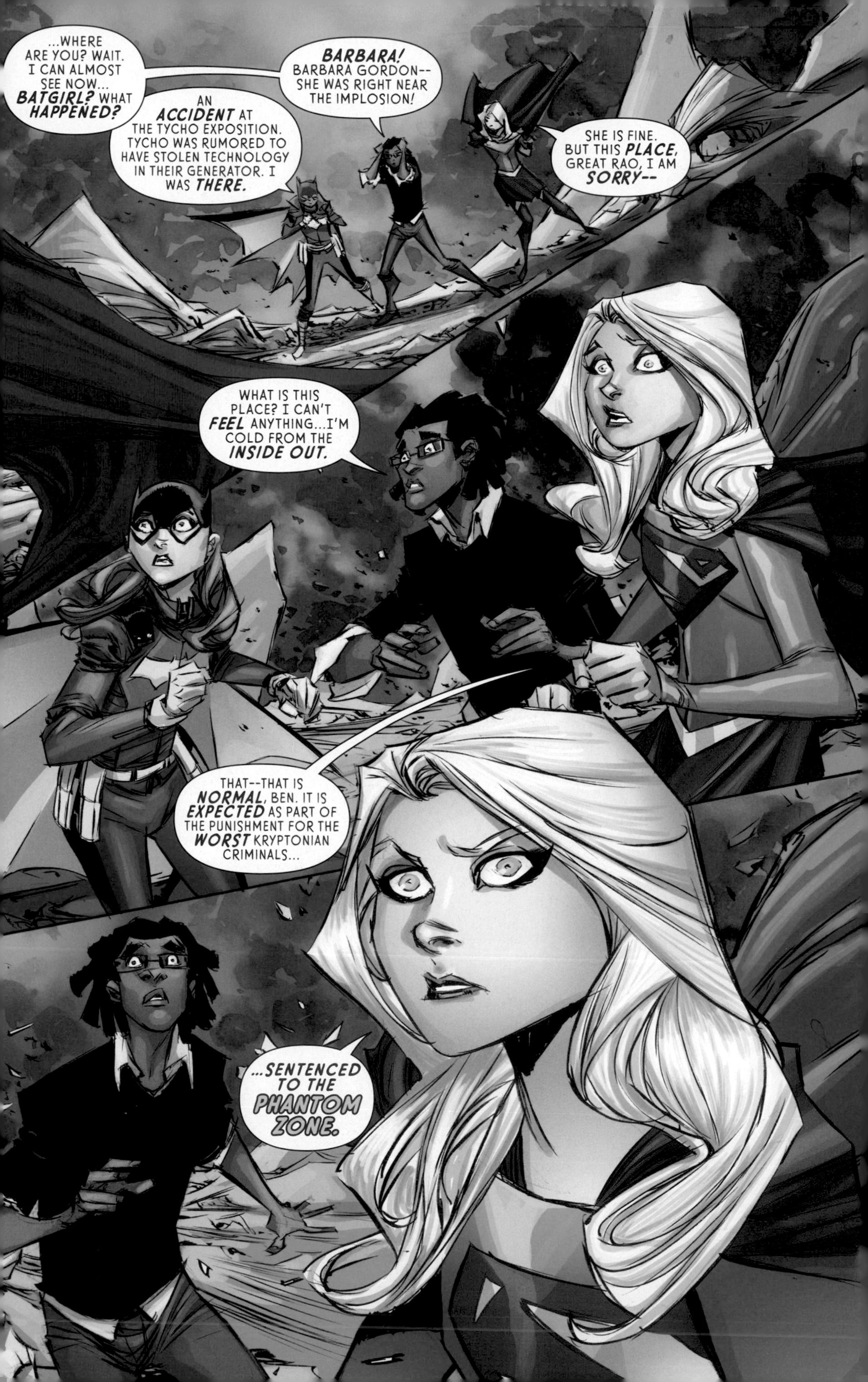

...WHERE ARE YOU? WAIT. I CAN ALMOST SEE NOW... BATGIRL? WHAT HAPPENED?
BARBARA! BARBARA GORDON-- SHE WAS RIGHT NEAR THE IMPLOSION!
AN ACCIDENT AT THE TYCHO EXPOSITION. TYCHO WAS RUMORED TO HAVE STOLEN TECHNOLOGY IN THEIR GENERATOR. I WAS THERE.
SHE IS FINE. BUT THIS PLACE, GREAT RAO, I AM SORRY--
WHAT IS THIS PLACE? I CAN'T FEEL ANYTHING...I'M COLD FROM THE INSIDE OUT.
THAT--THAT IS NORMAL, BEN. IT IS EXPECTED AS PART OF THE PUNISHMENT FOR THE WORST KRYPTONIAN CRIMINALS...
...SENTENCED TO THE PHANTOM ZONE.

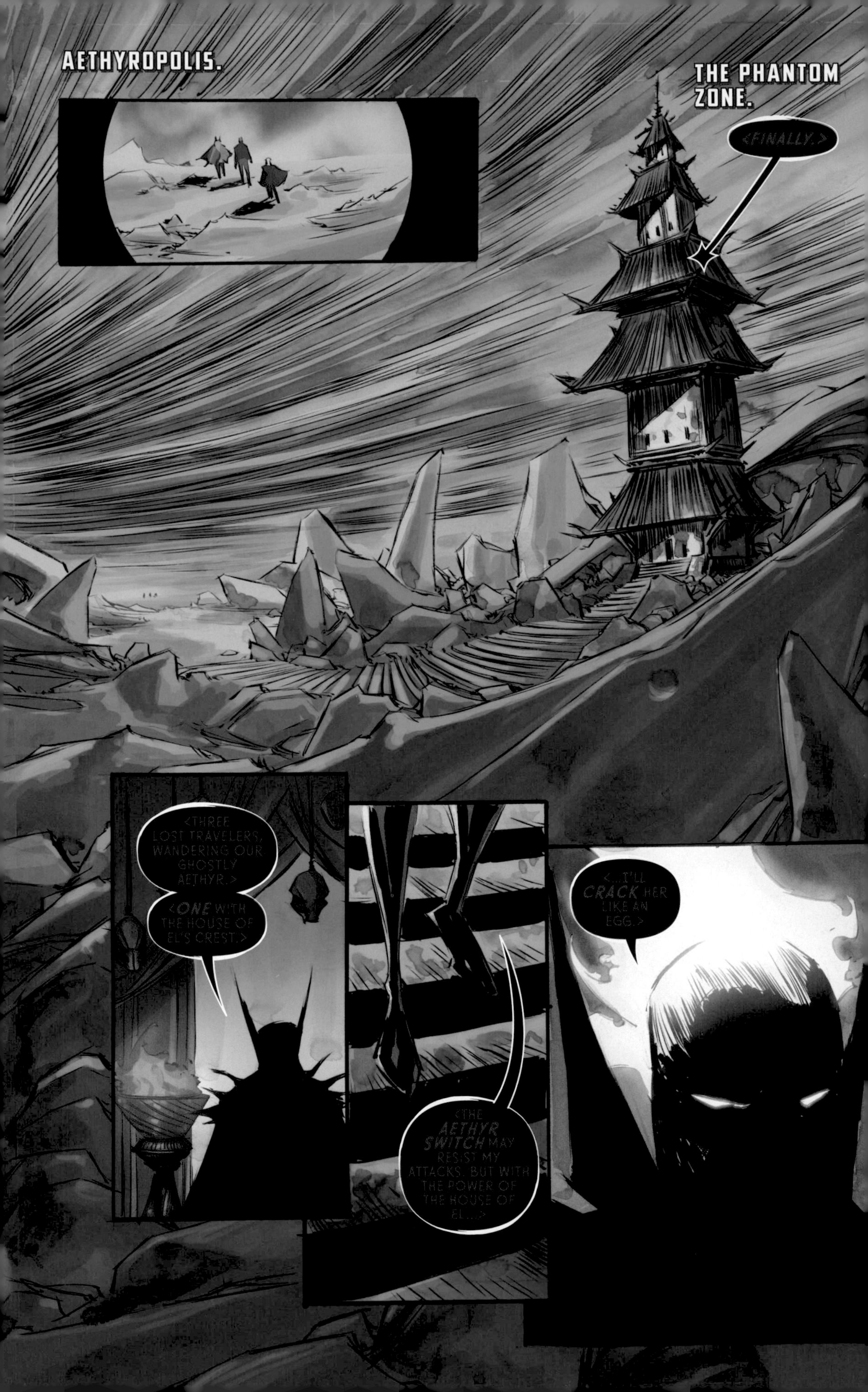
AETHYROPOLIS.
THE PHANTOM ZONE.
<FINALLY.>
<THREE LOST TRAVELERS, WANDERING OUR GHOSTLY AETHYR.>
<ONE WITH THE HOUSE OF EL'S CREST.>
<THE AETHYR SWITCH MAY RESIST MY ATTACKS, BUT WITH THE POWER OF THE HOUSE OF EL...>
<...I'LL CRACK HER LIKE AN EGG.>

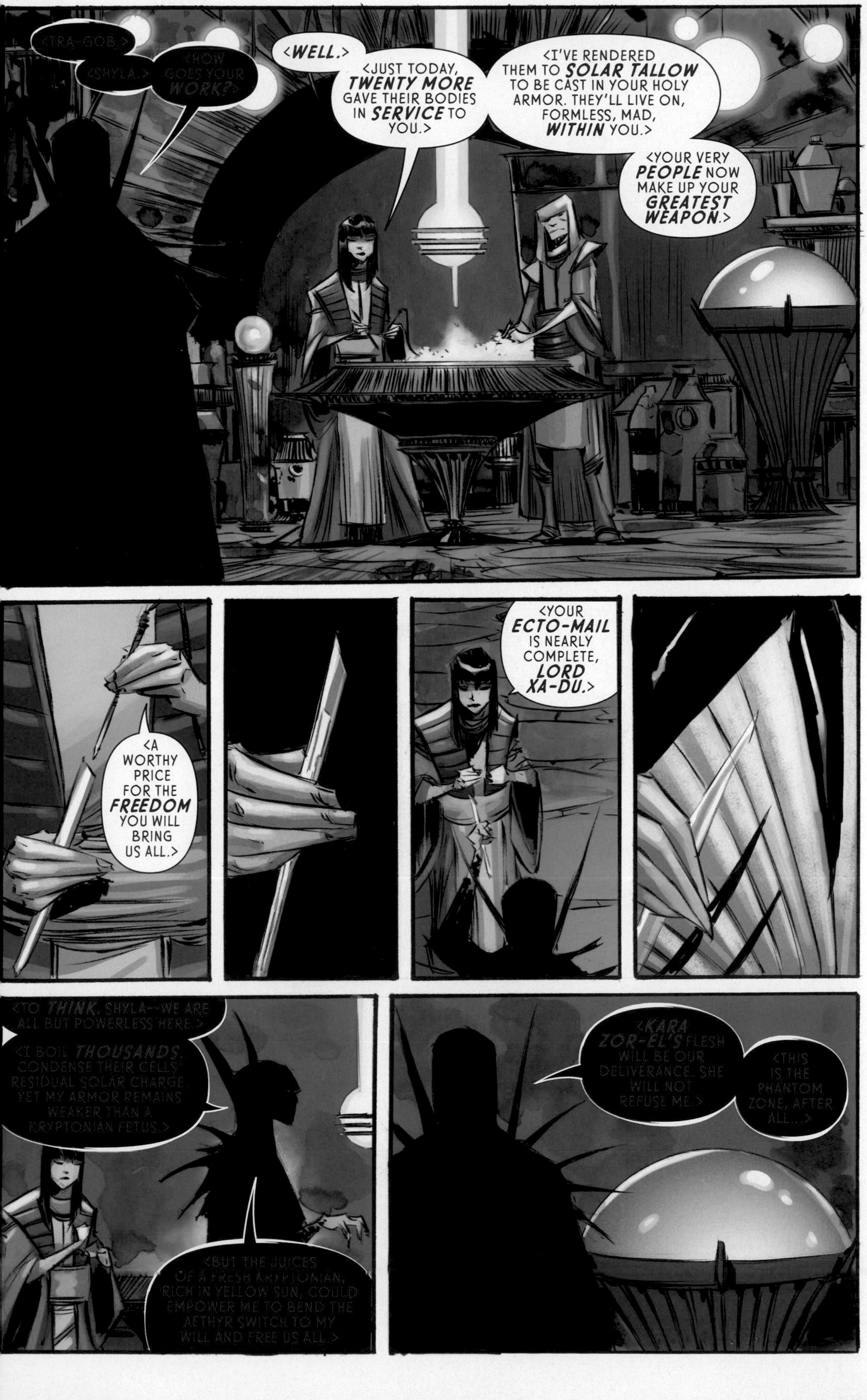

<TRA-GOB.>
<SHYLA.>
<HOW GOES YOUR WORK?>
<WELL.>
<JUST TODAY, TWENTY MORE GAVE THEIR BODIES IN SERVICE TO YOU.>
<I'VE RENDERED THEM TO SOLAR TALLOW TO BE CAST IN YOUR HOLY ARMOR. THEY'LL LIVE ON, FORMLESS, MAD, WITHIN YOU.>
<YOUR VERY PEOPLE NOW MAKE UP YOUR GREATEST WEAPON.>
<A WORTHY PRICE FOR THE FREEDOM YOU WILL BRING US ALL.>
<YOUR ECTO-MAIL IS NEARLY COMPLETE, LORD XA-DU.>
<TO THINK, SHYLA--WE ARE ALL BUT POWERLESS HERE.>
<I BOIL THOUSANDS, CONDENSE THEIR CELLS' RESIDUAL SOLAR CHARGE. YET MY ARMOR REMAINS WEAKER THAN A KRYPTONIAN FETUS.>
<BUT THE JUICES OF A FRESH KRYPTONIAN, RICH IN YELLOW SUN, COULD EMPOWER ME TO BEND THE AETHYR SWITCH TO MY WILL AND FREE US ALL.>
<KARA ZOR-EL'S FLESH WILL BE OUR DELIVERANCE. SHE WILL NOT REFUSE ME.>
<THIS IS THE PHANTOM ZONE, AFTER ALL...>

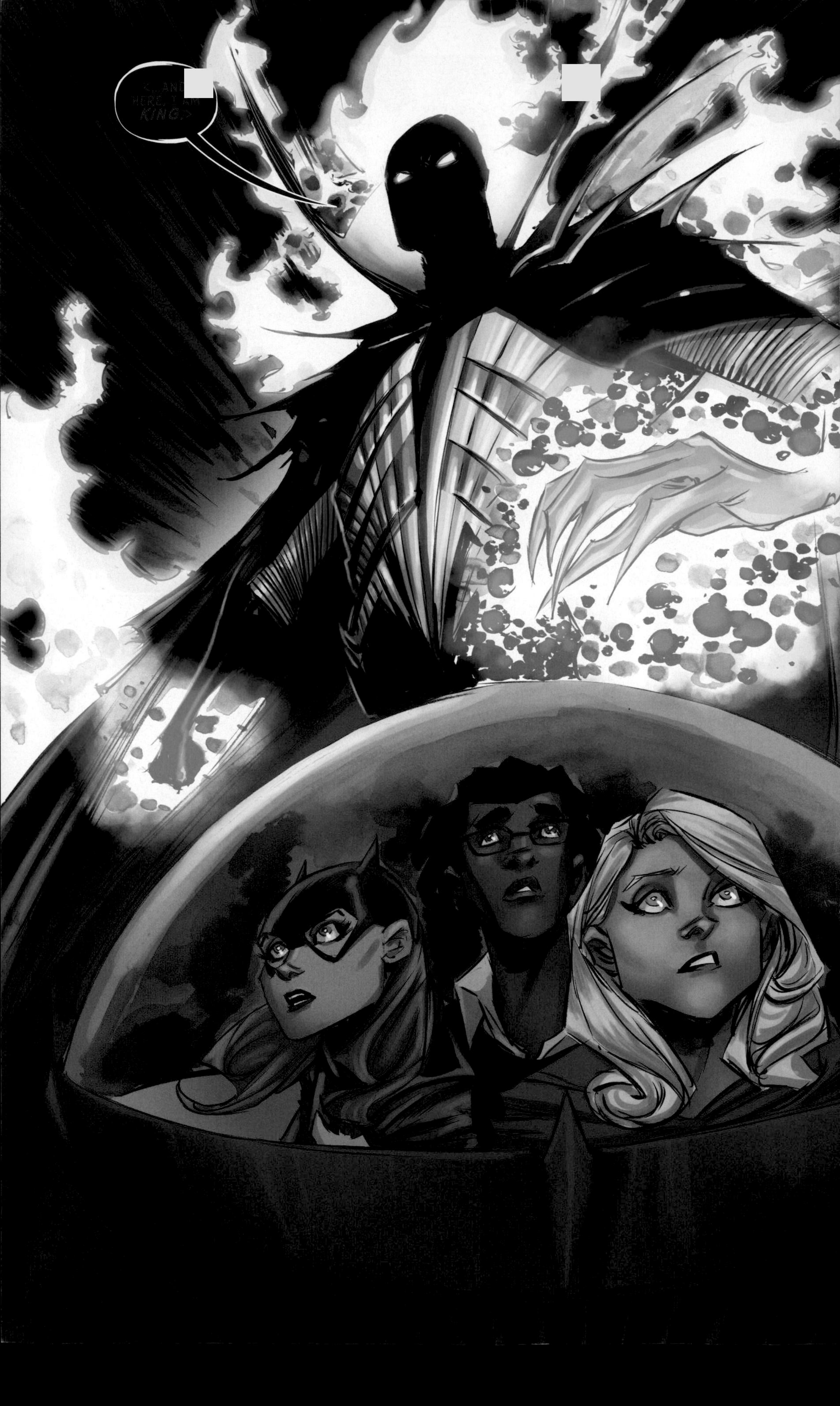
<...AND HERE, I AM KING.>

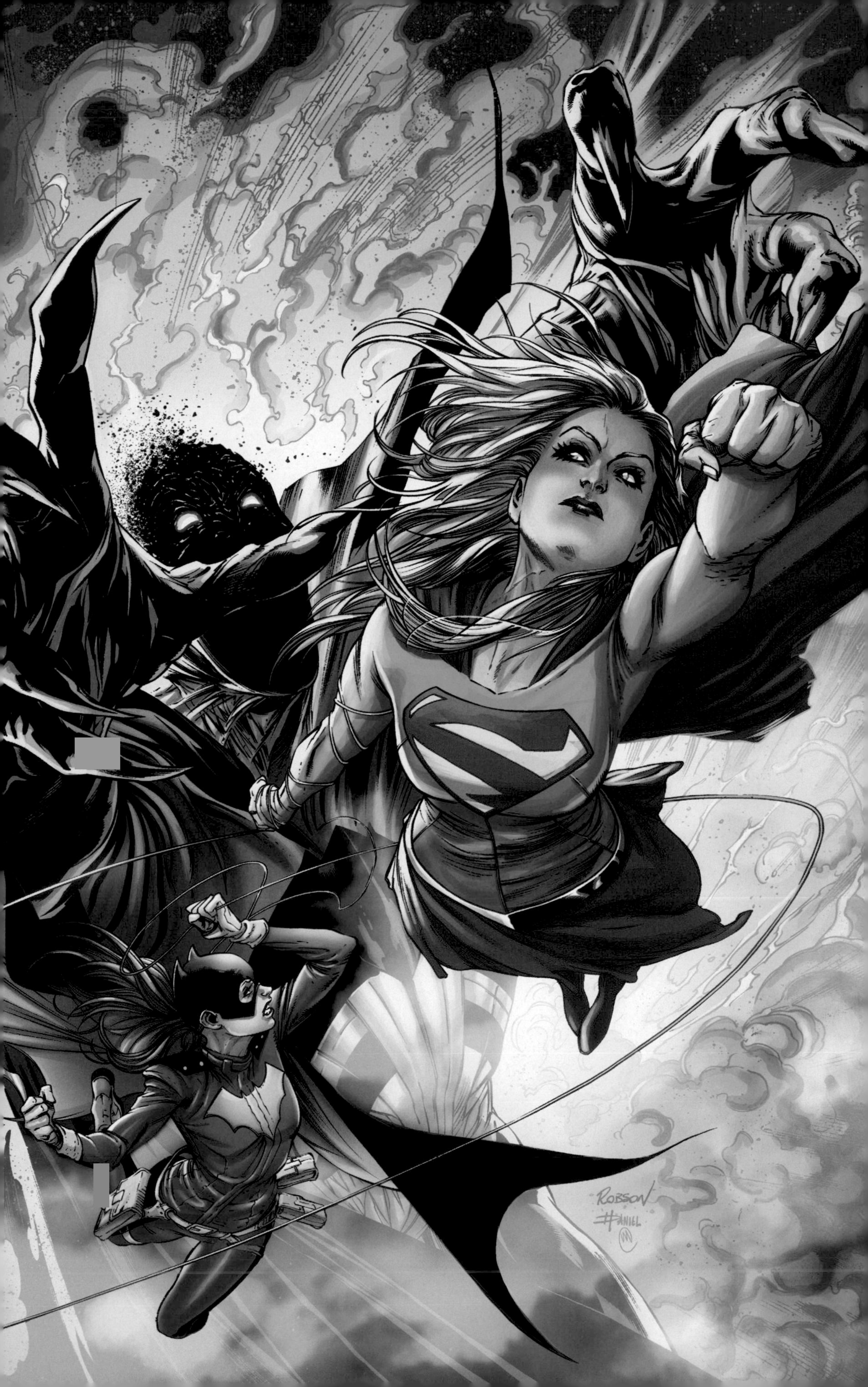
ROBSON
DANIEL

"ESCAPE FROM THE PHANTOM ZONE PART TWO"

STEVE ORLANDO writer * BRIAN CHING artist * MICHAEL ATIYEH colorist
cover by ROBSON ROCHA, DANIEL HENRIQUES and MICHAEL ATIYEH

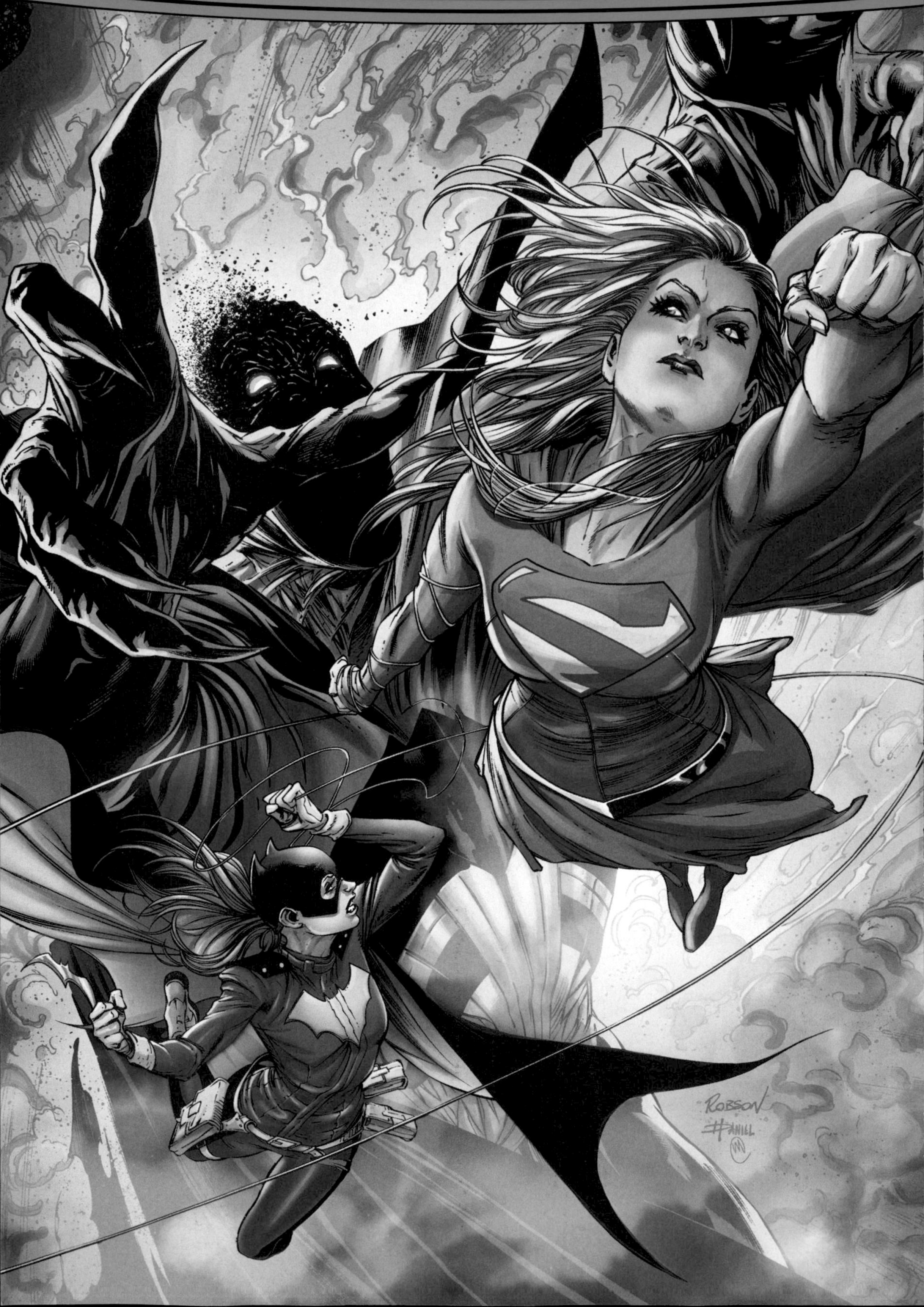
ROBSON

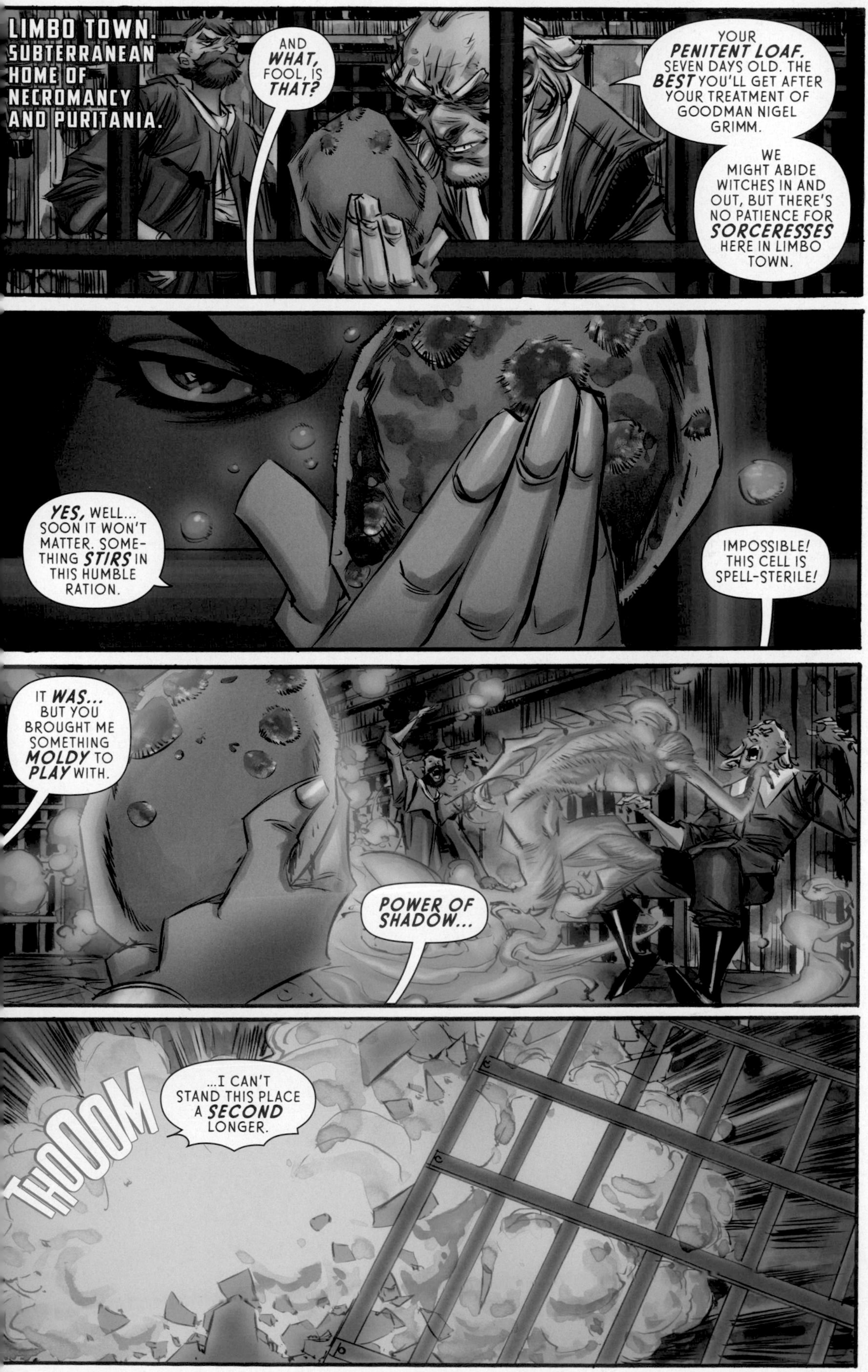

LIMBO TOWN. SUBTERRANEAN HOME OF NECROMANCY AND PURITANIA.
AND WHAT, FOOL, IS THAT?
YOUR PENITENT LOAF. SEVEN DAYS OLD. THE BEST YOU'LL GET AFTER YOUR TREATMENT OF GOODMAN NIGEL GRIMM.
WE MIGHT ABIDE WITCHES IN AND OUT, BUT THERE'S NO PATIENCE FOR SORCERESSES HERE IN LIMBO TOWN.
YES, WELL... SOON IT WON'T MATTER. SOME-THING STIRS IN THIS HUMBLE RATION.
IMPOSSIBLE! THIS CELL IS SPELL-STERILE!
IT WAS... BUT YOU BROUGHT ME SOMETHING MOLDY TO PLAY WITH.
POWER OF SHADOW...
THOOOM
...I CAN'T STAND THIS PLACE A SECOND LONGER.

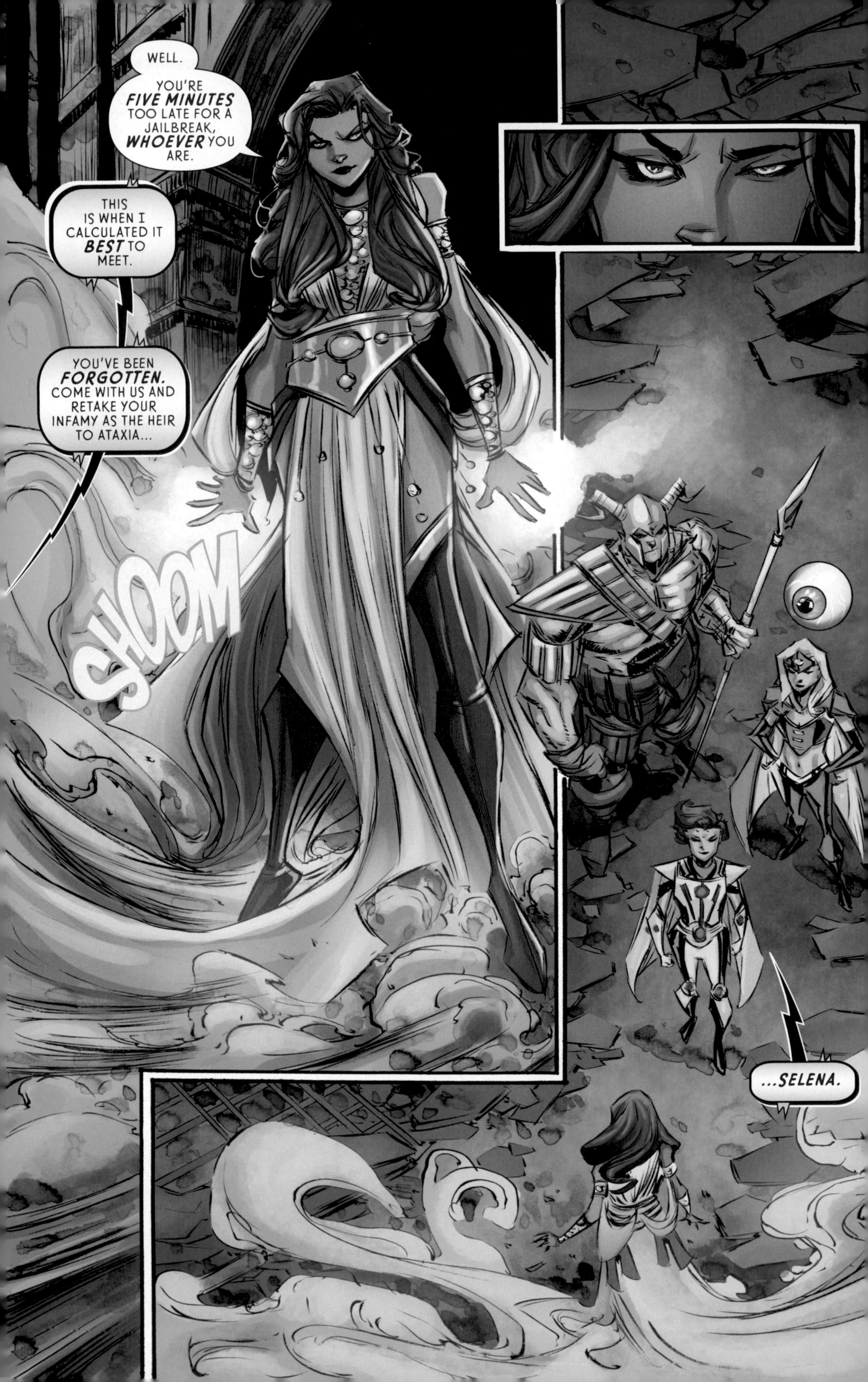
WELL.
YOU'RE FIVE MINUTES TOO LATE FOR A JAILBREAK, WHOEVER YOU ARE.
THIS IS WHEN I CALCULATED IT BEST TO MEET.
YOU'VE BEEN FORGOTTEN. COME WITH US AND RETAKE YOUR INFAMY AS THE HEIR TO ATAXIA...
SHOOM
...SELENA.

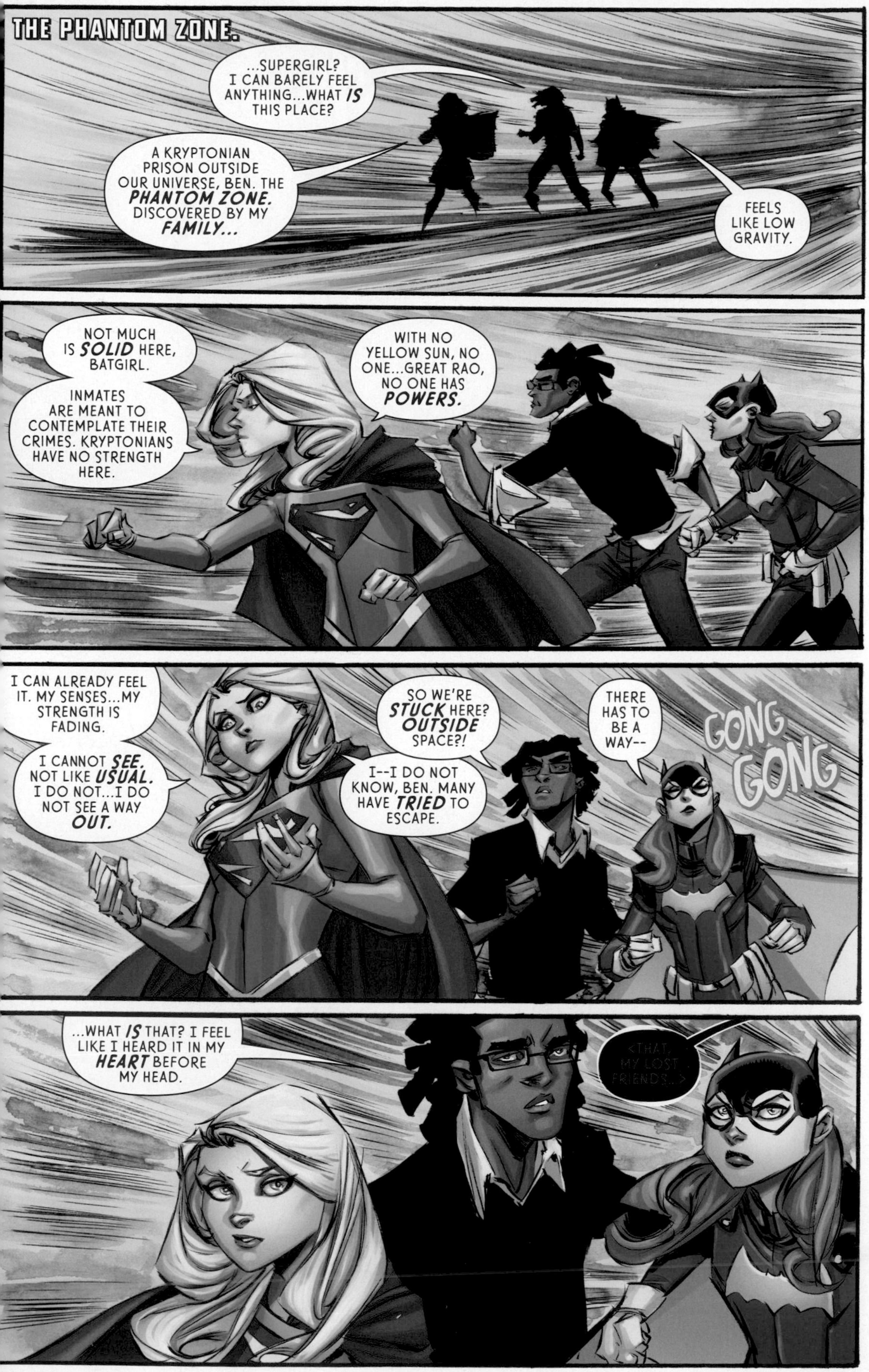
THE PHANTOM ZONE.
...SUPERGIRL? I CAN BARELY FEEL ANYTHING...WHAT IS THIS PLACE?
A KRYPTONIAN PRISON OUTSIDE OUR UNIVERSE, BEN. THE PHANTOM ZONE. DISCOVERED BY MY FAMILY...
FEELS LIKE LOW GRAVITY.
NOT MUCH IS SOLID HERE, BATGIRL.
INMATES ARE MEANT TO CONTEMPLATE THEIR CRIMES. KRYPTONIANS HAVE NO STRENGTH HERE.
WITH NO YELLOW SUN, NO ONE...GREAT RAO, NO ONE HAS POWERS.
I CAN ALREADY FEEL IT. MY SENSES...MY STRENGTH IS FADING.
I CANNOT SEE. NOT LIKE USUAL. I DO NOT...I DO NOT SEE A WAY OUT.
SO WE'RE STUCK HERE? OUTSIDE SPACE?!
I--I DO NOT KNOW, BEN. MANY HAVE TRIED TO ESCAPE.
THERE HAS TO BE A WAY--
GONG GONG
...WHAT IS THAT? I FEEL LIKE I HEARD IT IN MY HEART BEFORE MY HEAD.
<THAT, MY LOST FRIENDS...>

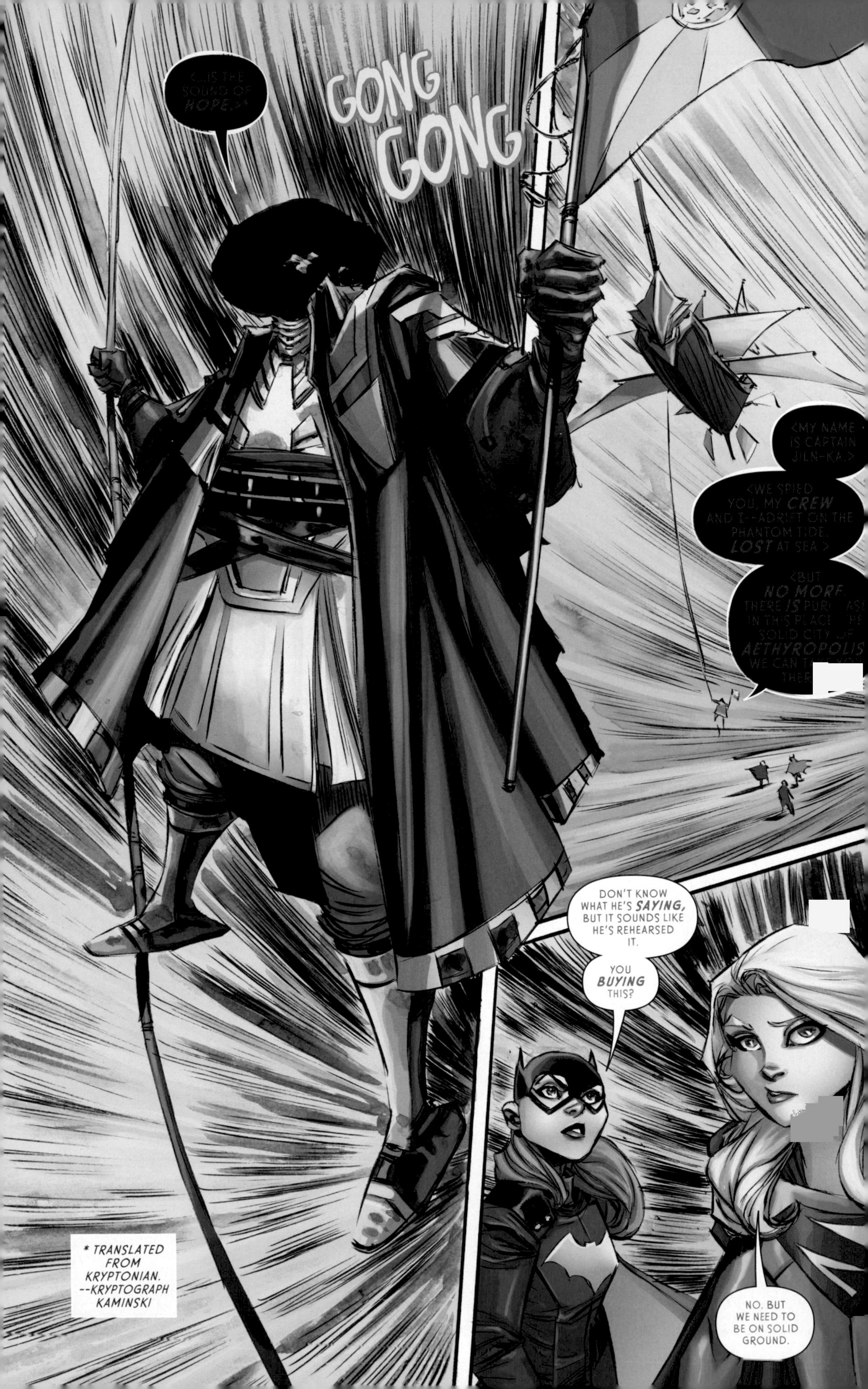
GONG GONG
<...IS THE SOUND OF HOPE.>*
<MY NAME IS CAPTAIN JILN-KA.>
<WE SPIED YOU, MY CREW AND I--ADRIFT ON THE PHANTOM TIDE. LOST AT SEA.>
<BUT NO MORE. THERE IS PUR… IN THIS PLACE… SOLID CITY OF AETHYROPOLIS. WE CAN T… THER…
DON'T KNOW WHAT HE'S SAYING, BUT IT SOUNDS LIKE HE'S REHEARSED IT.
YOU BUYING THIS?
NO. BUT WE NEED TO BE ON SOLID GROUND.
* TRANSLATED FROM KRYPTONIAN. --KRYPTOGRAPH KAMINSKI

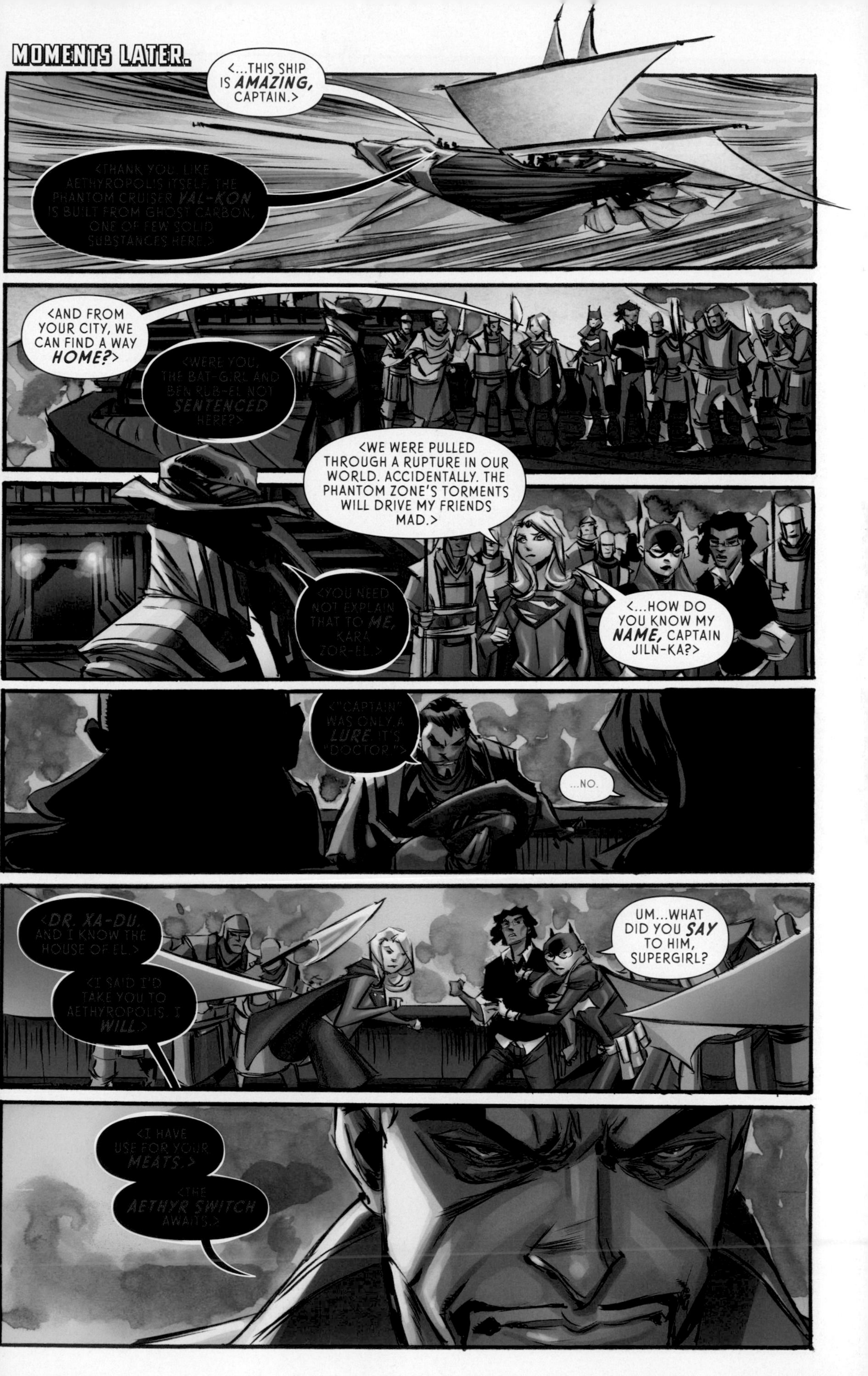
MOMENTS LATER.
<...THIS SHIP IS AMAZING, CAPTAIN.>
<THANK YOU. LIKE AETHYROPOLIS ITSELF, THE PHANTOM CRUISER VAL-KON IS BUILT FROM GHOST CARBON, ONE OF FEW SOLID SUBSTANCES HERE.>
<AND FROM YOUR CITY, WE CAN FIND A WAY HOME?>
<WERE YOU, THE BAT-GIRL AND BEN RUB-EL NOT SENTENCED HERE?>
<WE WERE PULLED THROUGH A RUPTURE IN OUR WORLD. ACCIDENTALLY. THE PHANTOM ZONE'S TORMENTS WILL DRIVE MY FRIENDS MAD.>
<YOU NEED NOT EXPLAIN THAT TO ME, KARA ZOR-EL.>
<...HOW DO YOU KNOW MY NAME, CAPTAIN JILN-KA?>
<"CAPTAIN" WAS ONLY A LURE. IT'S "DOCTOR.">
...NO.
<DR. XA-DU. AND I KNOW THE HOUSE OF EL.>
<I SAID I'D TAKE YOU TO AETHYROPOLIS. I WILL.>
UM...WHAT DID YOU SAY TO HIM, SUPERGIRL?
<I HAVE USE FOR YOUR MEATS.>
<THE AETHYR SWITCH AWAITS.>

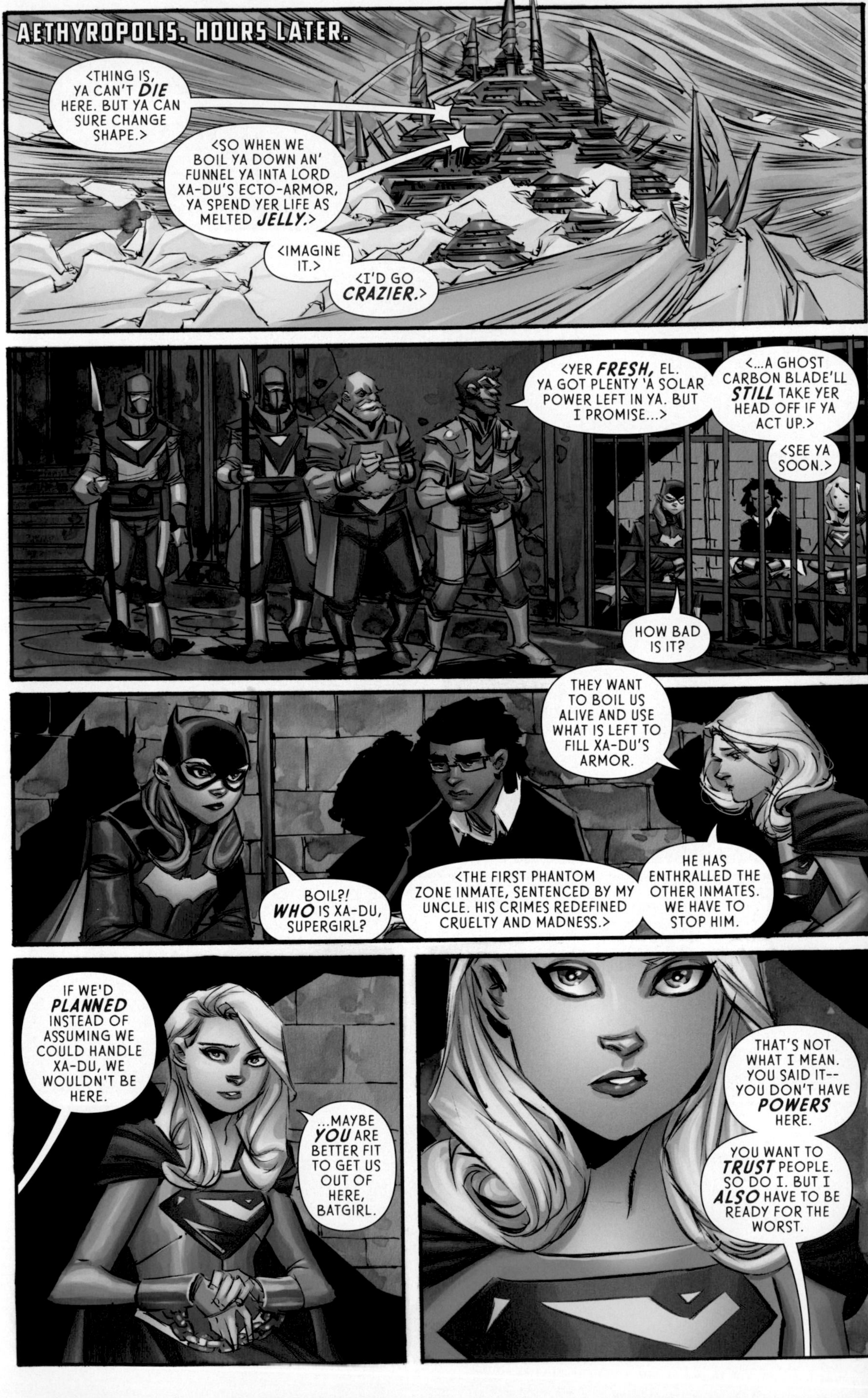
AETHYROPOLIS. HOURS LATER.
<THING IS, YA CAN'T DIE HERE. BUT YA CAN SURE CHANGE SHAPE.>
<SO WHEN WE BOIL YA DOWN AN' FUNNEL YA INTA LORD XA-DU'S ECTO-ARMOR, YA SPEND YER LIFE AS MELTED JELLY.>
<IMAGINE IT.>
<I'D GO CRAZIER.>
<YER FRESH, EL. YA GOT PLENTY 'A SOLAR POWER LEFT IN YA. BUT I PROMISE...>
<...A GHOST CARBON BLADE'LL STILL TAKE YER HEAD OFF IF YA ACT UP.>
<SEE YA SOON.>
HOW BAD IS IT?
THEY WANT TO BOIL US ALIVE AND USE WHAT IS LEFT TO FILL XA-DU'S ARMOR.
BOIL?! WHO IS XA-DU, SUPERGIRL?
<THE FIRST PHANTOM ZONE INMATE, SENTENCED BY MY UNCLE. HIS CRIMES REDEFINED CRUELTY AND MADNESS.>
HE HAS ENTHRALLED THE OTHER INMATES. WE HAVE TO STOP HIM.
IF WE'D PLANNED INSTEAD OF ASSUMING WE COULD HANDLE XA-DU, WE WOULDN'T BE HERE.
...MAYBE YOU ARE BETTER FIT TO GET US OUT OF HERE, BATGIRL.
THAT'S NOT WHAT I MEAN. YOU SAID IT-- YOU DON'T HAVE POWERS HERE.
YOU WANT TO TRUST PEOPLE. SO DO I. BUT I ALSO HAVE TO BE READY FOR THE WORST.

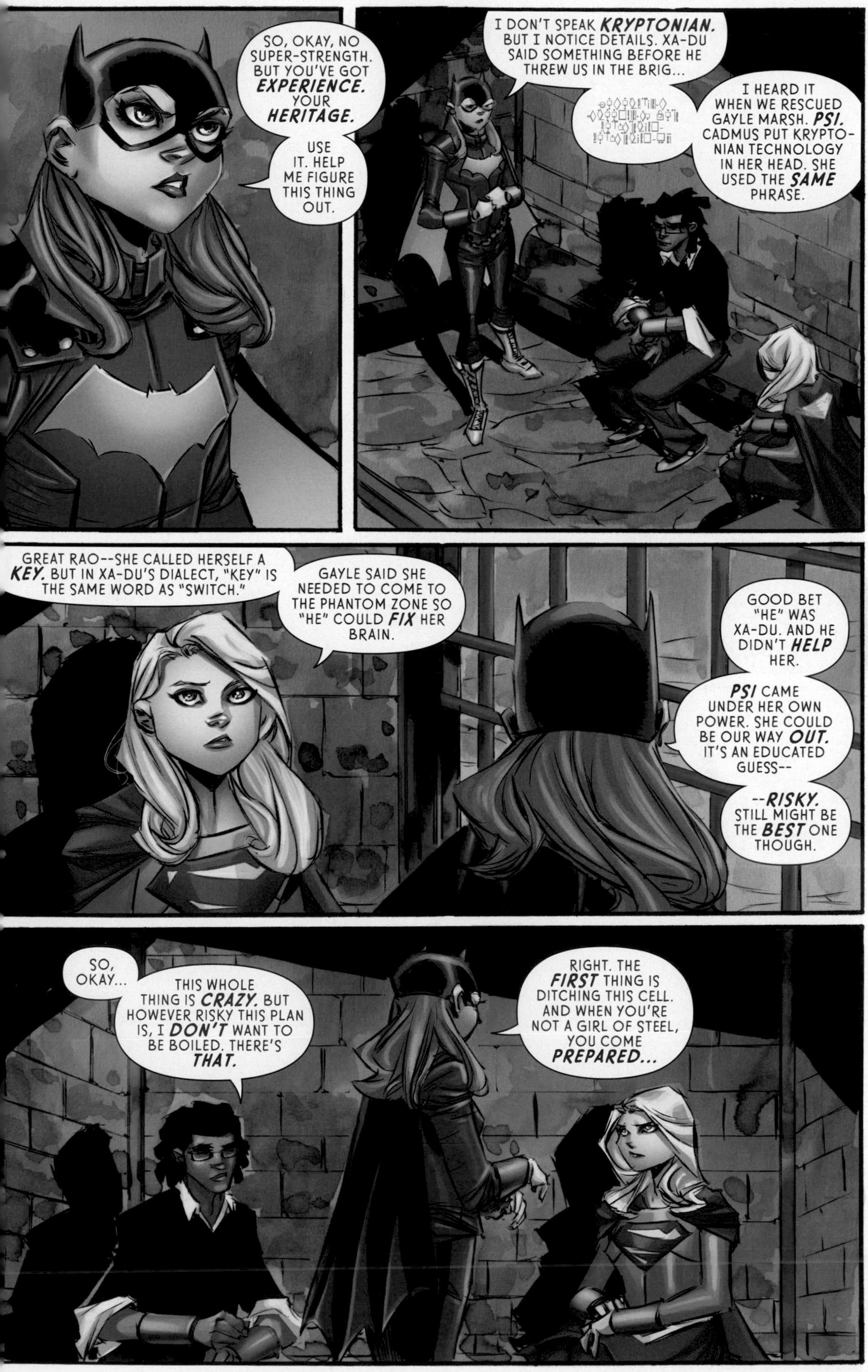
SO, OKAY, NO SUPER-STRENGTH. BUT YOU'VE GOT EXPERIENCE. YOUR HERITAGE.
USE IT. HELP ME FIGURE THIS THING OUT.
I DON'T SPEAK KRYPTONIAN. BUT I NOTICE DETAILS. XA-DU SAID SOMETHING BEFORE HE THREW US IN THE BRIG...
I HEARD IT WHEN WE RESCUED GAYLE MARSH. PSI. CADMUS PUT KRYPTONIAN TECHNOLOGY IN HER HEAD. SHE USED THE SAME PHRASE.
GREAT RAO--SHE CALLED HERSELF A KEY. BUT IN XA-DU'S DIALECT, "KEY" IS THE SAME WORD AS "SWITCH."
GAYLE SAID SHE NEEDED TO COME TO THE PHANTOM ZONE SO "HE" COULD FIX HER BRAIN.
GOOD BET "HE" WAS XA-DU. AND HE DIDN'T HELP HER.
PSI CAME UNDER HER OWN POWER. SHE COULD BE OUR WAY OUT. IT'S AN EDUCATED GUESS--
--RISKY. STILL MIGHT BE THE BEST ONE THOUGH.
SO, OKAY...
THIS WHOLE THING IS CRAZY. BUT HOWEVER RISKY THIS PLAN IS, I DON'T WANT TO BE BOILED. THERE'S THAT.
RIGHT. THE FIRST THING IS DITCHING THIS CELL. AND WHEN YOU'RE NOT A GIRL OF STEEL, YOU COME PREPARED...

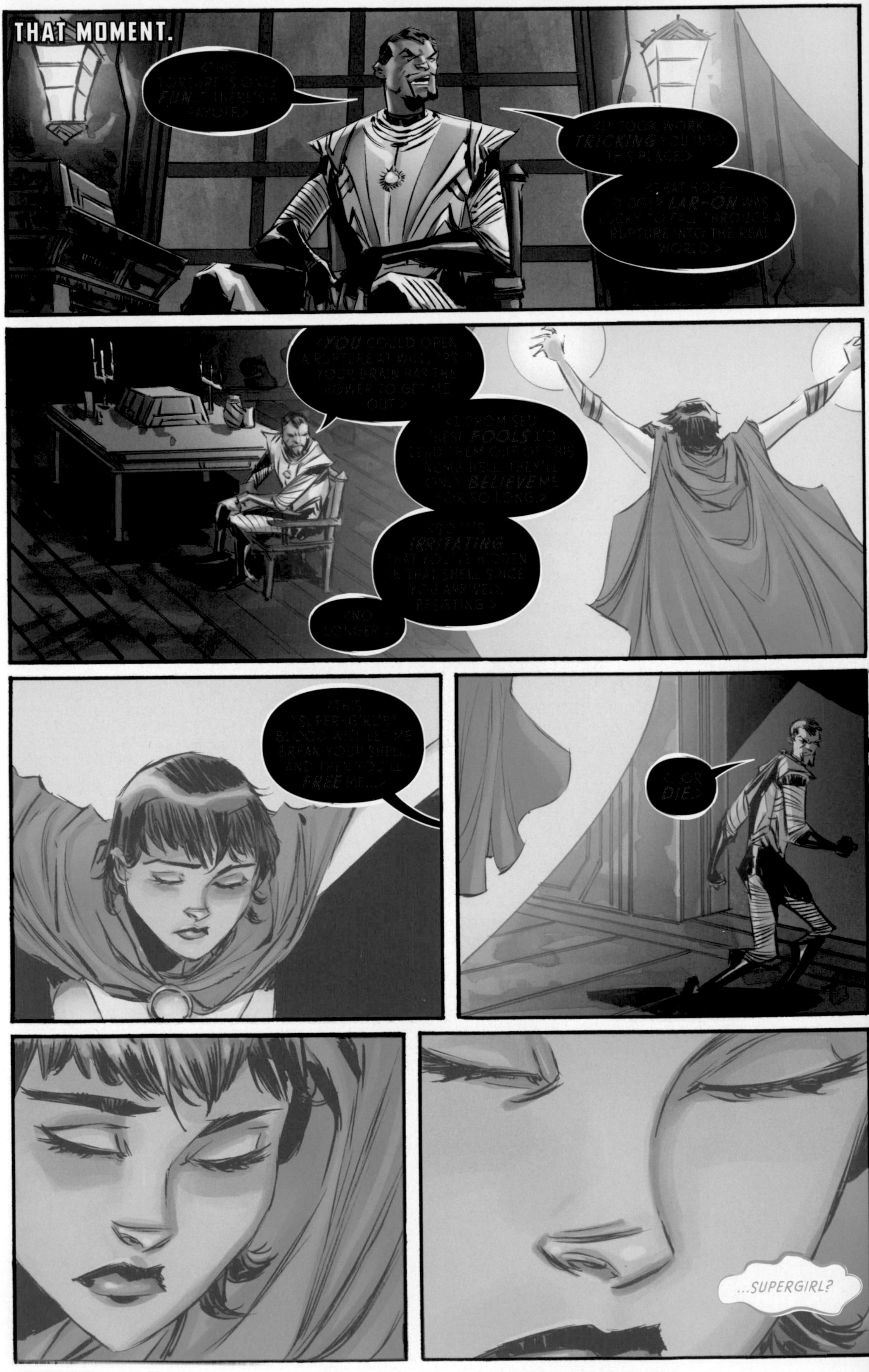
THAT MOMENT.
<THIS TORTURE IS ONLY FUN IF THERE'S A PAYOFF>
<IT TOOK WORK TRICKING YOU INTO THIS PLACE>
<THAT HOLE-DIGGER LAR-ON WAS LUCKY TO FALL THROUGH A RUPTURE INTO THE REAL WORLD>
<YOU COULD OPEN A RUPTURE AT WILL. YES, YOUR BRAIN HAS THE POWER TO GET ME OUT>
<I PROMISED THESE FOOLS I'D LEAD THEM OUT OF THIS NUMB HELL. THEY'LL ONLY BELIEVE ME FOR SO LONG>
<SO IT'S IRRITATING THAT YOU'VE HIDDEN IN THAT SHELL SINCE YOU ARRIVED, RESISTING>
<NO LONGER>
<THIS "SUPER-GIRL'S" BLOOD WILL LET ME BREAK YOUR SHELL. AND THEN YOU'LL FREE ME...>
<...OR DIE>
...SUPERGIRL?

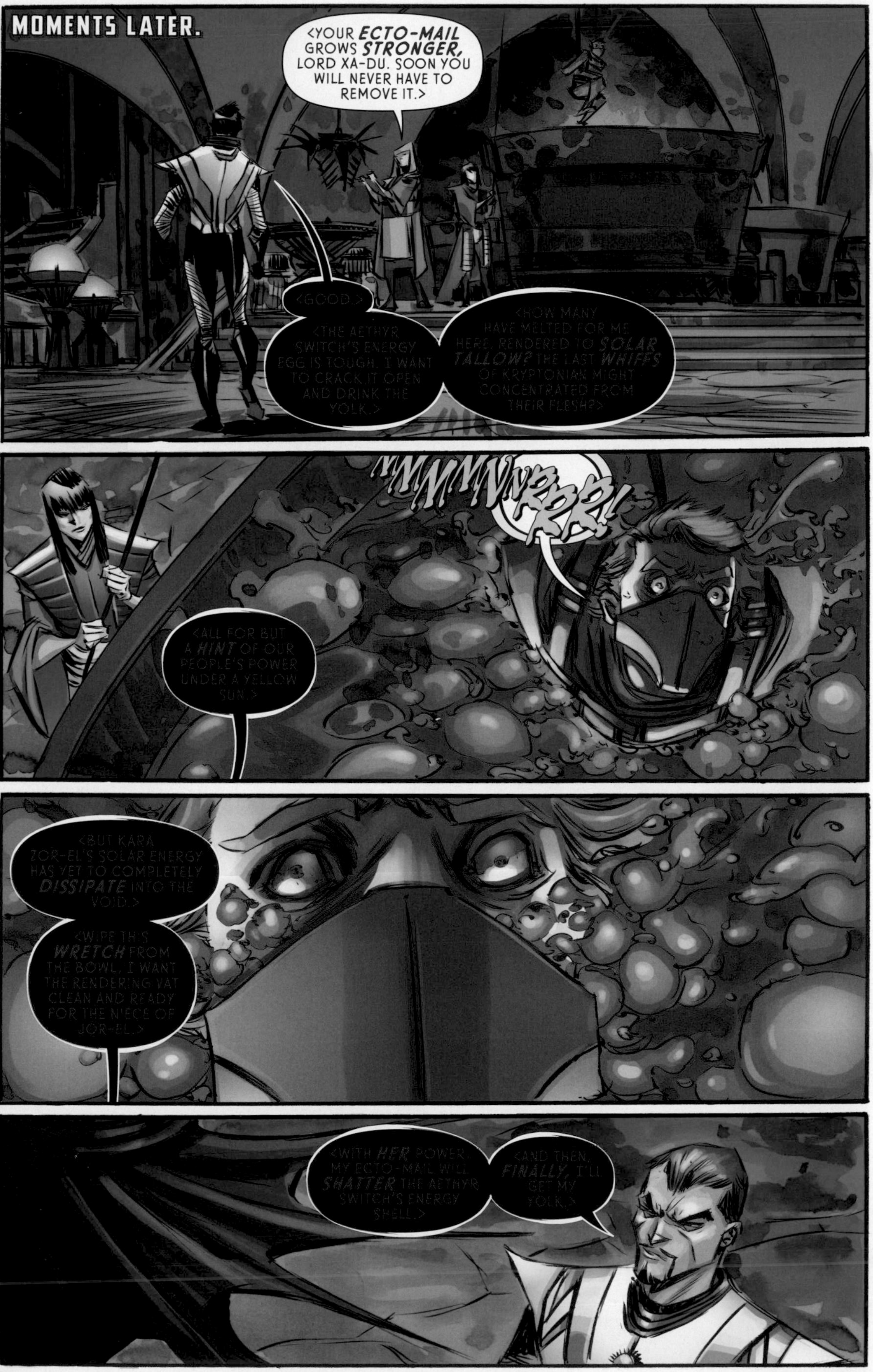
MOMENTS LATER.
<YOUR ECTO-MAIL GROWS STRONGER, LORD XA-DU. SOON YOU WILL NEVER HAVE TO REMOVE IT.>
<GOOD.>
<THE AETHYR SWITCH'S ENERGY EGG IS TOUGH. I WANT TO CRACK IT OPEN AND DRINK THE YOLK.>
<HOW MANY HAVE MELTED FOR ME HERE, RENDERED TO SOLAR TALLOW? THE LAST WHIFFS OF KRYPTONIAN MIGHT CONCENTRATED FROM THEIR FLESH?>
NNMMMNNNRRR!
<ALL FOR BUT A HINT OF OUR PEOPLE'S POWER UNDER A YELLOW SUN.>
<BUT KARA ZOR-EL'S SOLAR ENERGY HAS YET TO COMPLETELY DISSIPATE INTO THE VOID.>
<WIPE THIS WRETCH FROM THE BOWL. I WANT THE RENDERING VAT CLEAN AND READY FOR THE NIECE OF JOR-EL.>
<WITH HER POWER, MY ECTO-MAIL WILL SHATTER THE AETHYR SWITCH'S ENERGY SHELL.>
<AND THEN, FINALLY, I'LL GET MY YOLK.>

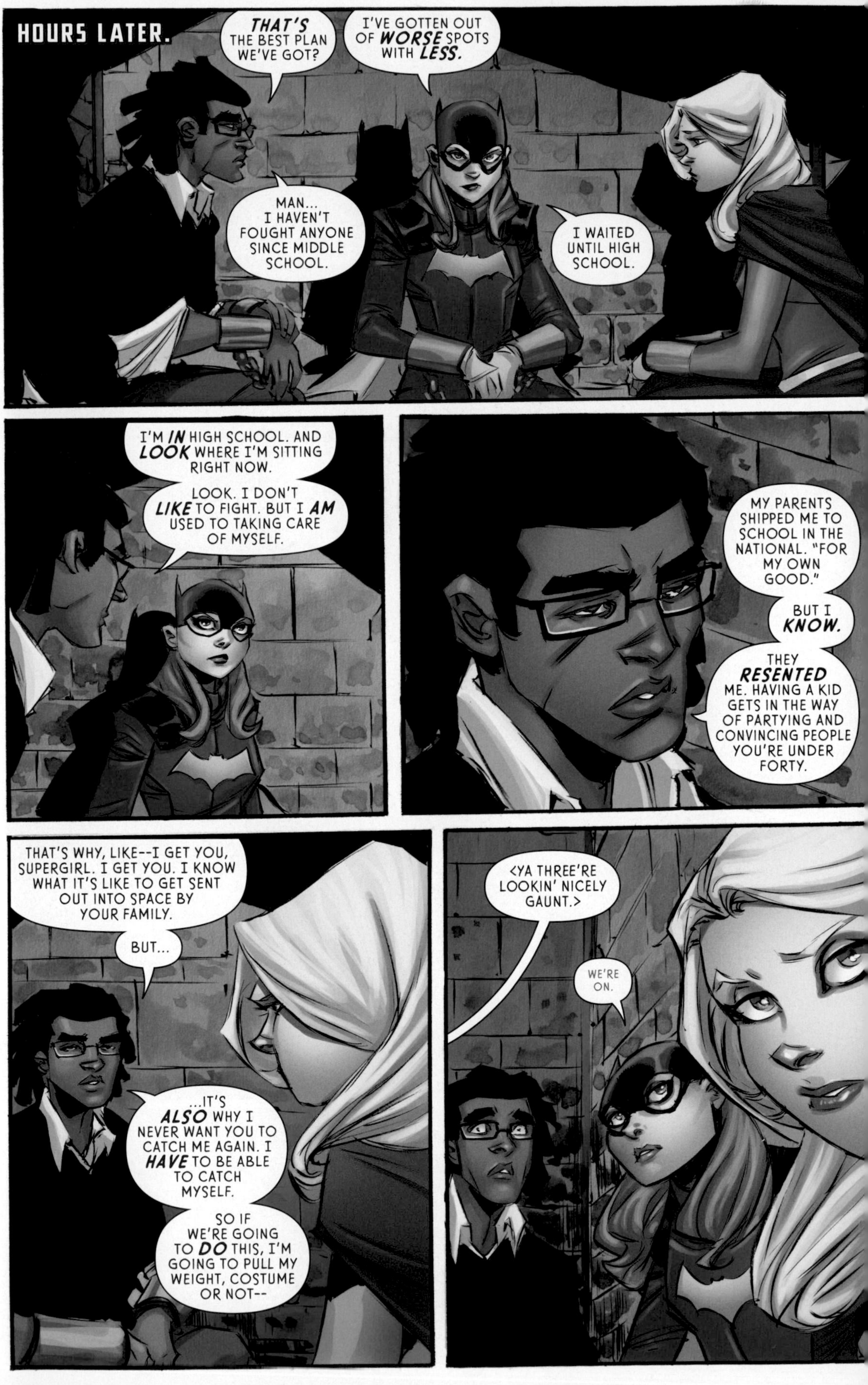
HOURS LATER.
THAT'S THE BEST PLAN WE'VE GOT?
I'VE GOTTEN OUT OF WORSE SPOTS WITH LESS.
MAN... I HAVEN'T FOUGHT ANYONE SINCE MIDDLE SCHOOL.
I WAITED UNTIL HIGH SCHOOL.
I'M IN HIGH SCHOOL. AND LOOK WHERE I'M SITTING RIGHT NOW.
LOOK. I DON'T LIKE TO FIGHT. BUT I AM USED TO TAKING CARE OF MYSELF.
MY PARENTS SHIPPED ME TO SCHOOL IN THE NATIONAL. "FOR MY OWN GOOD."
BUT I KNOW.
THEY RESENTED ME. HAVING A KID GETS IN THE WAY OF PARTYING AND CONVINCING PEOPLE YOU'RE UNDER FORTY.
THAT'S WHY, LIKE--I GET YOU, SUPERGIRL. I GET YOU. I KNOW WHAT IT'S LIKE TO GET SENT OUT INTO SPACE BY YOUR FAMILY.
BUT...
...IT'S ALSO WHY I NEVER WANT YOU TO CATCH ME AGAIN. I HAVE TO BE ABLE TO CATCH MYSELF.
SO IF WE'RE GOING TO DO THIS, I'M GOING TO PULL MY WEIGHT, COSTUME OR NOT--
<YA THREE'RE LOOKIN' NICELY GAUNT.>
WE'RE ON.

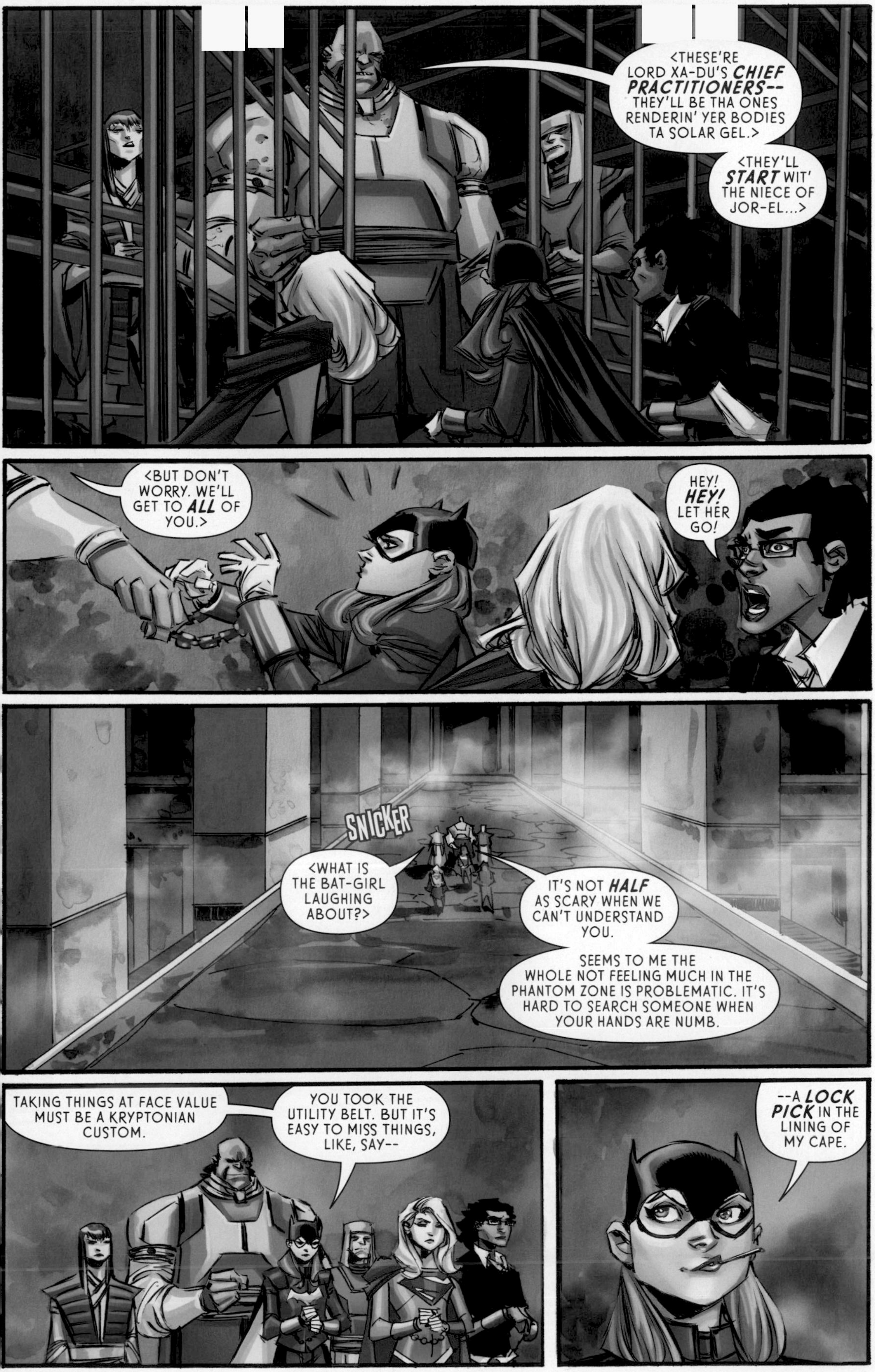
<THESE'RE LORD XA-DU'S CHIEF PRACTITIONERS-- THEY'LL BE THA ONES RENDERIN' YER BODIES TA SOLAR GEL.>
<THEY'LL START WIT' THE NIECE OF JOR-EL...>
<BUT DON'T WORRY. WE'LL GET TO ALL OF YOU.>
HEY! HEY! LET HER GO!
SNICKER
<WHAT IS THE BAT-GIRL LAUGHING ABOUT?>
IT'S NOT HALF AS SCARY WHEN WE CAN'T UNDERSTAND YOU.
SEEMS TO ME THE WHOLE NOT FEELING MUCH IN THE PHANTOM ZONE IS PROBLEMATIC. IT'S HARD TO SEARCH SOMEONE WHEN YOUR HANDS ARE NUMB.
TAKING THINGS AT FACE VALUE MUST BE A KRYPTONIAN CUSTOM.
YOU TOOK THE UTILITY BELT. BUT IT'S EASY TO MISS THINGS, LIKE, SAY--
--A LOCK PICK IN THE LINING OF MY CAPE.

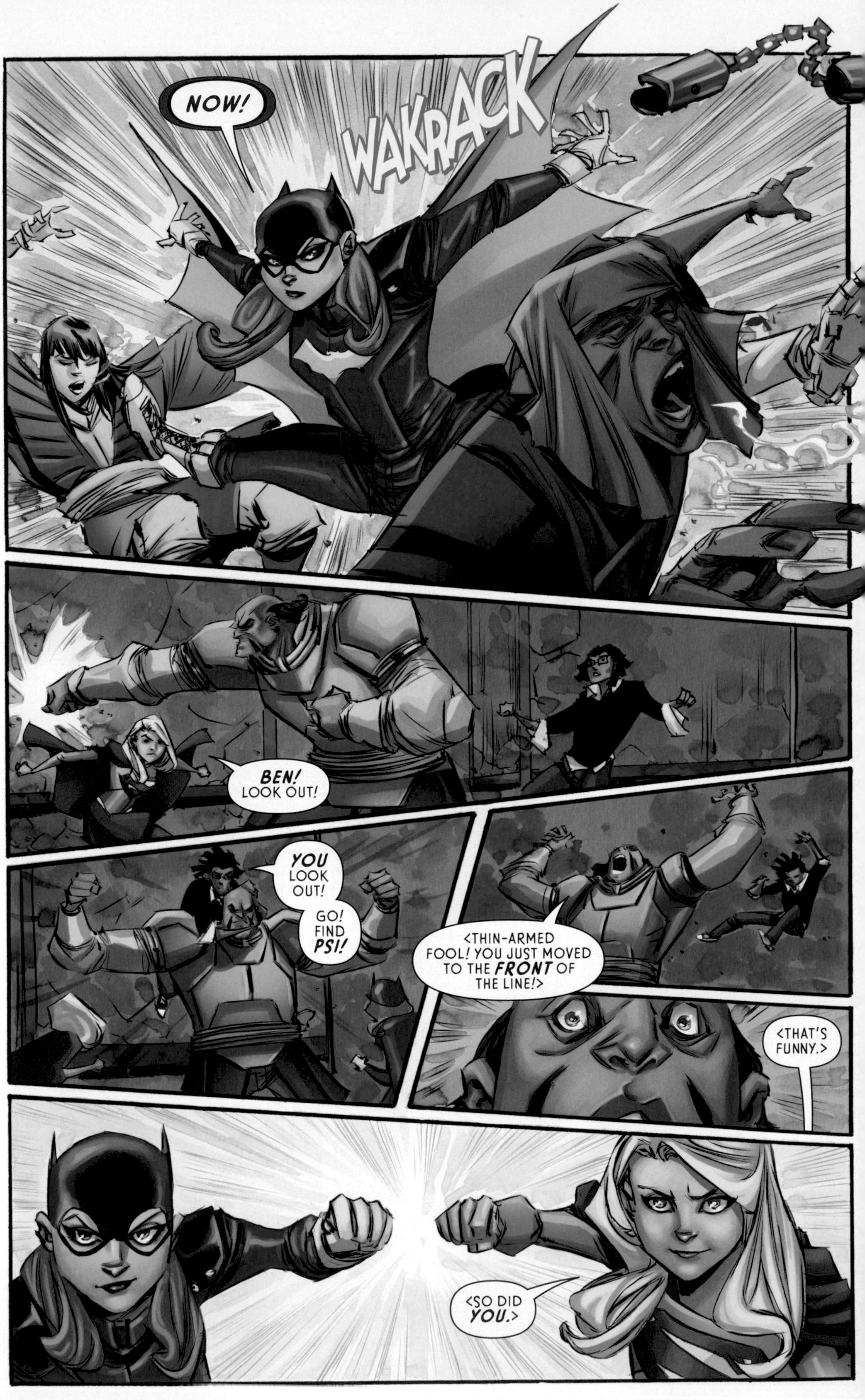
NOW!
WAKRACK
BEN! LOOK OUT!
YOU LOOK OUT!
GO! FIND PSI!
<THIN-ARMED FOOL! YOU JUST MOVED TO THE FRONT OF THE LINE!>
<THAT'S FUNNY.>
<SO DID YOU.>

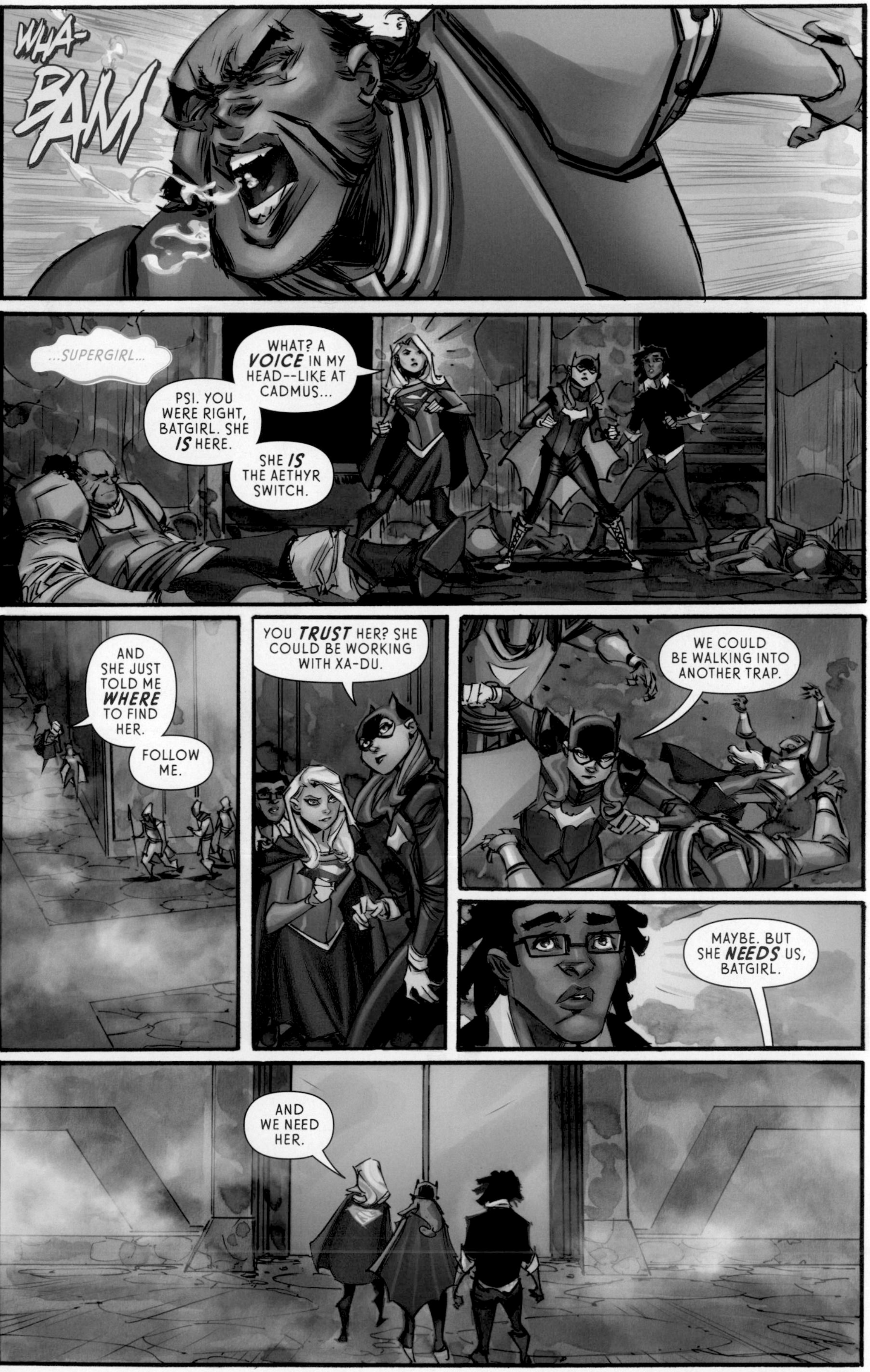
WHA-BAM
...SUPERGIRL...
WHAT? A VOICE IN MY HEAD--LIKE AT CADMUS...
PSI. YOU WERE RIGHT, BATGIRL. SHE IS HERE.
SHE IS THE AETHYR SWITCH.
AND SHE JUST TOLD ME WHERE TO FIND HER.
FOLLOW ME.
YOU TRUST HER? SHE COULD BE WORKING WITH XA-DU.
WE COULD BE WALKING INTO ANOTHER TRAP.
MAYBE. BUT SHE NEEDS US, BATGIRL.
AND WE NEED HER.

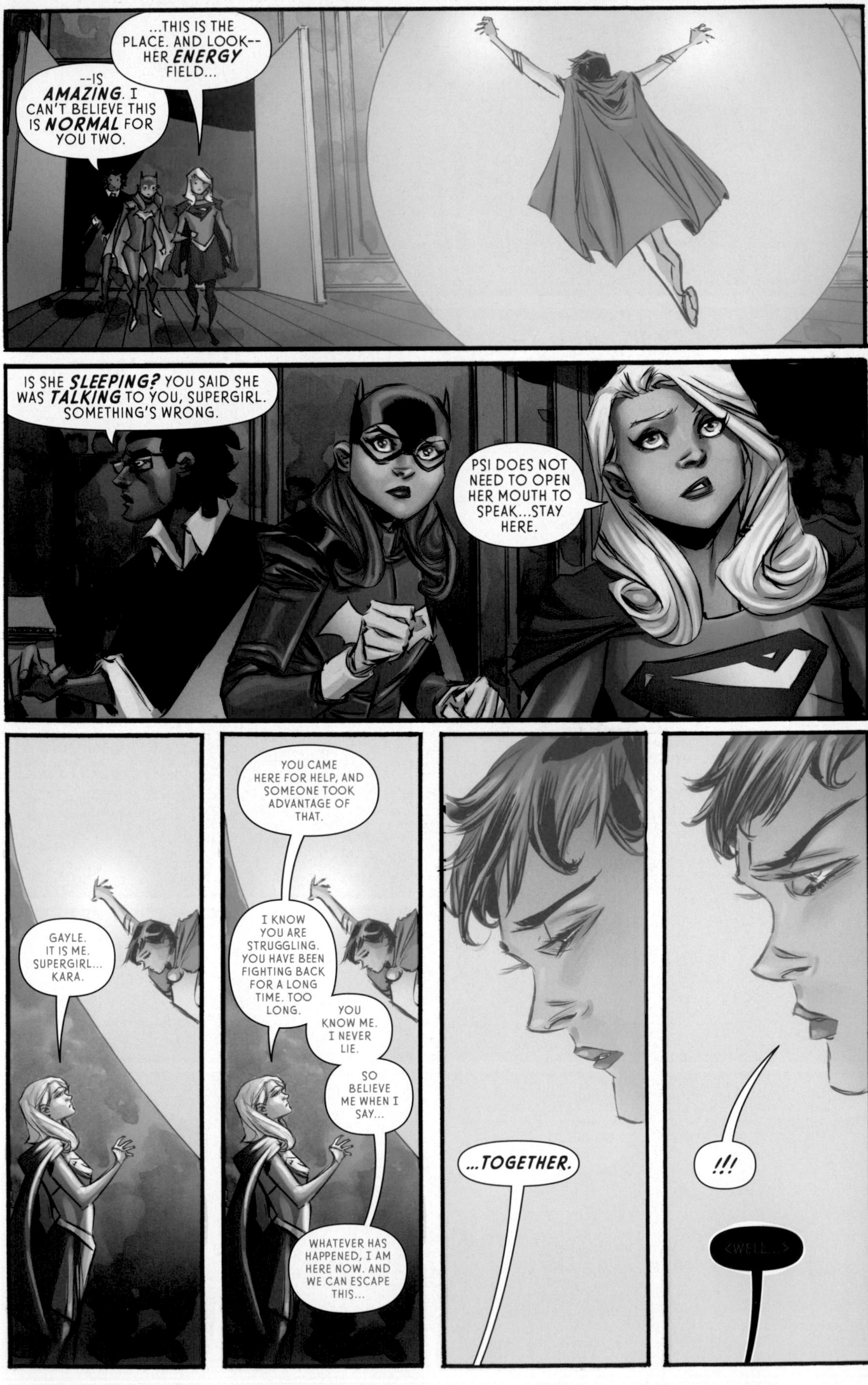
...THIS IS THE PLACE. AND LOOK-- HER ENERGY FIELD...
--IS AMAZING. I CAN'T BELIEVE THIS IS NORMAL FOR YOU TWO.
IS SHE SLEEPING? YOU SAID SHE WAS TALKING TO YOU, SUPERGIRL. SOMETHING'S WRONG.
PSI DOES NOT NEED TO OPEN HER MOUTH TO SPEAK...STAY HERE.
GAYLE. IT IS ME. SUPERGIRL... KARA.
YOU CAME HERE FOR HELP, AND SOMEONE TOOK ADVANTAGE OF THAT.
I KNOW YOU ARE STRUGGLING. YOU HAVE BEEN FIGHTING BACK FOR A LONG TIME. TOO LONG.
YOU KNOW ME. I NEVER LIE.
SO BELIEVE ME WHEN I SAY...
WHATEVER HAS HAPPENED, I AM HERE NOW. AND WE CAN ESCAPE THIS...
...TOGETHER.
!!!
<WELL...>

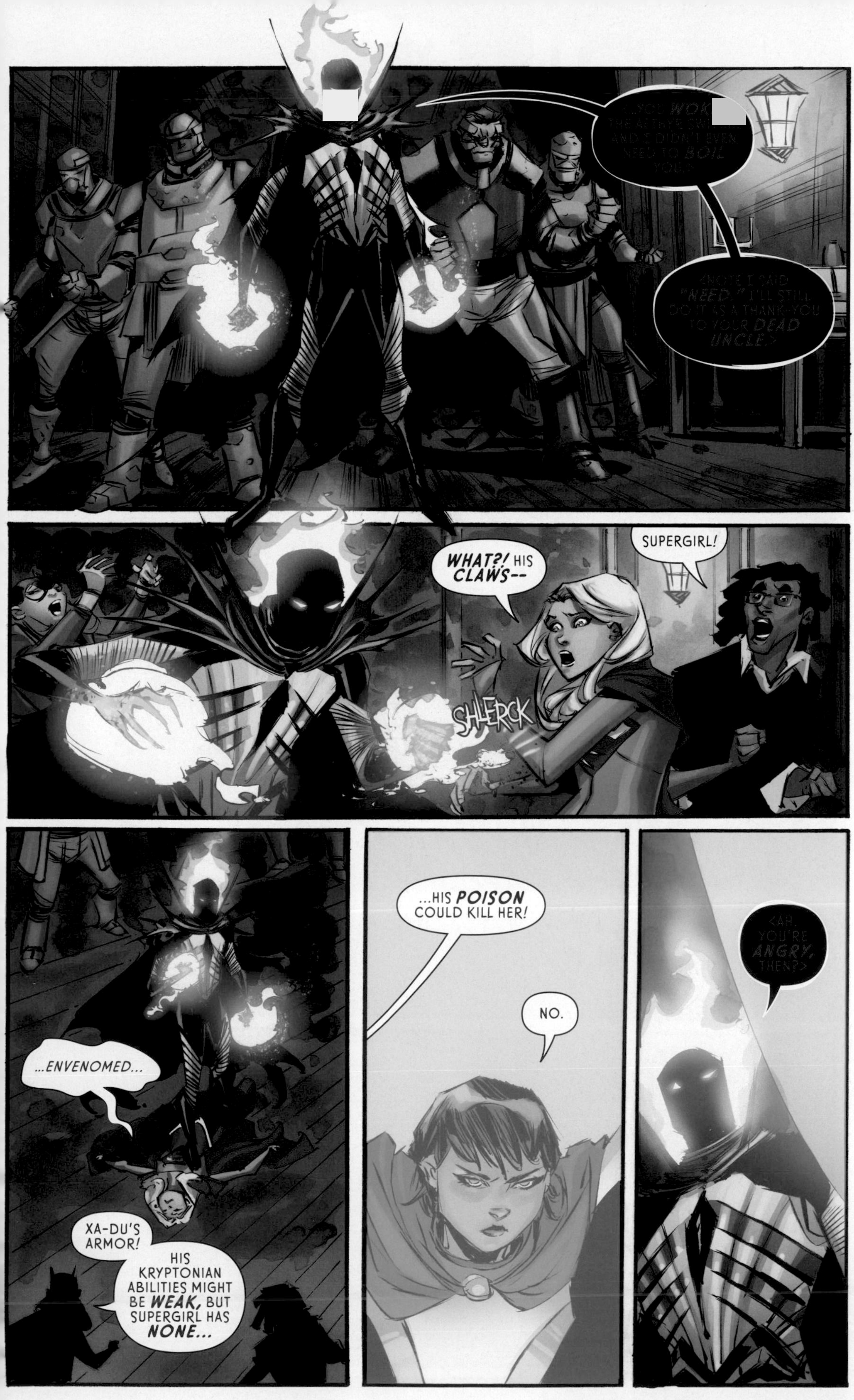
AND I DIDN'T EVEN NEED TO BOIL YOU.>
<NOTE I SAID "NEED." I'LL STILL DO IT AS A THANK-YOU TO YOUR DEAD UNCLE.>
WHAT?! HIS CLAWS--
SUPERGIRL!
SHLERCK
...ENVENOMED...
XA-DU'S ARMOR!
HIS KRYPTONIAN ABILITIES MIGHT BE WEAK, BUT SUPERGIRL HAS NONE...
...HIS POISON COULD KILL HER!
NO.
<AH. YOU'RE ANGRY, THEN?>

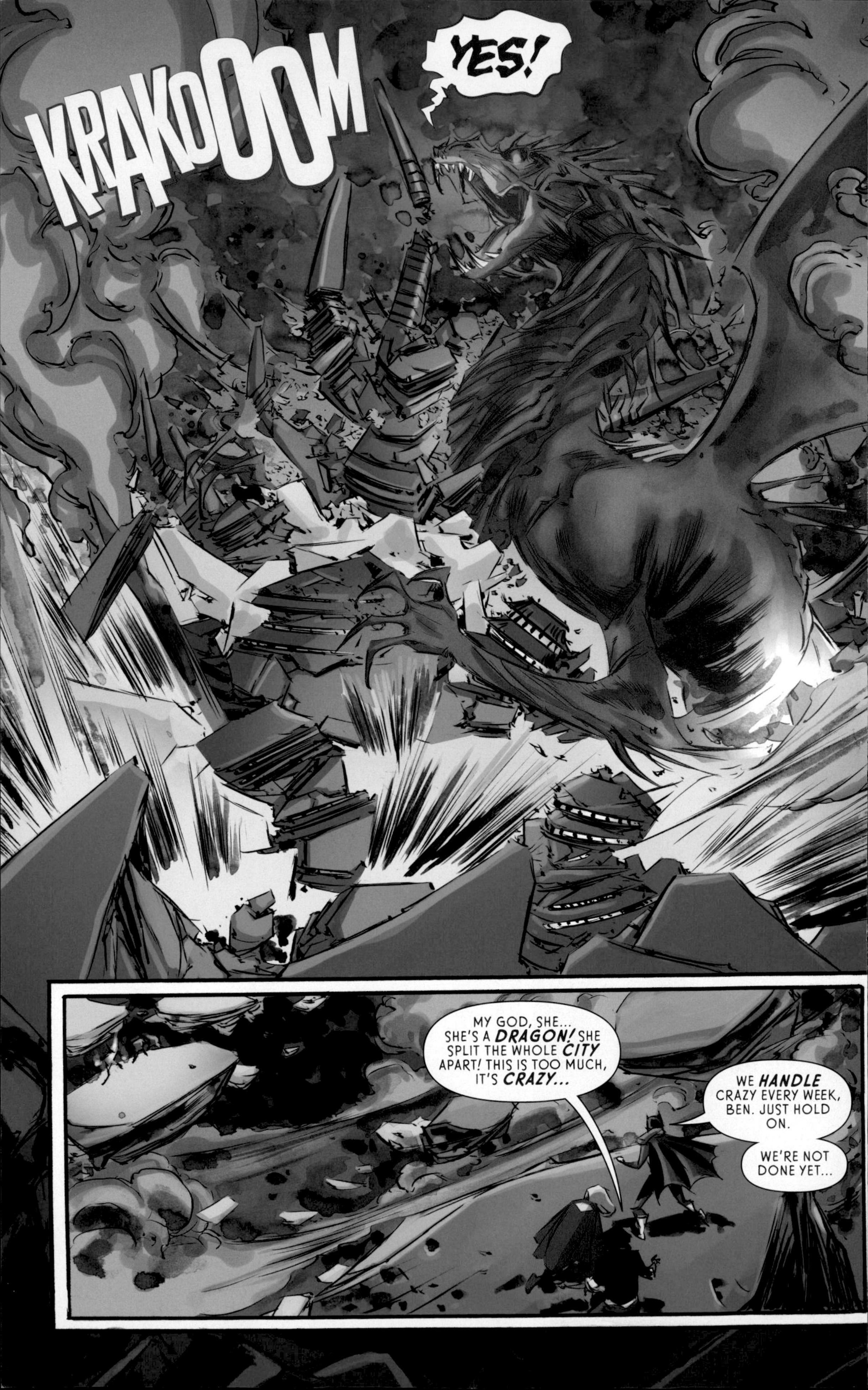
KRAKOOOOM
YES!
MY GOD, SHE... SHE'S A DRAGON! SHE SPLIT THE WHOLE CITY APART! THIS IS TOO MUCH, IT'S CRAZY...
WE HANDLE CRAZY EVERY WEEK, BEN. JUST HOLD ON.
WE'RE NOT DONE YET...

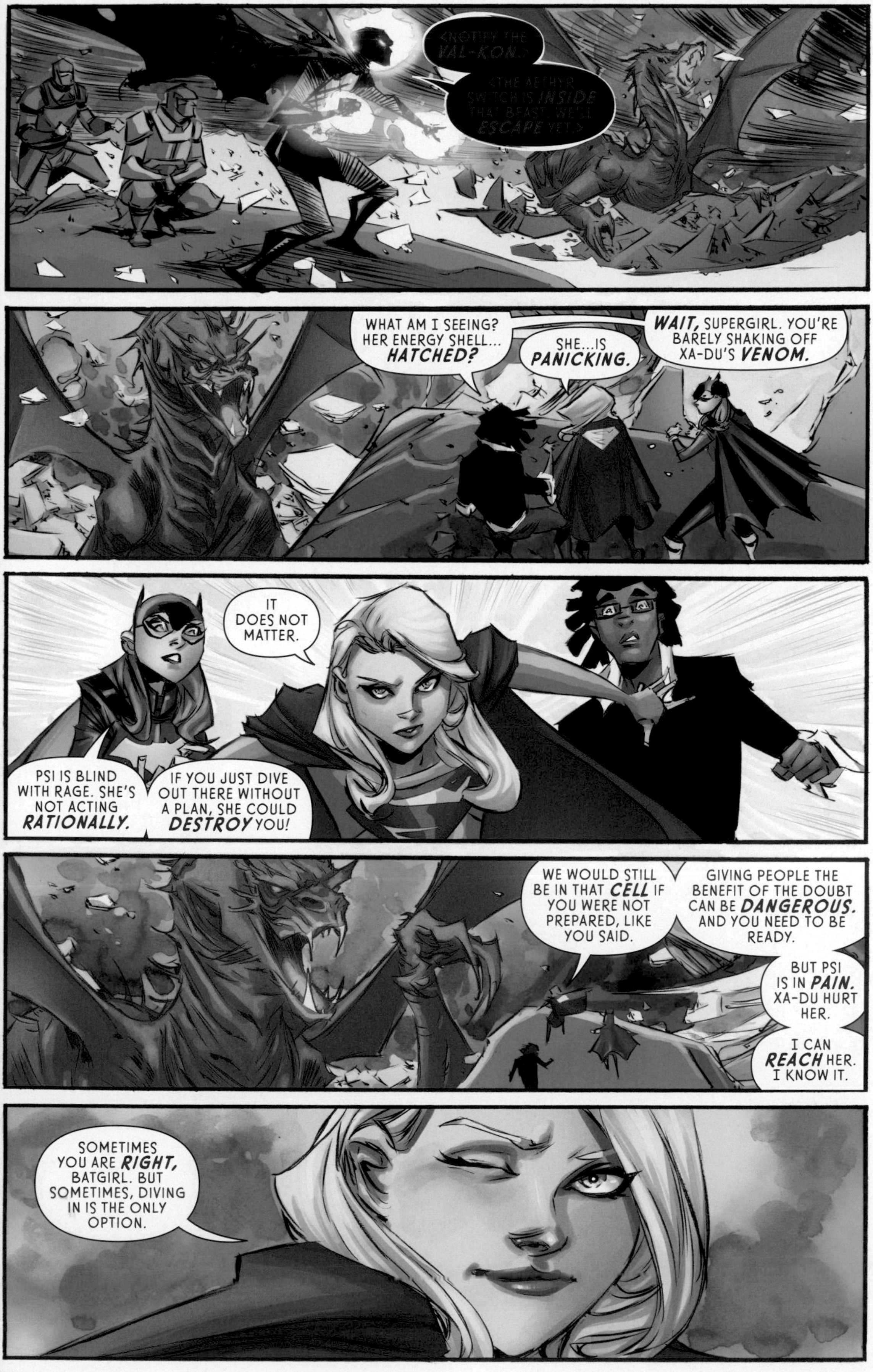

<NOTIFY THE VAL-KON.>
<THE AETHYR SWITCH IS INSIDE THAT BEAST. WE'LL ESCAPE YET.>
WHAT AM I SEEING? HER ENERGY SHELL... HATCHED?
SHE...IS PANICKING.
WAIT, SUPERGIRL. YOU'RE BARELY SHAKING OFF XA-DU'S VENOM.
IT DOES NOT MATTER.
PSI IS BLIND WITH RAGE. SHE'S NOT ACTING RATIONALLY.
IF YOU JUST DIVE OUT THERE WITHOUT A PLAN, SHE COULD DESTROY YOU!
GIVING PEOPLE THE BENEFIT OF THE DOUBT CAN BE DANGEROUS. AND YOU NEED TO BE READY.
WE WOULD STILL BE IN THAT CELL IF YOU WERE NOT PREPARED, LIKE YOU SAID.
BUT PSI IS IN PAIN. XA-DU HURT HER.
I CAN REACH HER. I KNOW IT.
SOMETIMES YOU ARE RIGHT, BATGIRL. BUT SOMETIMES, DIVING IN IS THE ONLY OPTION.

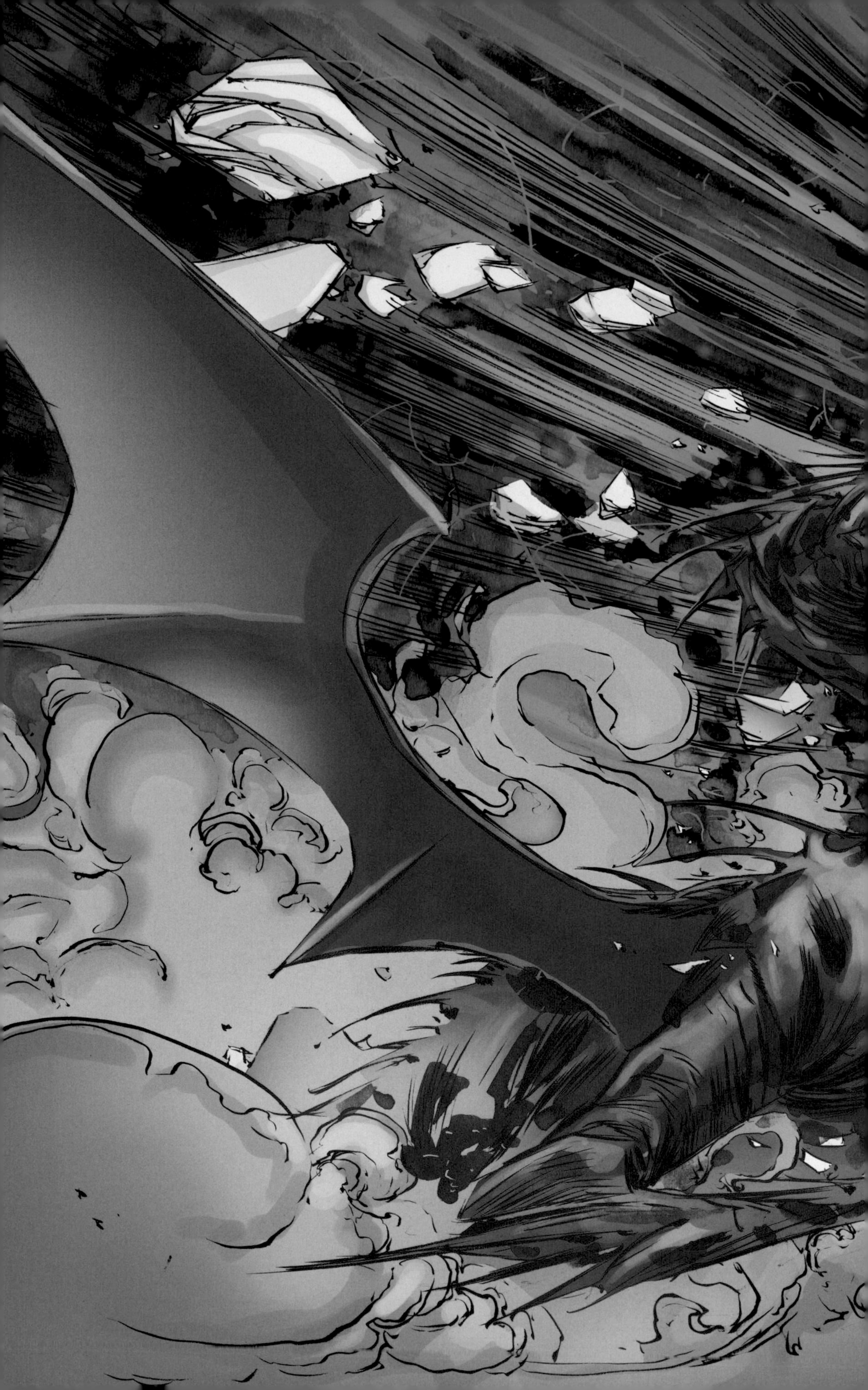

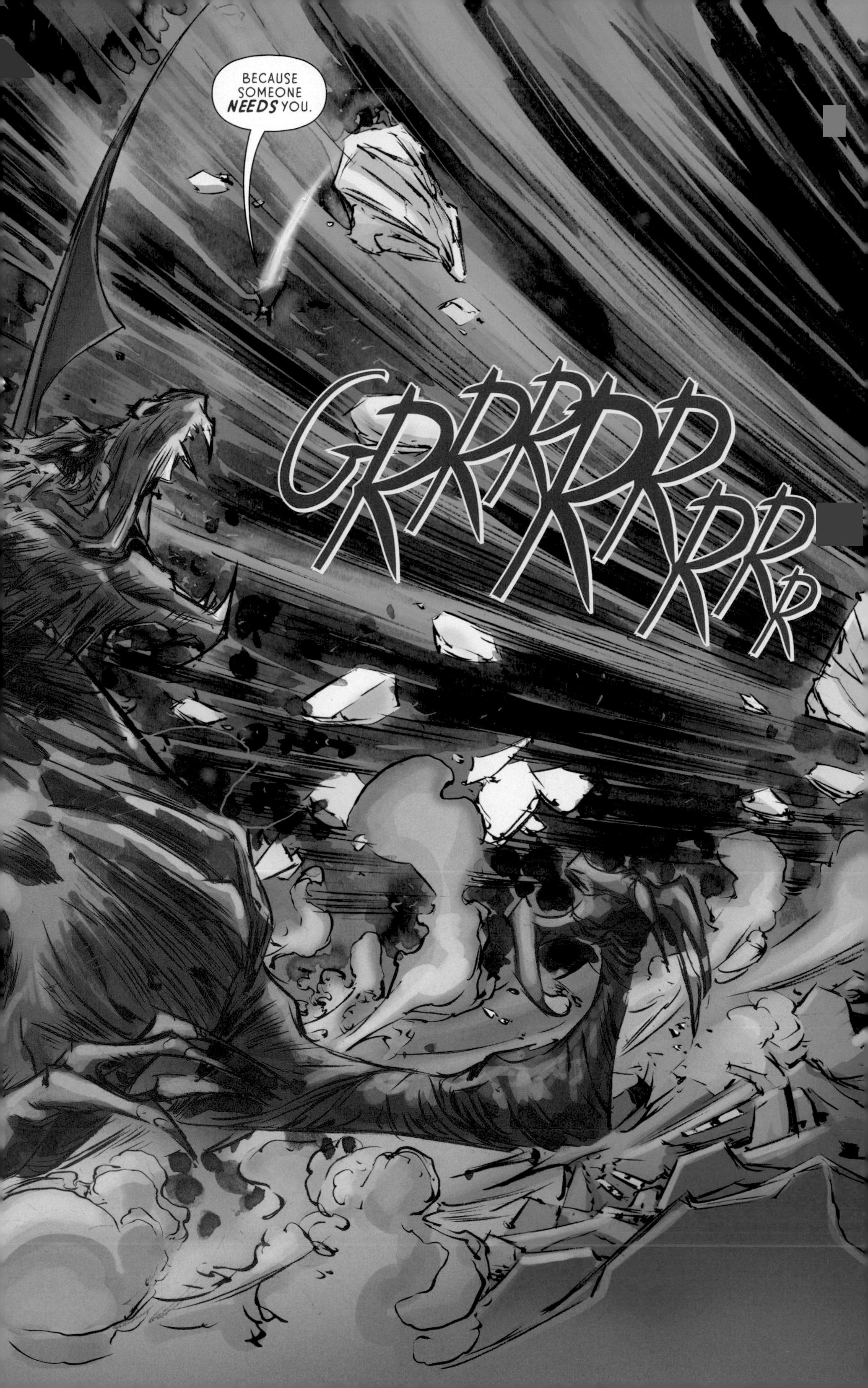
BECAUSE SOMEONE **NEEDS** YOU.
GRRRRRRRRRRR

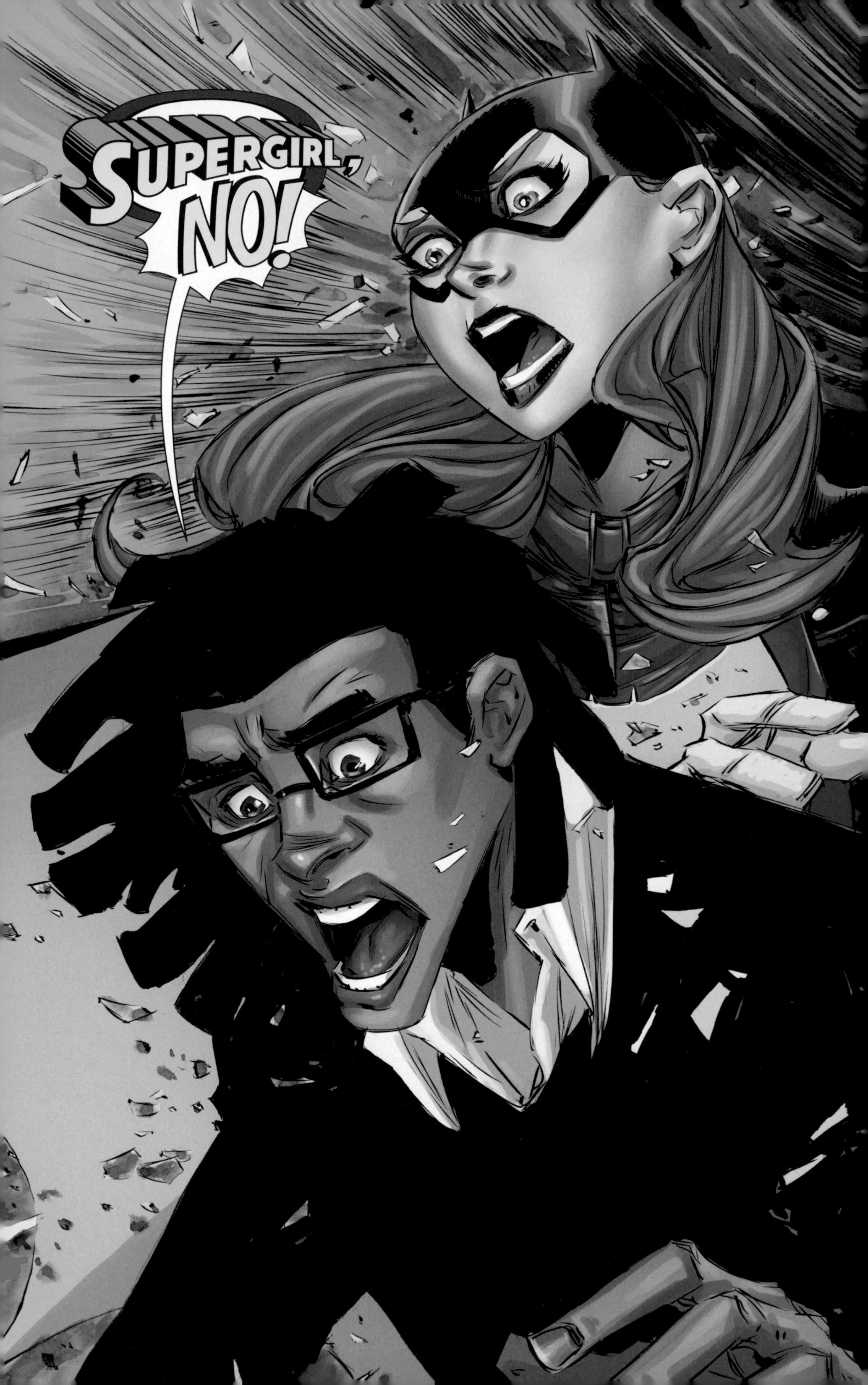
SUPERGIRL, NO!

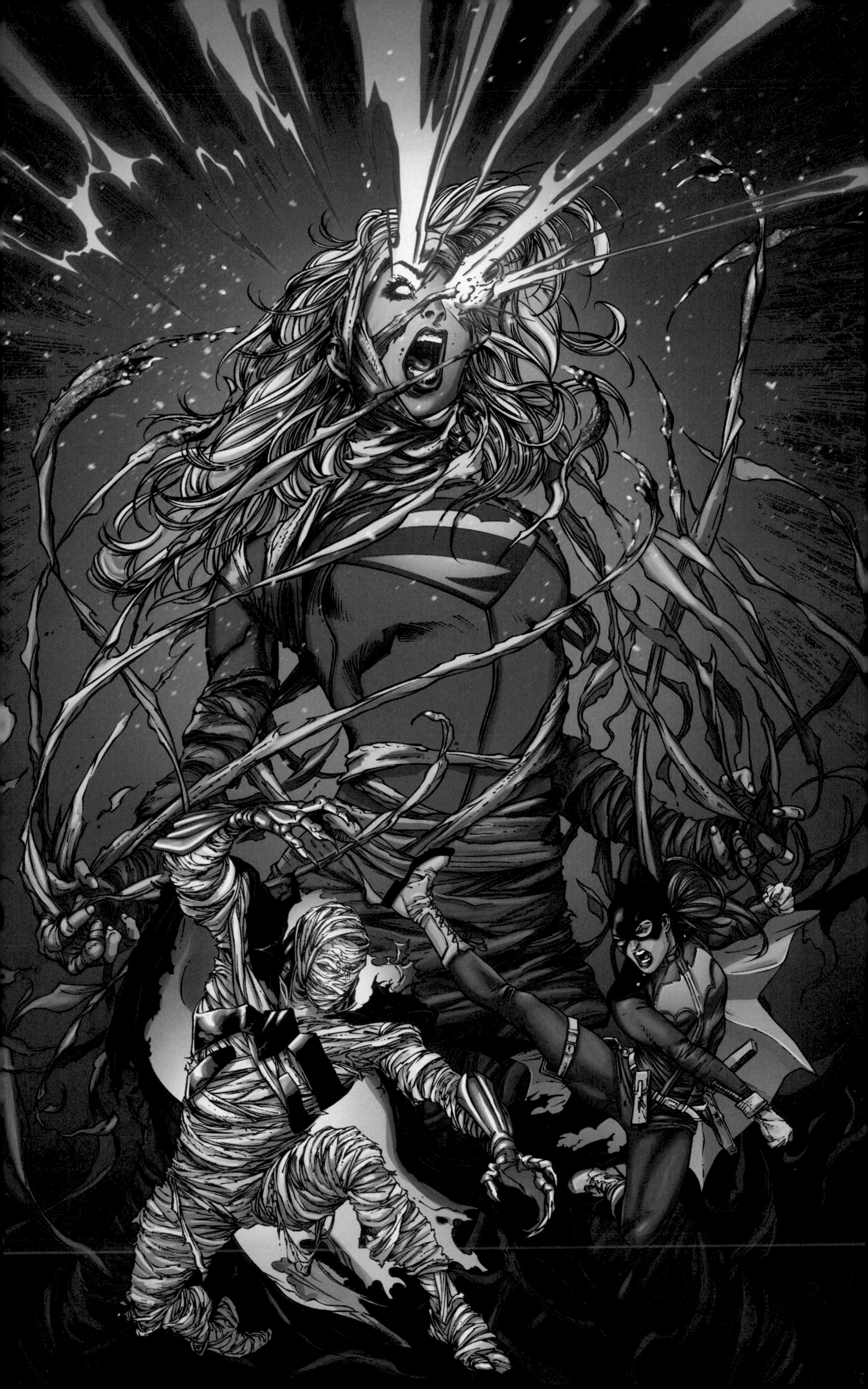

"ESCAPE FROM THE PHANTOM ZONE FINALE"

STEVE ORLANDO writer * BRIAN CHING artist * MICHAEL ATIYEH colorist
cover by ROBSON ROCHA, DANIEL HENRIQUES and MICHAEL ATIYEH

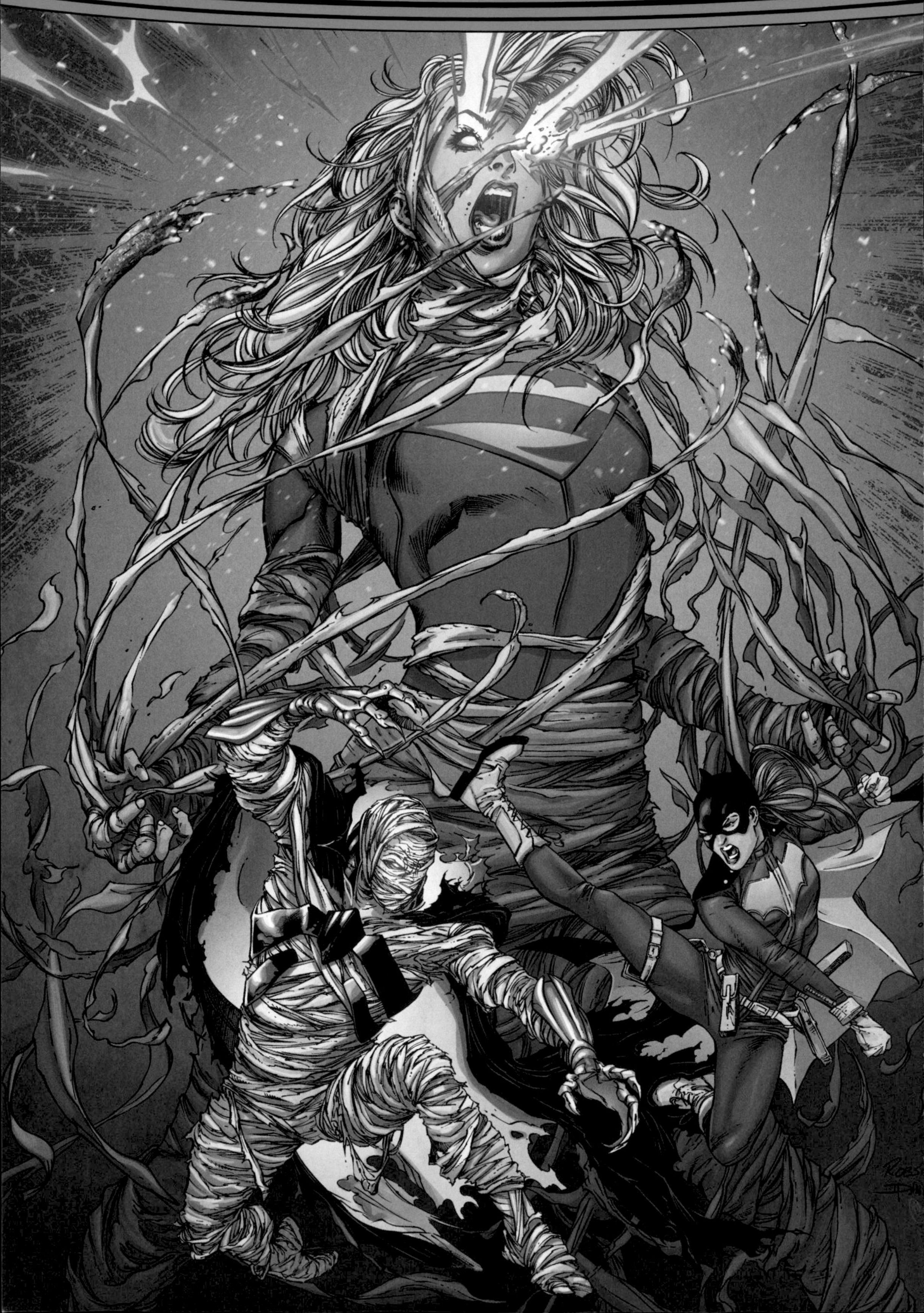

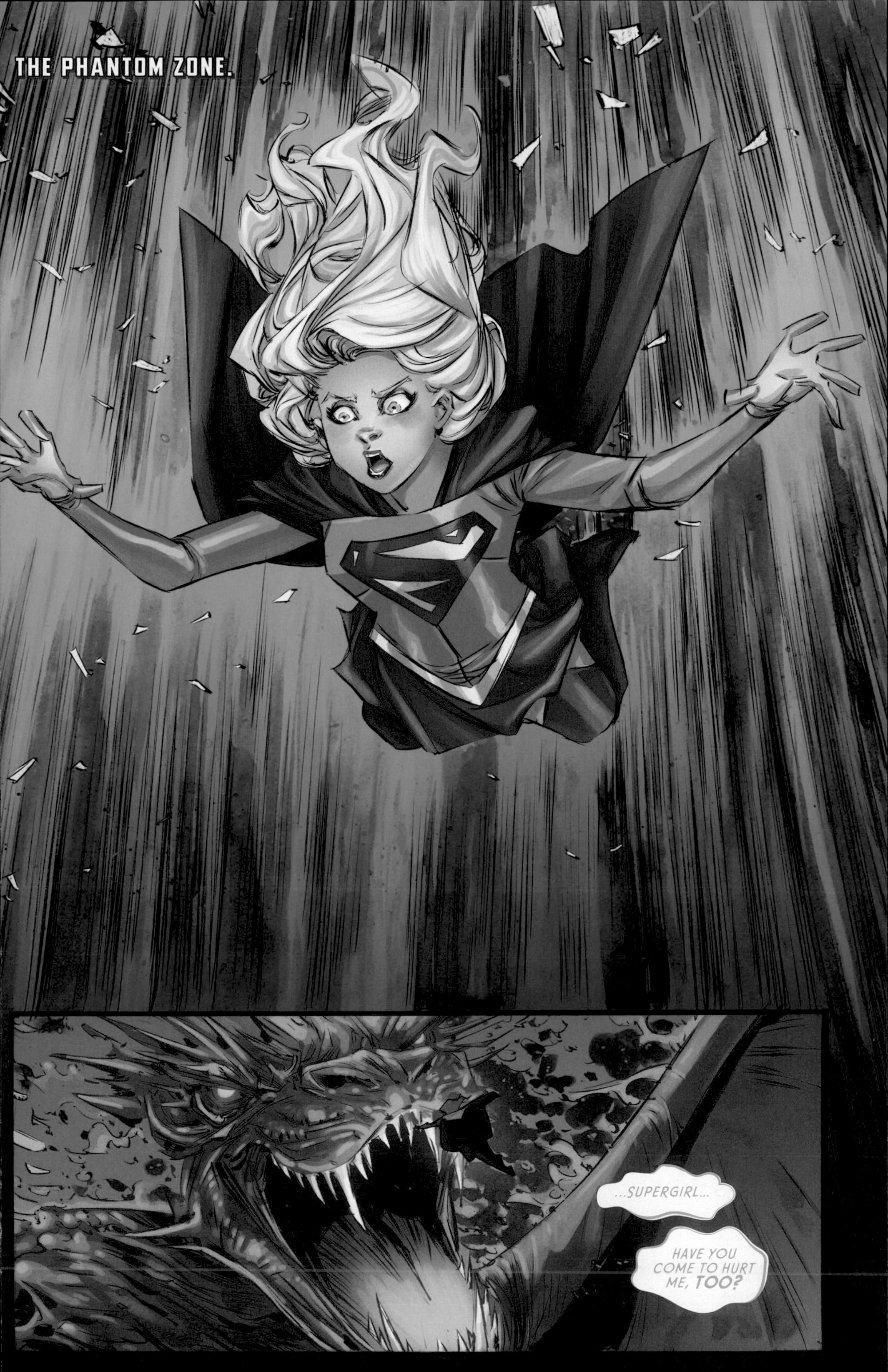
THE PHANTOM ZONE.
...SUPERGIRL...
HAVE YOU COME TO HURT ME, TOO?

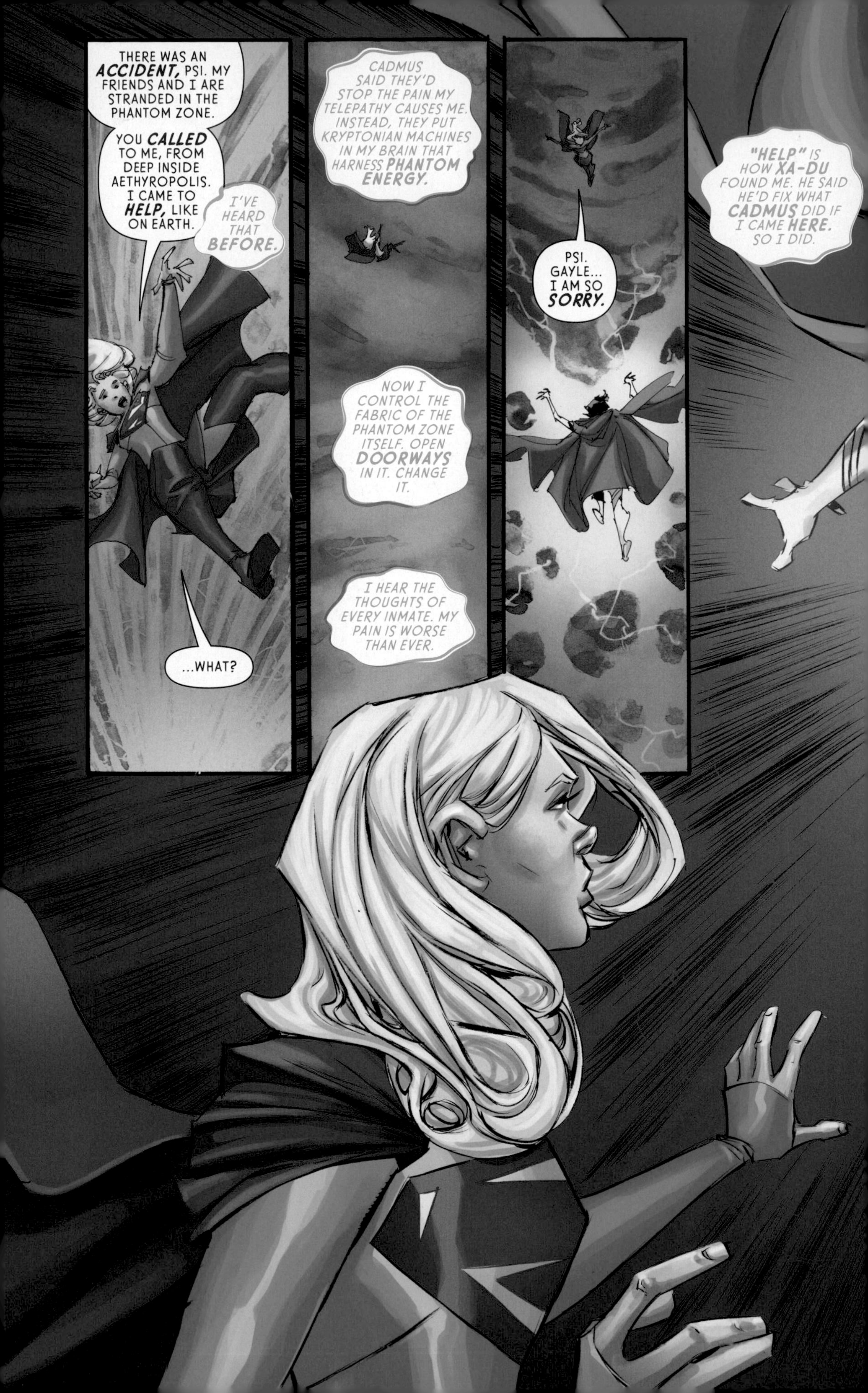
THERE WAS AN ACCIDENT, PSI. MY FRIENDS AND I ARE STRANDED IN THE PHANTOM ZONE.
YOU CALLED TO ME, FROM DEEP INSIDE AETHYROPOLIS. I CAME TO HELP, LIKE ON EARTH.
I'VE HEARD THAT BEFORE.
...WHAT?
CADMUS SAID THEY'D STOP THE PAIN MY TELEPATHY CAUSES ME. INSTEAD, THEY PUT KRYPTONIAN MACHINES IN MY BRAIN THAT HARNESS PHANTOM ENERGY.
NOW I CONTROL THE FABRIC OF THE PHANTOM ZONE ITSELF. OPEN DOORWAYS IN IT. CHANGE IT.
I HEAR THE THOUGHTS OF EVERY INMATE. MY PAIN IS WORSE THAN EVER.
PSI. GAYLE... I AM SO SORRY.
"HELP" IS HOW XA-DU FOUND ME. HE SAID HE'D FIX WHAT CADMUS DID IF I CAME HERE. SO I DID.

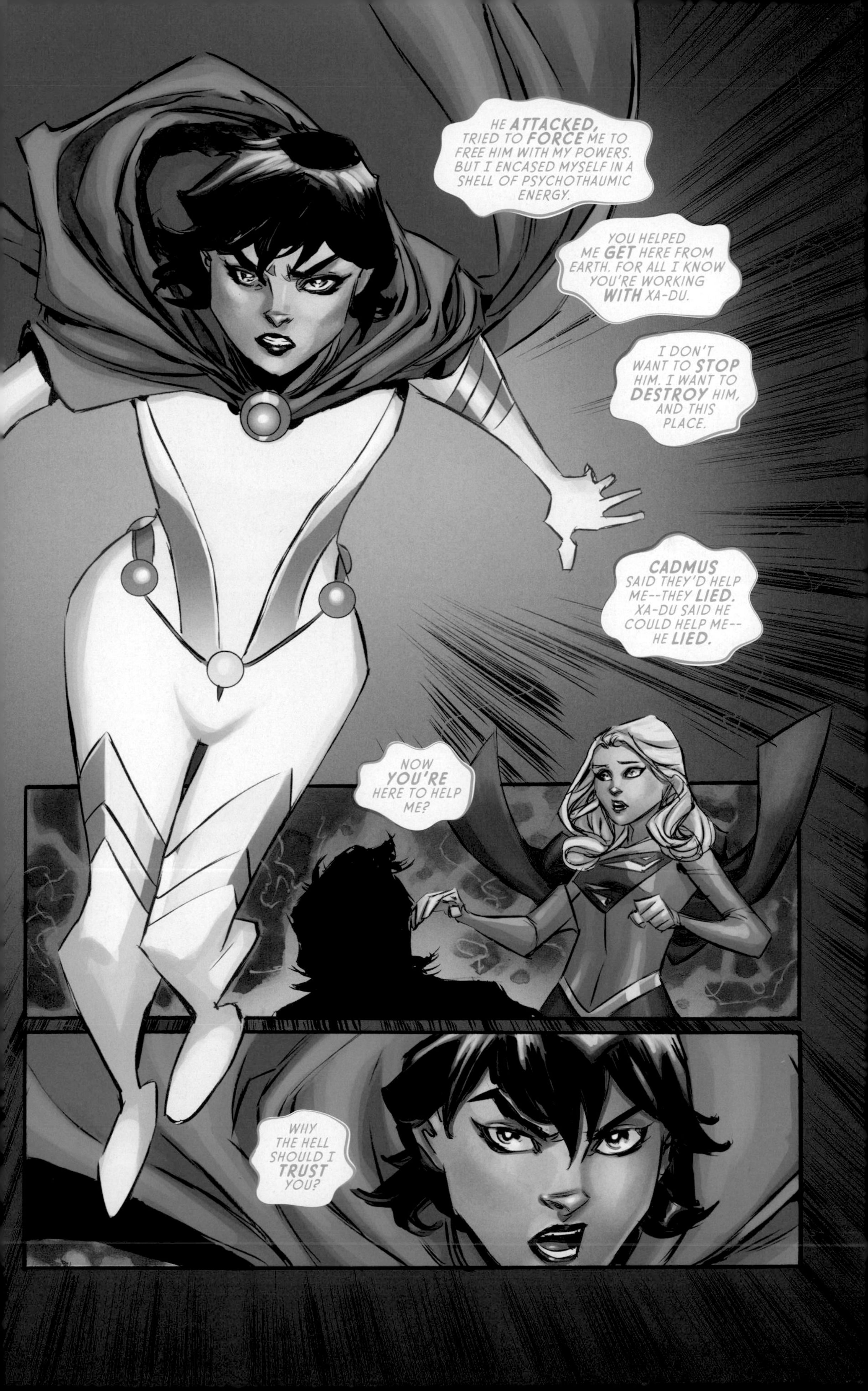
HE ATTACKED, TRIED TO FORCE ME TO FREE HIM WITH MY POWERS. BUT I ENCASED MYSELF IN A SHELL OF PSYCHOTHAUMIC ENERGY.
YOU HELPED ME GET HERE FROM EARTH. FOR ALL I KNOW YOU'RE WORKING WITH XA-DU.
I DON'T WANT TO STOP HIM. I WANT TO DESTROY HIM, AND THIS PLACE.
CADMUS SAID THEY'D HELP ME--THEY LIED. XA-DU SAID HE COULD HELP ME--HE LIED.
NOW YOU'RE HERE TO HELP ME?
WHY THE HELL SHOULD I TRUST YOU?

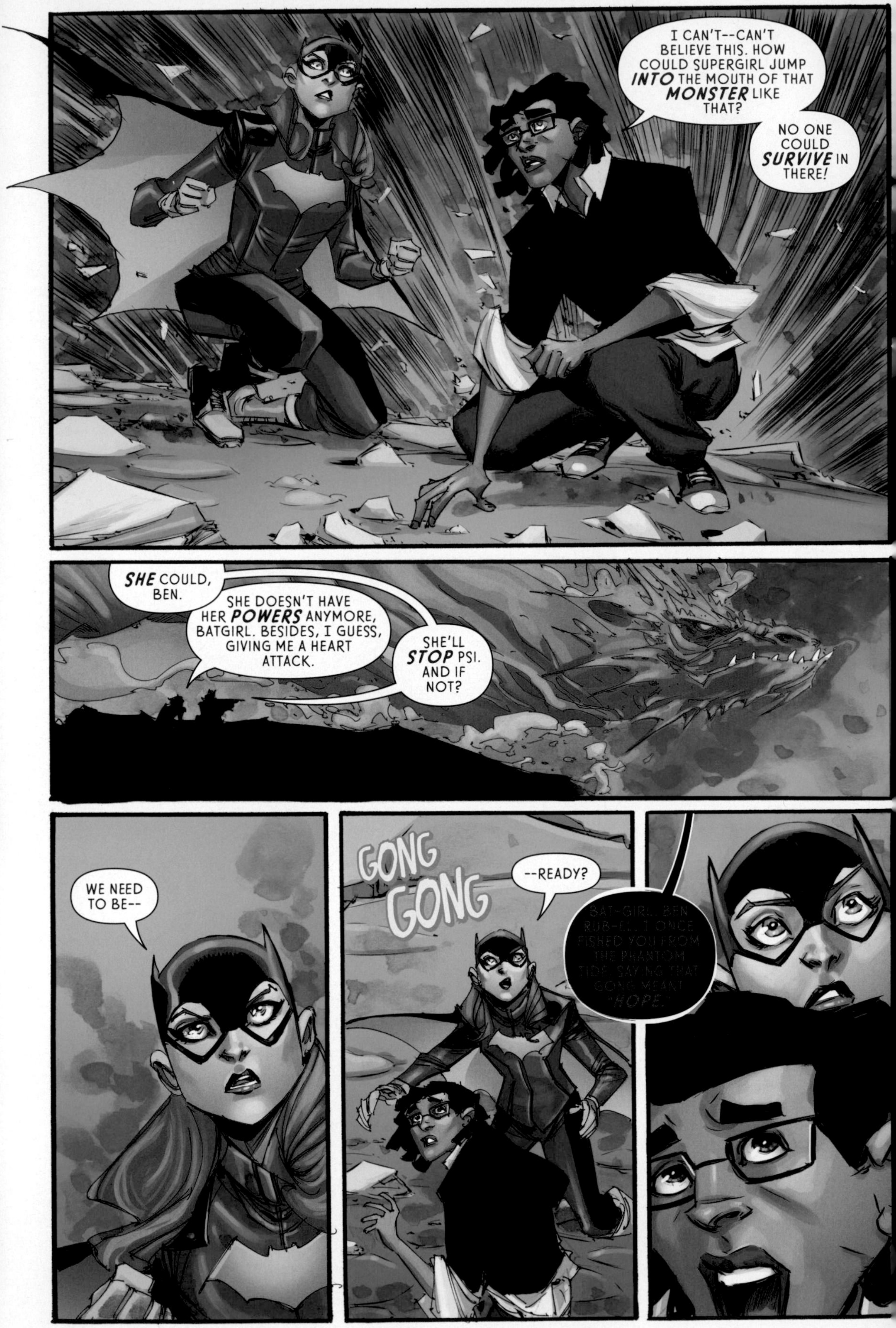
I CAN'T--CAN'T BELIEVE THIS. HOW COULD SUPERGIRL JUMP INTO THE MOUTH OF THAT MONSTER LIKE THAT?
NO ONE COULD SURVIVE IN THERE!
SHE COULD, BEN.
SHE DOESN'T HAVE HER POWERS ANYMORE, BATGIRL. BESIDES, I GUESS, GIVING ME A HEART ATTACK.
SHE'LL STOP PSI. AND IF NOT?
WE NEED TO BE--
GONG GONG
--READY?
BAT-GIRL. BEN RUB-EL. I ONCE FISHED YOU FROM THE PHANTOM TIDE, SAYING THAT GONG MEANT "HOPE."

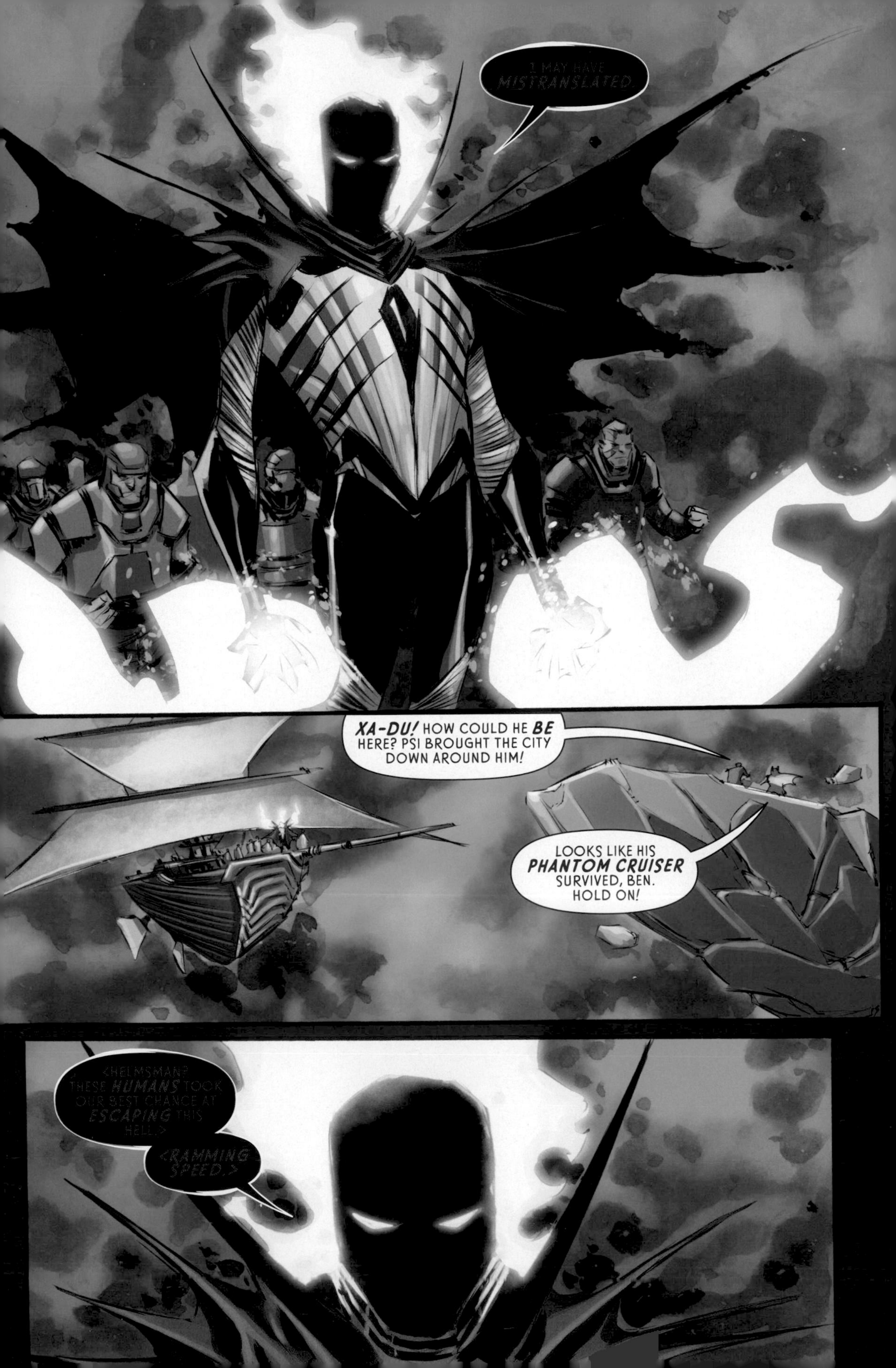
I MAY HAVE MISTRANSLATED.
XA-DU! HOW COULD HE BE HERE? PSI BROUGHT THE CITY DOWN AROUND HIM!
LOOKS LIKE HIS PHANTOM CRUISER SURVIVED, BEN. HOLD ON!
<HELMSMAN? THESE HUMANS TOOK OUR BEST CHANCE AT ESCAPING THIS HELL.>
<RAMMING SPEED.>

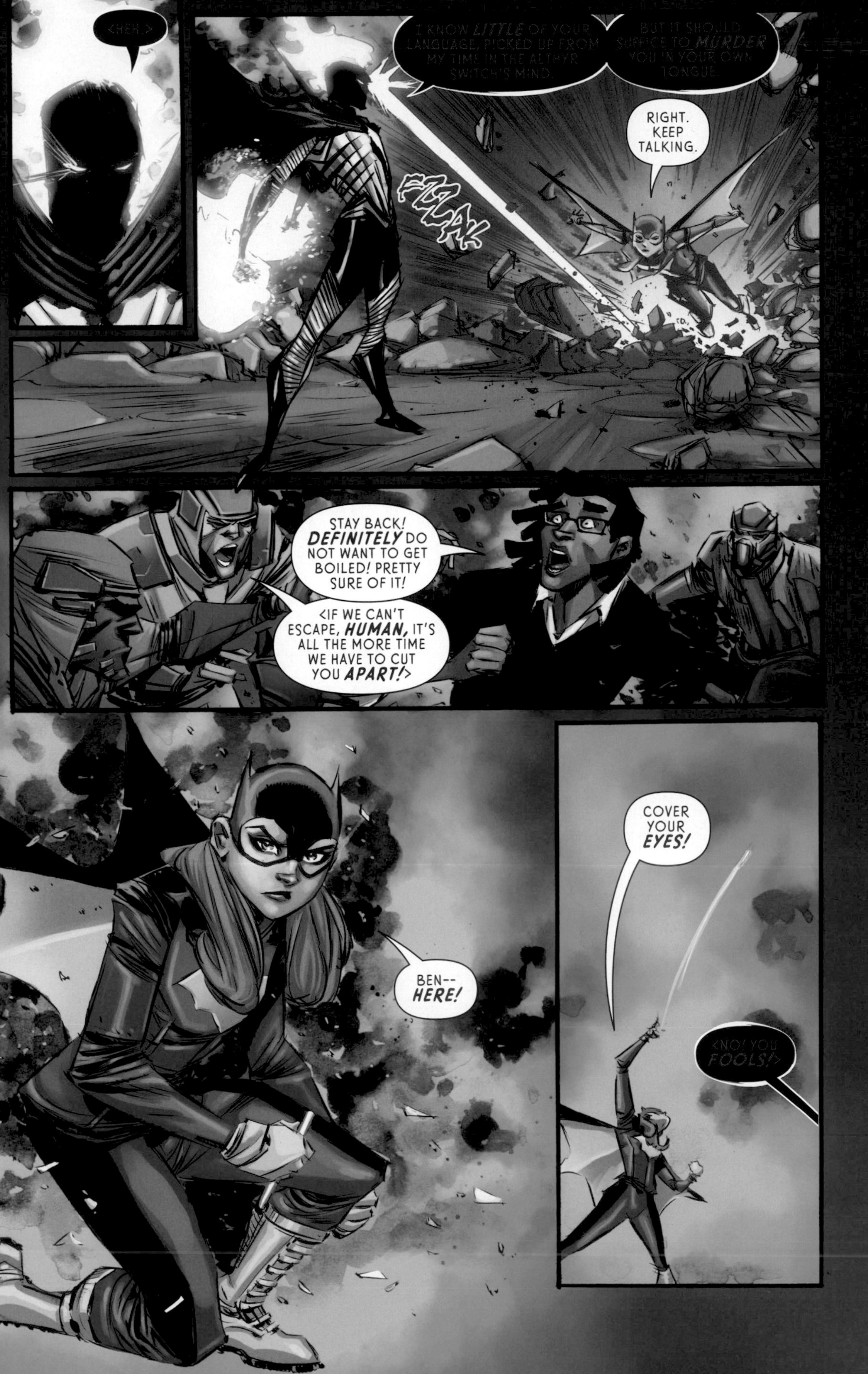
<HEH.>
I KNOW LITTLE OF YOUR LANGUAGE, PICKED UP FROM MY TIME IN THE ALTHYR SWITCH'S MIND.
BUT IT SHOULD SUFFICE TO MURDER YOU IN YOUR OWN TONGUE.
RIGHT. KEEP TALKING.
FZZAK
STAY BACK! DEFINITELY DO NOT WANT TO GET BOILED! PRETTY SURE OF IT!
<IF WE CAN'T ESCAPE, HUMAN, IT'S ALL THE MORE TIME WE HAVE TO CUT YOU APART!>
BEN-- HERE!
COVER YOUR EYES!
<NO! YOU FOOLS!>

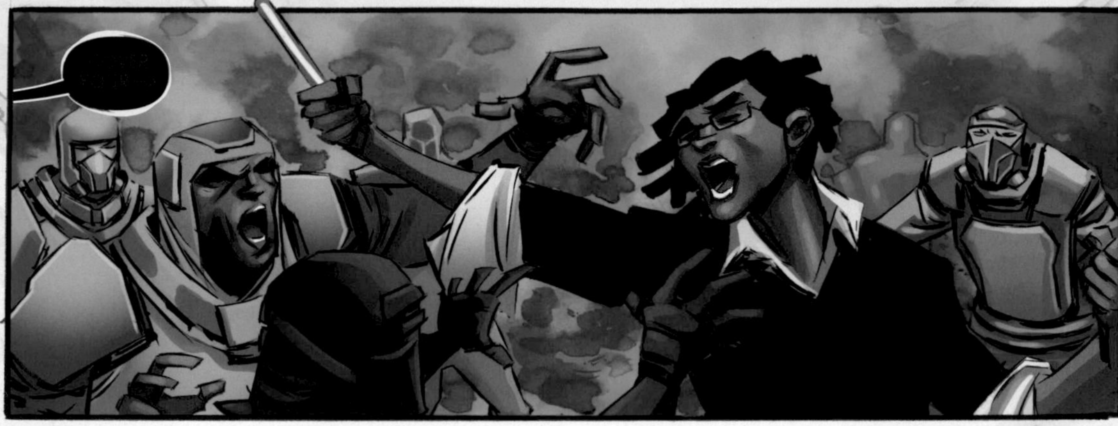

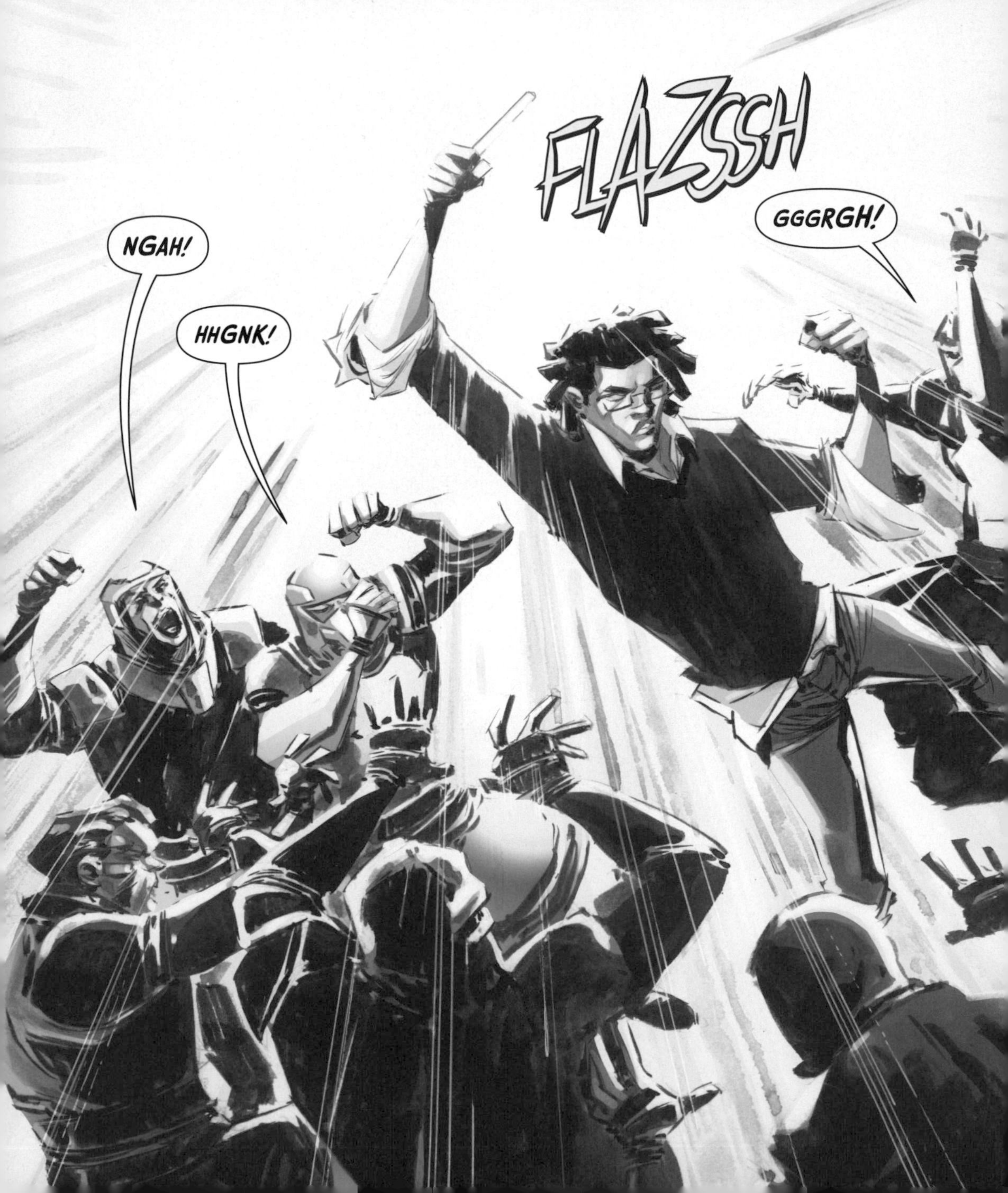
FLAZSSH
GGGRGH!
NGAH!
HHGNK!

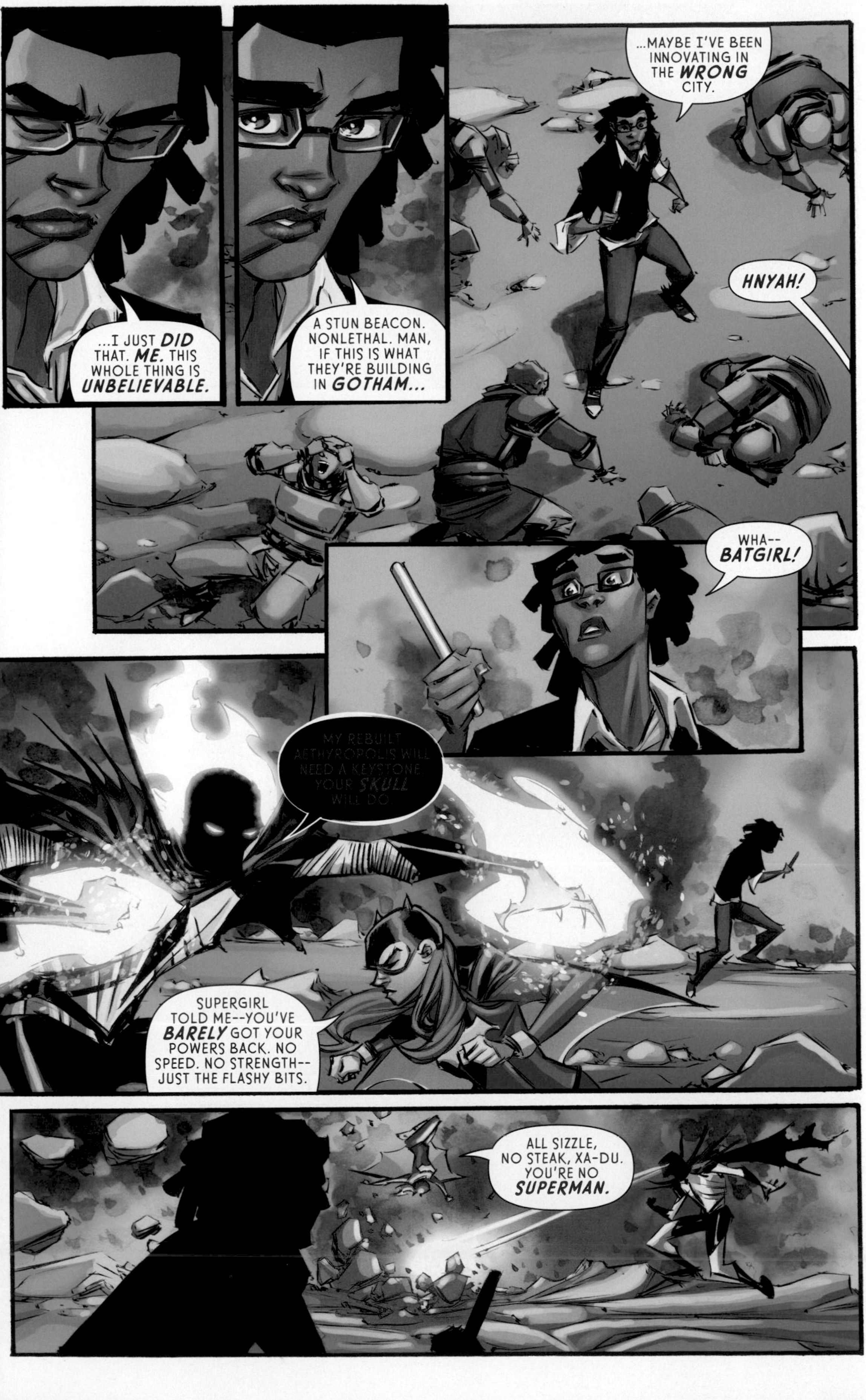
...I JUST DID THAT. ME. THIS WHOLE THING IS UNBELIEVABLE.
A STUN BEACON. NONLETHAL. MAN, IF THIS IS WHAT THEY'RE BUILDING IN GOTHAM...
...MAYBE I'VE BEEN INNOVATING IN THE WRONG CITY.
HNYAH!
WHA-- BATGIRL!
MY REBUILT AETHYROPOLIS WILL NEED A KEYSTONE. YOUR SKULL WILL DO.
SUPERGIRL TOLD ME--YOU'VE BARELY GOT YOUR POWERS BACK. NO SPEED. NO STRENGTH-- JUST THE FLASHY BITS.
ALL SIZZLE, NO STEAK, XA-DU. YOU'RE NO SUPERMAN.

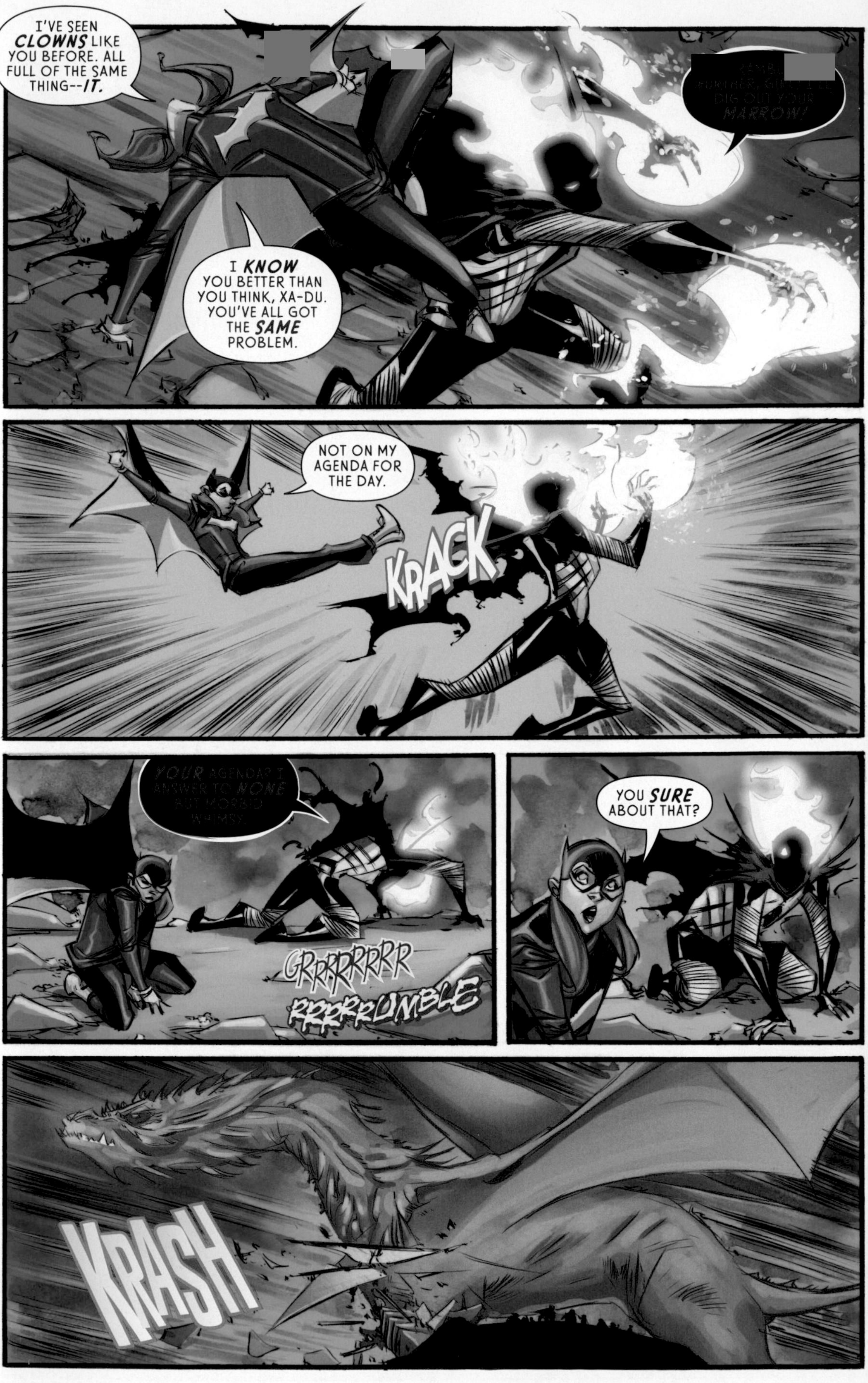
I'VE SEEN CLOWNS LIKE YOU BEFORE. ALL FULL OF THE SAME THING--IT.
[redacted] REMBL [redacted] FURTHER, GIRL? I'LL DIG OUT YOUR MARROW!
I KNOW YOU BETTER THAN YOU THINK, XA-DU. YOU'VE ALL GOT THE SAME PROBLEM.
NOT ON MY AGENDA FOR THE DAY.
KRACK
YOUR AGENDA? I ANSWER TO NONE BUT MORBID WHIMSY.
GRRRRRRRR
RRRRRUMBLE
YOU SURE ABOUT THAT?
KRASH

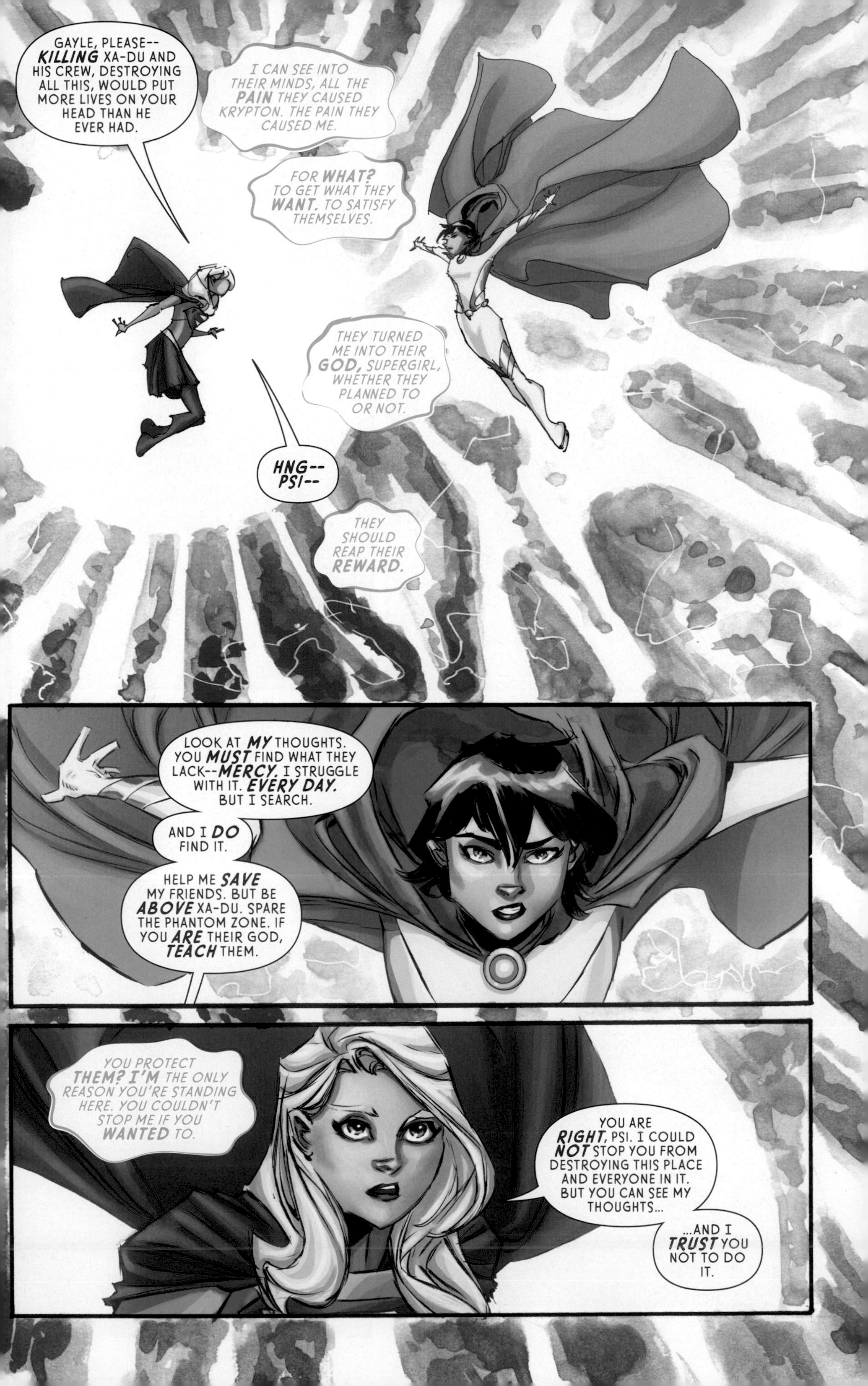

GAYLE, PLEASE-- KILLING XA-DU AND HIS CREW, DESTROYING ALL THIS, WOULD PUT MORE LIVES ON YOUR HEAD THAN HE EVER HAD.
I CAN SEE INTO THEIR MINDS, ALL THE PAIN THEY CAUSED KRYPTON. THE PAIN THEY CAUSED ME.
FOR WHAT? TO GET WHAT THEY WANT. TO SATISFY THEMSELVES.
THEY TURNED ME INTO THEIR GOD, SUPERGIRL, WHETHER THEY PLANNED TO OR NOT.
HNG-- PSI--
THEY SHOULD REAP THEIR REWARD.
LOOK AT MY THOUGHTS. YOU MUST FIND WHAT THEY LACK--MERCY. I STRUGGLE WITH IT. EVERY DAY. BUT I SEARCH.
AND I DO FIND IT.
HELP ME SAVE MY FRIENDS. BUT BE ABOVE XA-DU. SPARE THE PHANTOM ZONE. IF YOU ARE THEIR GOD, TEACH THEM.
YOU PROTECT THEM? I'M THE ONLY REASON YOU'RE STANDING HERE. YOU COULDN'T STOP ME IF YOU WANTED TO.
YOU ARE RIGHT, PSI. I COULD NOT STOP YOU FROM DESTROYING THIS PLACE AND EVERYONE IN IT. BUT YOU CAN SEE MY THOUGHTS...
...AND I TRUST YOU NOT TO DO IT.

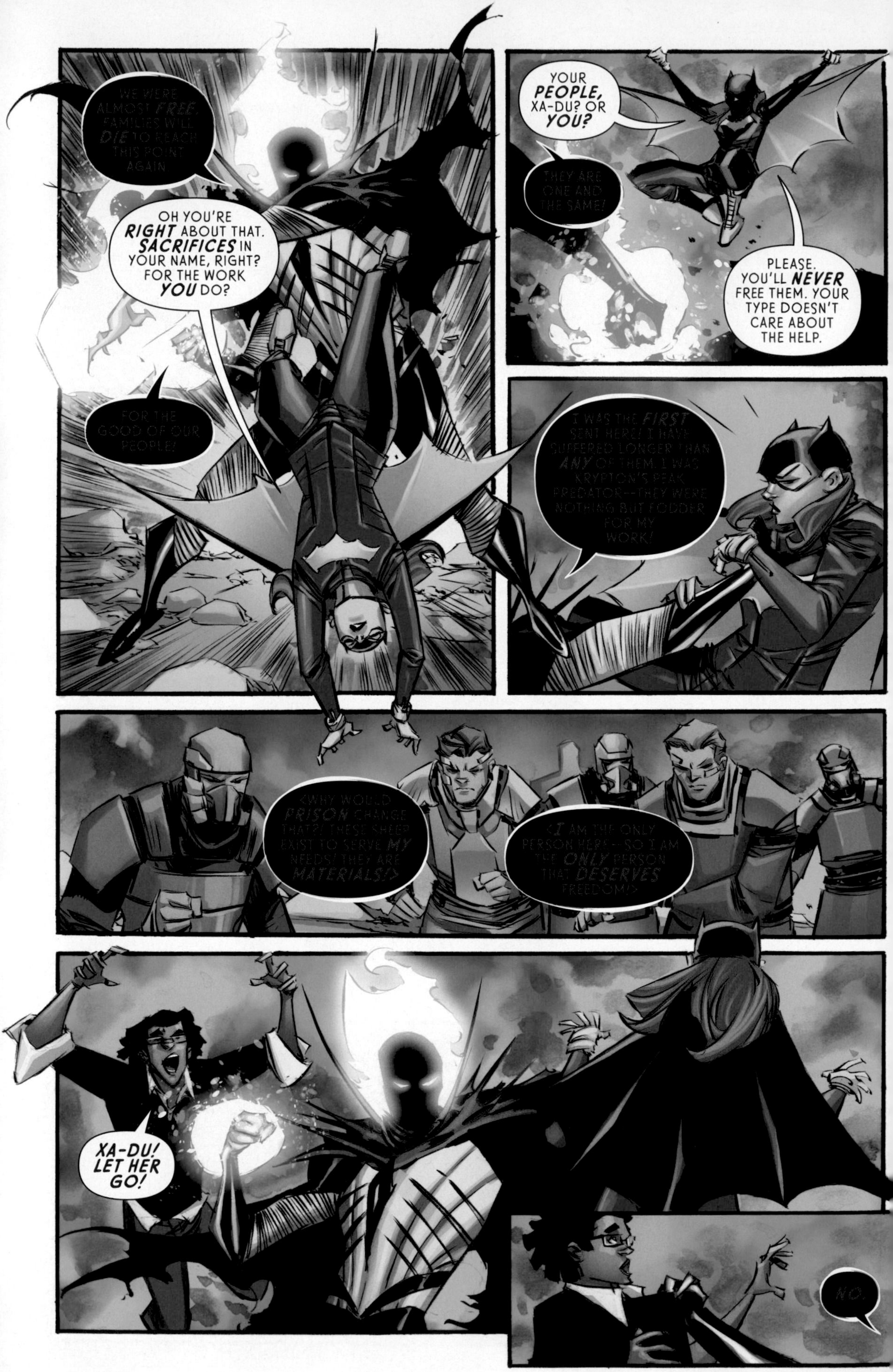
WE WERE ALMOST FREE. FAMILIES WILL DIE TO REACH THIS POINT AGAIN.
OH YOU'RE RIGHT ABOUT THAT. SACRIFICES IN YOUR NAME, RIGHT? FOR THE WORK YOU DO?
FOR THE GOOD OF OUR PEOPLE!
YOUR PEOPLE, XA-DU? OR YOU?
THEY ARE ONE AND THE SAME!
PLEASE. YOU'LL NEVER FREE THEM. YOUR TYPE DOESN'T CARE ABOUT THE HELP.
I WAS THE FIRST SENT HERE! I HAVE SUFFERED LONGER THAN ANY OF THEM. I WAS KRYPTON'S PEAK PREDATOR--THEY WERE NOTHING BUT FODDER FOR MY WORK!
<WHY WOULD PRISON CHANGE THAT?! THESE SHEEP EXIST TO SERVE MY NEEDS! THEY ARE MATERIALS!>
<I AM THE ONLY PERSON HERE--SO I AM THE ONLY PERSON THAT DESERVES FREEDOM!>
XA-DU! LET HER GO!
NO.

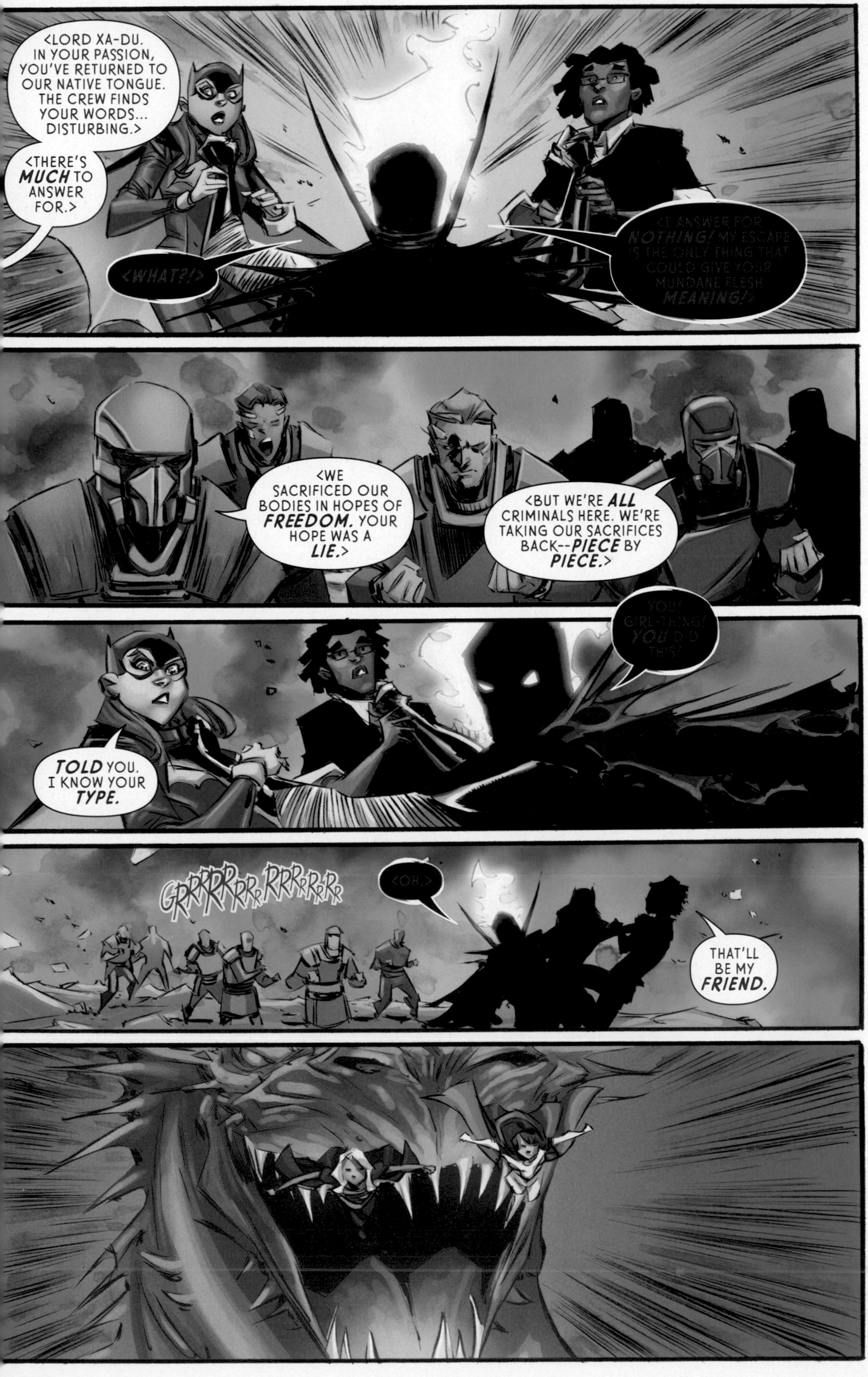

<LORD XA-DU. IN YOUR PASSION, YOU'VE RETURNED TO OUR NATIVE TONGUE. THE CREW FINDS YOUR WORDS... DISTURBING.>
<THERE'S **MUCH** TO ANSWER FOR.>
<*WHAT?!*>
<I ANSWER FOR *NOTHING!* MY ESCAPE IS THE ONLY THING THAT COULD GIVE YOUR MUNDANE FLESH *MEANING!*>
<WE SACRIFICED OUR BODIES IN HOPES OF **FREEDOM.** YOUR HOPE WAS A ***LIE.***>
<BUT WE'RE ***ALL*** CRIMINALS HERE. WE'RE TAKING OUR SACRIFICES BACK--***PIECE*** BY ***PIECE.***>
YOU! GIRL-THING! *YOU* DID THIS!
TOLD YOU. I KNOW YOUR ***TYPE.***
GRRRRRRRRRRRRRR
<OH.>
THAT'LL BE MY ***FRIEND.***

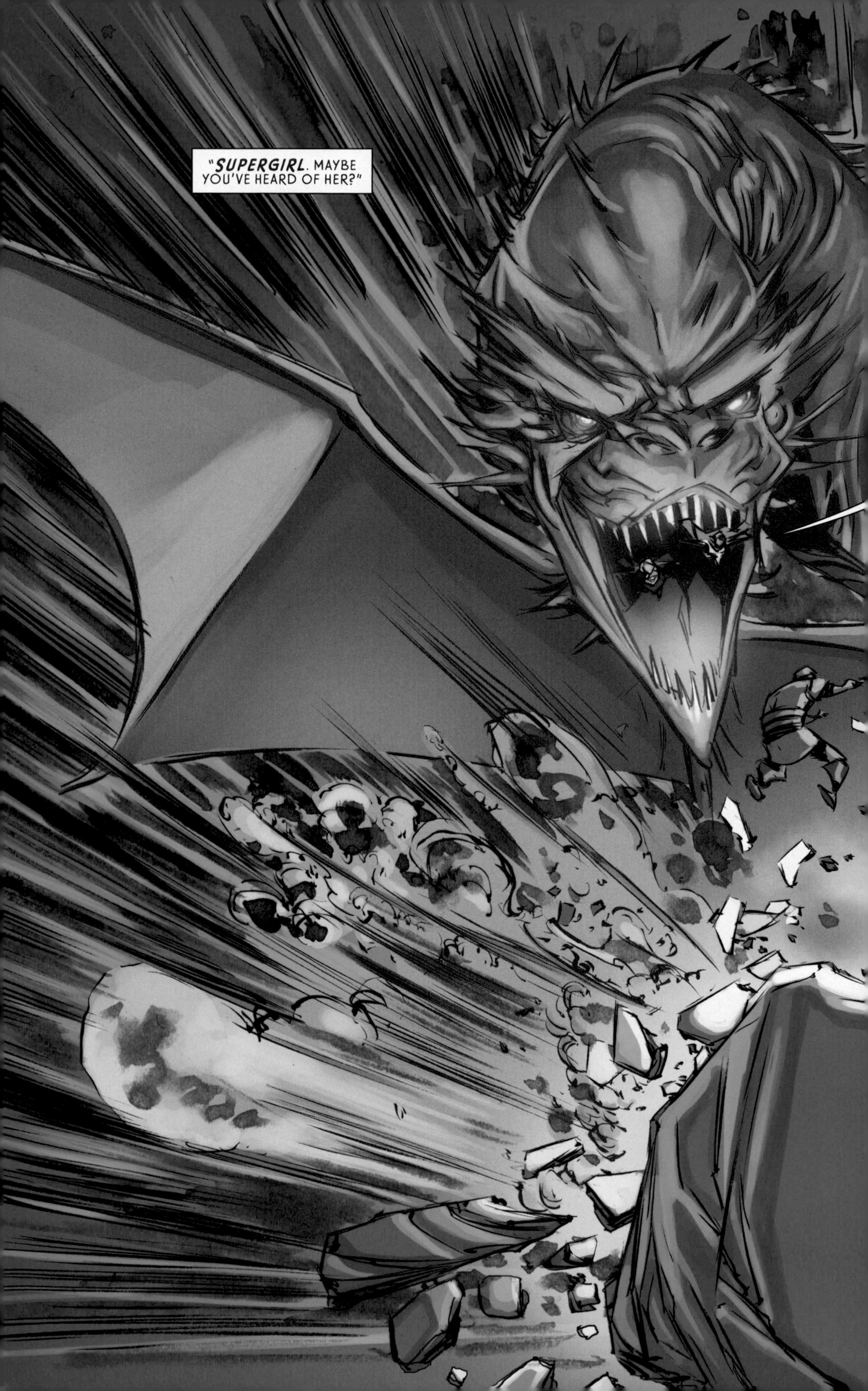
"SUPERGIRL. MAYBE YOU'VE HEARD OF HER?"

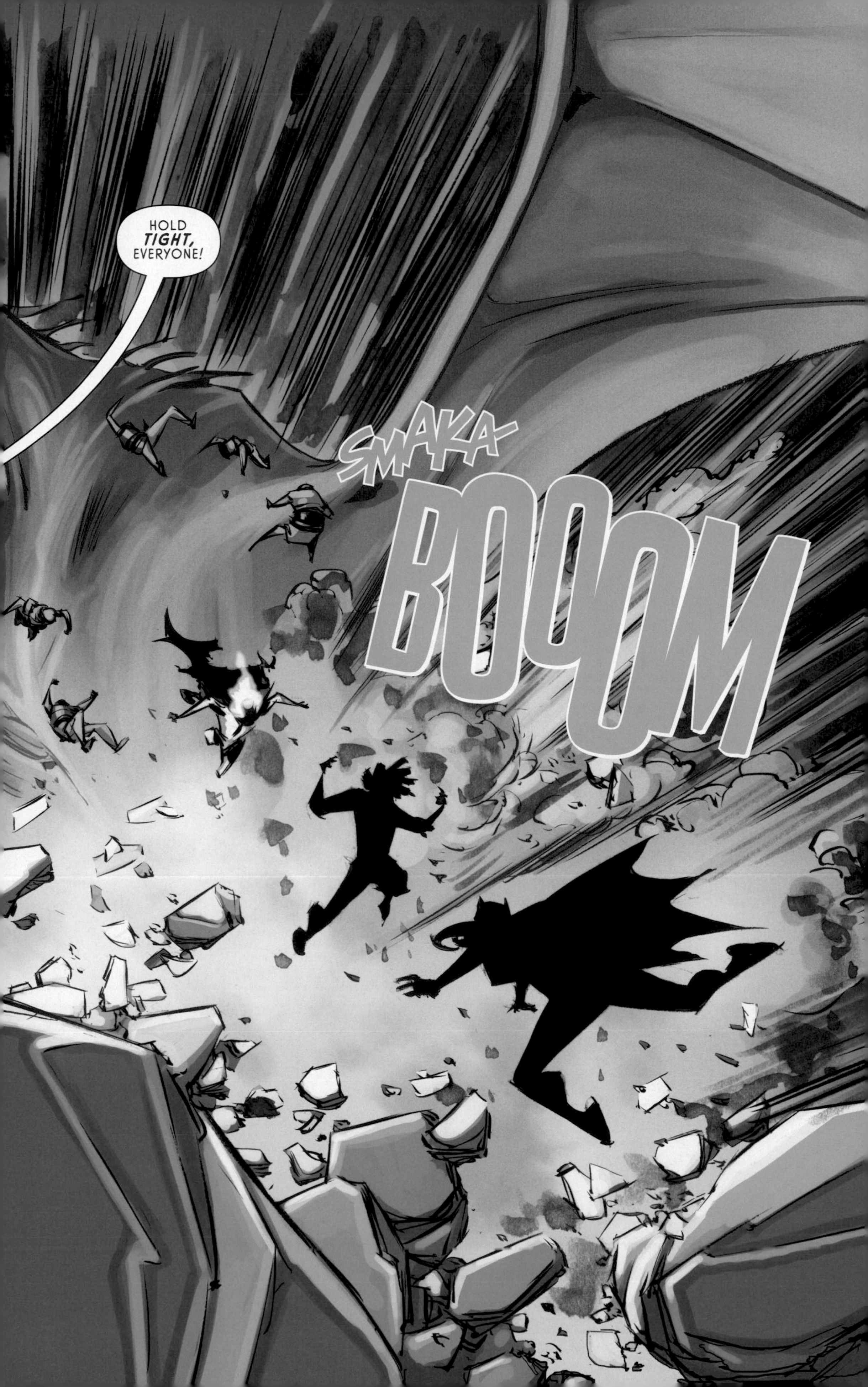
HOLD TIGHT, EVERYONE!
SMAKA-
BOOOOM

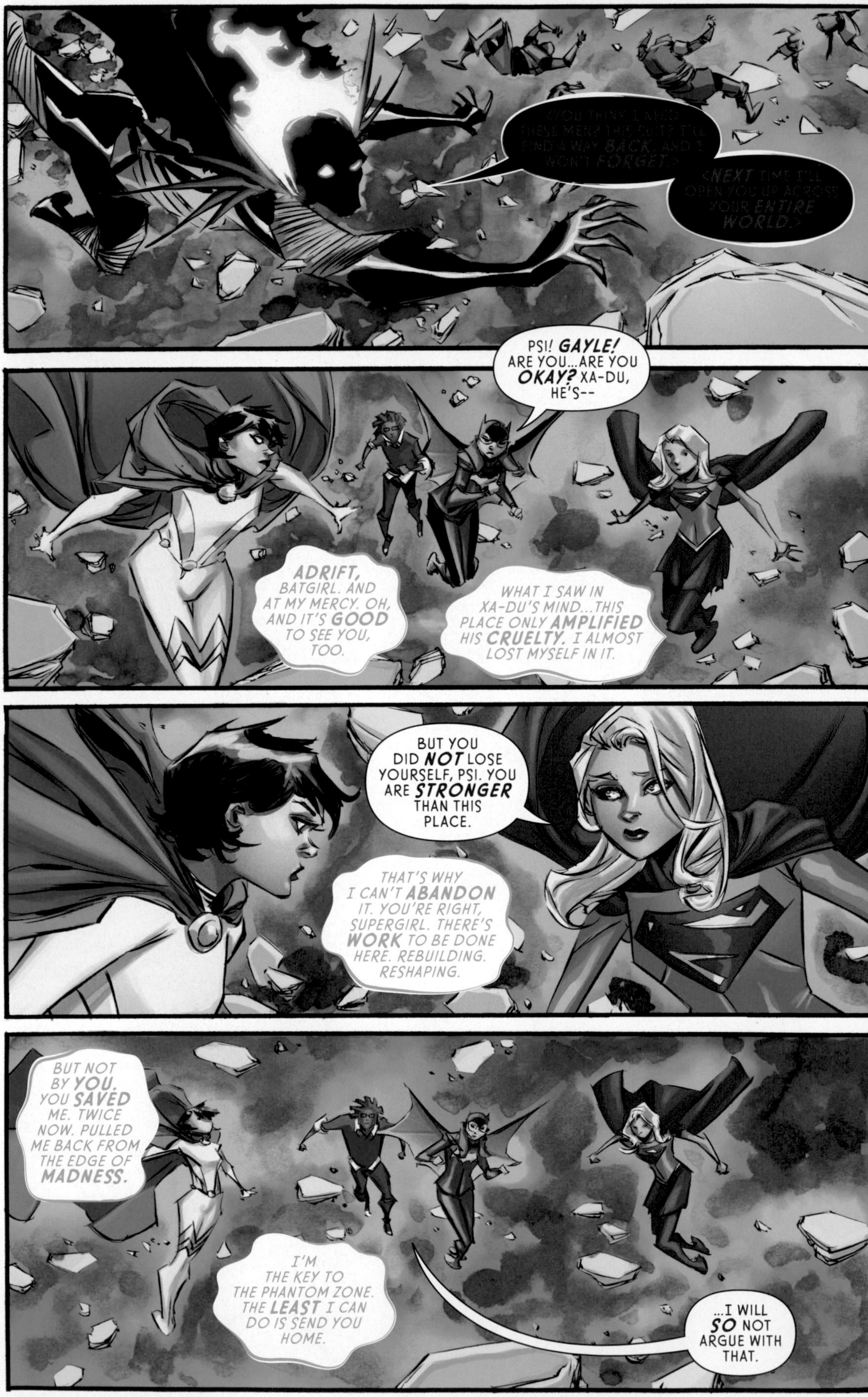
<YOU THINK I NEED THESE MEN? THIS SUIT? I'LL FIND A WAY BACK, AND I WON'T FORGET.>
<NEXT TIME I'LL OPEN YOU UP ACROSS YOUR ENTIRE WORLD.>
PSI! GAYLE! ARE YOU...ARE YOU OKAY? XA-DU, HE'S--
ADRIFT, BATGIRL. AND AT MY MERCY. OH, AND IT'S GOOD TO SEE YOU, TOO.
WHAT I SAW IN XA-DU'S MIND...THIS PLACE ONLY AMPLIFIED HIS CRUELTY. I ALMOST LOST MYSELF IN IT.
BUT YOU DID NOT LOSE YOURSELF, PSI. YOU ARE STRONGER THAN THIS PLACE.
THAT'S WHY I CAN'T ABANDON IT. YOU'RE RIGHT, SUPERGIRL. THERE'S WORK TO BE DONE HERE. REBUILDING. RESHAPING.
BUT NOT BY YOU. YOU SAVED ME. TWICE NOW. PULLED ME BACK FROM THE EDGE OF MADNESS.
I'M THE KEY TO THE PHANTOM ZONE. THE LEAST I CAN DO IS SEND YOU HOME.
...I WILL SO NOT ARGUE WITH THAT.

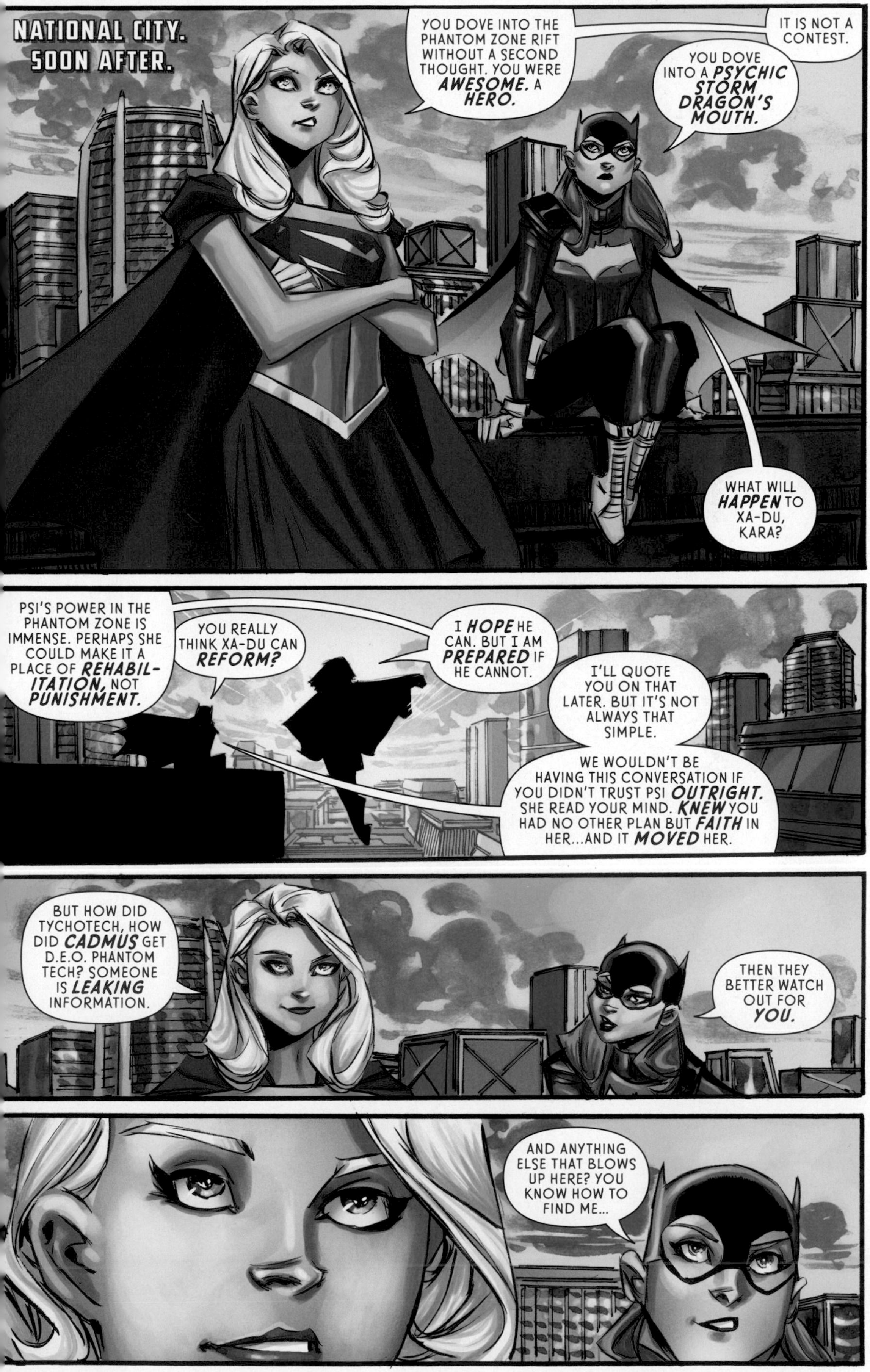
NATIONAL CITY. SOON AFTER.
YOU DOVE INTO THE PHANTOM ZONE RIFT WITHOUT A SECOND THOUGHT. YOU WERE AWESOME. A HERO.
IT IS NOT A CONTEST.
YOU DOVE INTO A PSYCHIC STORM DRAGON'S MOUTH.
WHAT WILL HAPPEN TO XA-DU, KARA?
PSI'S POWER IN THE PHANTOM ZONE IS IMMENSE. PERHAPS SHE COULD MAKE IT A PLACE OF REHABIL-ITATION, NOT PUNISHMENT.
YOU REALLY THINK XA-DU CAN REFORM?
I HOPE HE CAN. BUT I AM PREPARED IF HE CANNOT.
I'LL QUOTE YOU ON THAT LATER. BUT IT'S NOT ALWAYS THAT SIMPLE.
WE WOULDN'T BE HAVING THIS CONVERSATION IF YOU DIDN'T TRUST PSI OUTRIGHT. SHE READ YOUR MIND. KNEW YOU HAD NO OTHER PLAN BUT FAITH IN HER...AND IT MOVED HER.
BUT HOW DID TYCHOTECH, HOW DID CADMUS GET D.E.O. PHANTOM TECH? SOMEONE IS LEAKING INFORMATION.
THEN THEY BETTER WATCH OUT FOR YOU.
AND ANYTHING ELSE THAT BLOWS UP HERE? YOU KNOW HOW TO FIND ME...

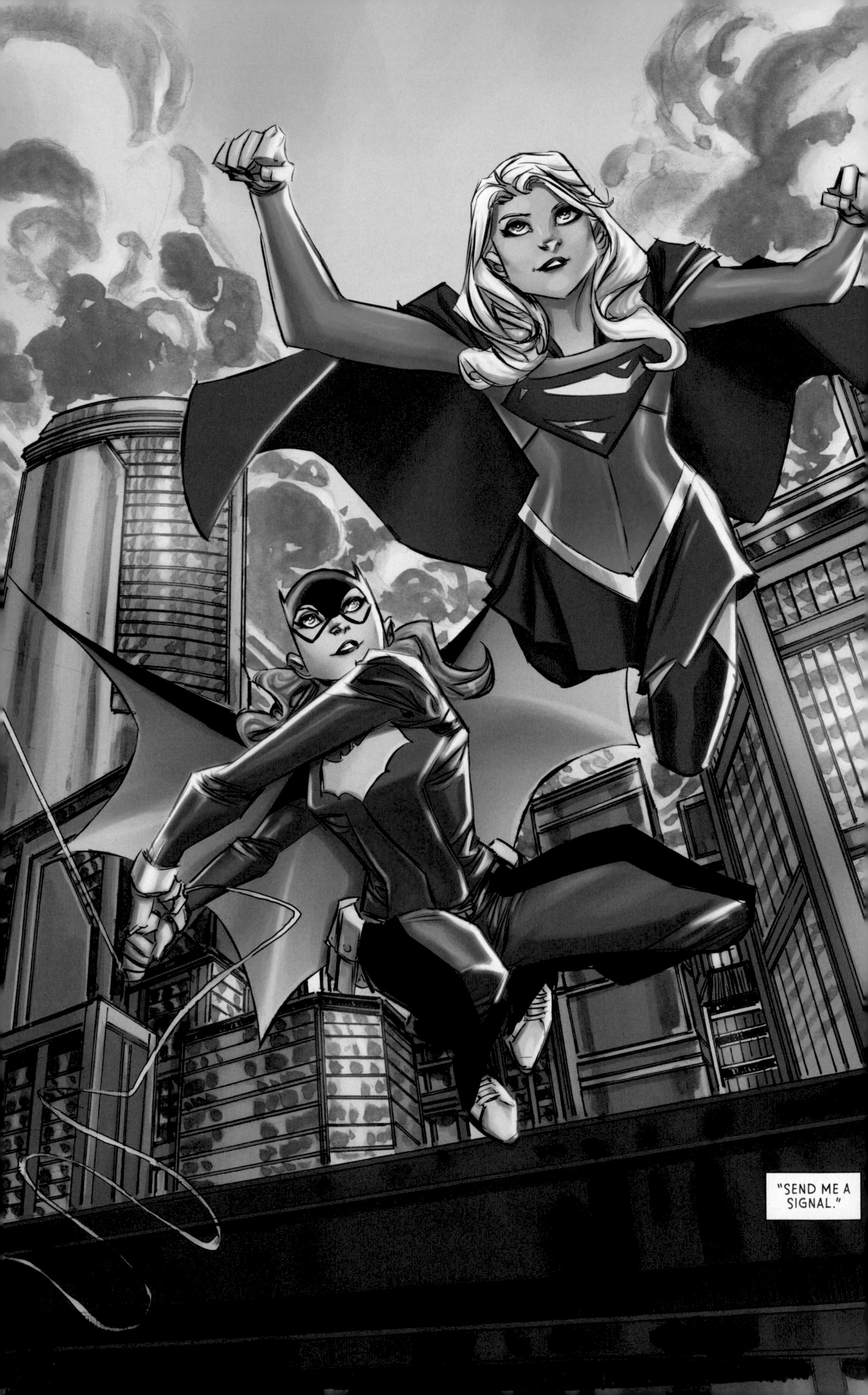
"SEND ME A SIGNAL."

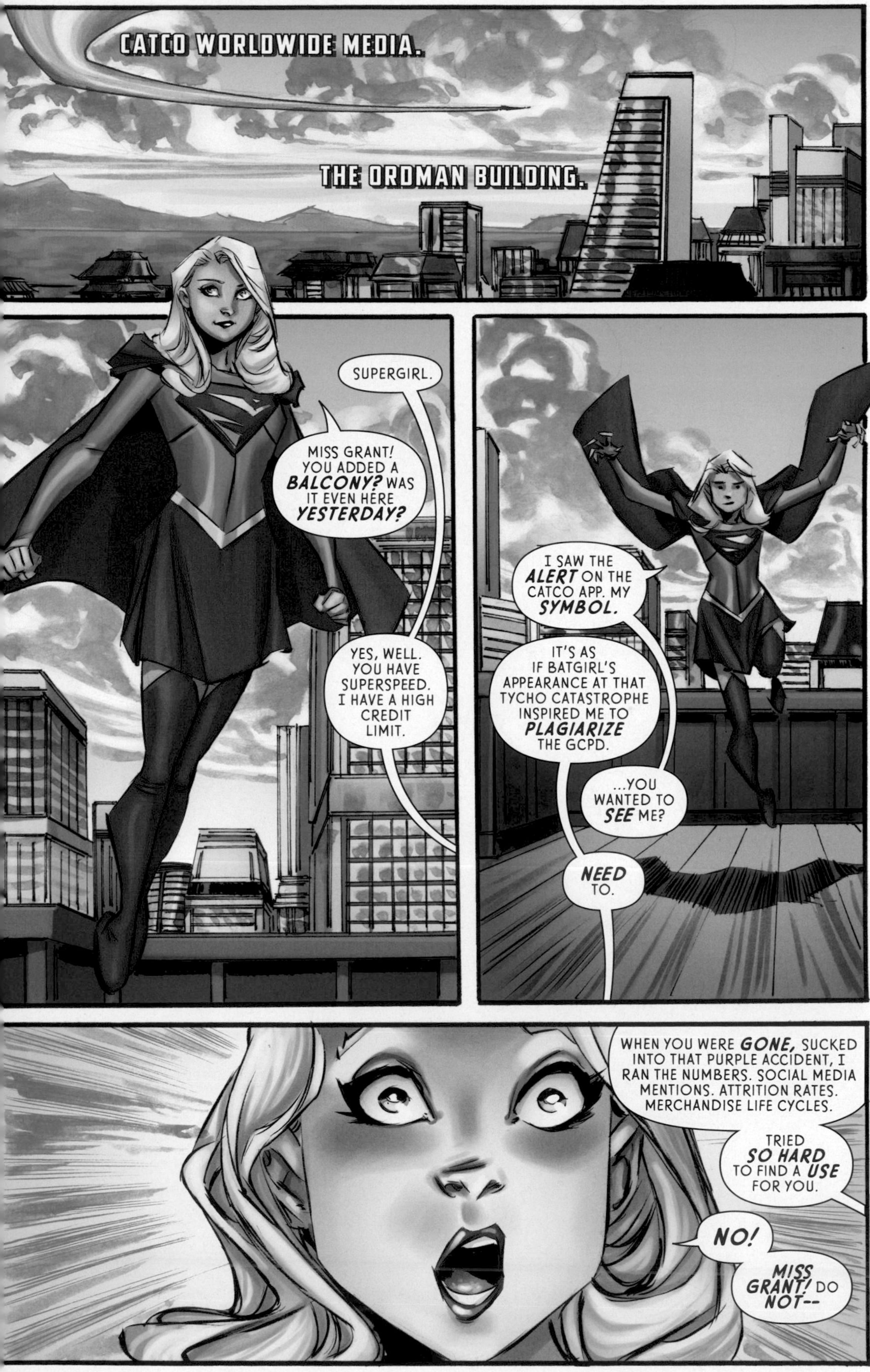
CATCO WORLDWIDE MEDIA.
THE ORDMAN BUILDING.
SUPERGIRL.
MISS GRANT! YOU ADDED A BALCONY? WAS IT EVEN HERE YESTERDAY?
YES, WELL. YOU HAVE SUPERSPEED. I HAVE A HIGH CREDIT LIMIT.
I SAW THE ALERT ON THE CATCO APP. MY SYMBOL.
IT'S AS IF BATGIRL'S APPEARANCE AT THAT TYCHO CATASTROPHE INSPIRED ME TO PLAGIARIZE THE GCPD.
...YOU WANTED TO SEE ME?
NEED TO.
WHEN YOU WERE GONE, SUCKED INTO THAT PURPLE ACCIDENT, I RAN THE NUMBERS. SOCIAL MEDIA MENTIONS. ATTRITION RATES. MERCHANDISE LIFE CYCLES.
TRIED SO HARD TO FIND A USE FOR YOU.
NO!
MISS GRANT! DO NOT--

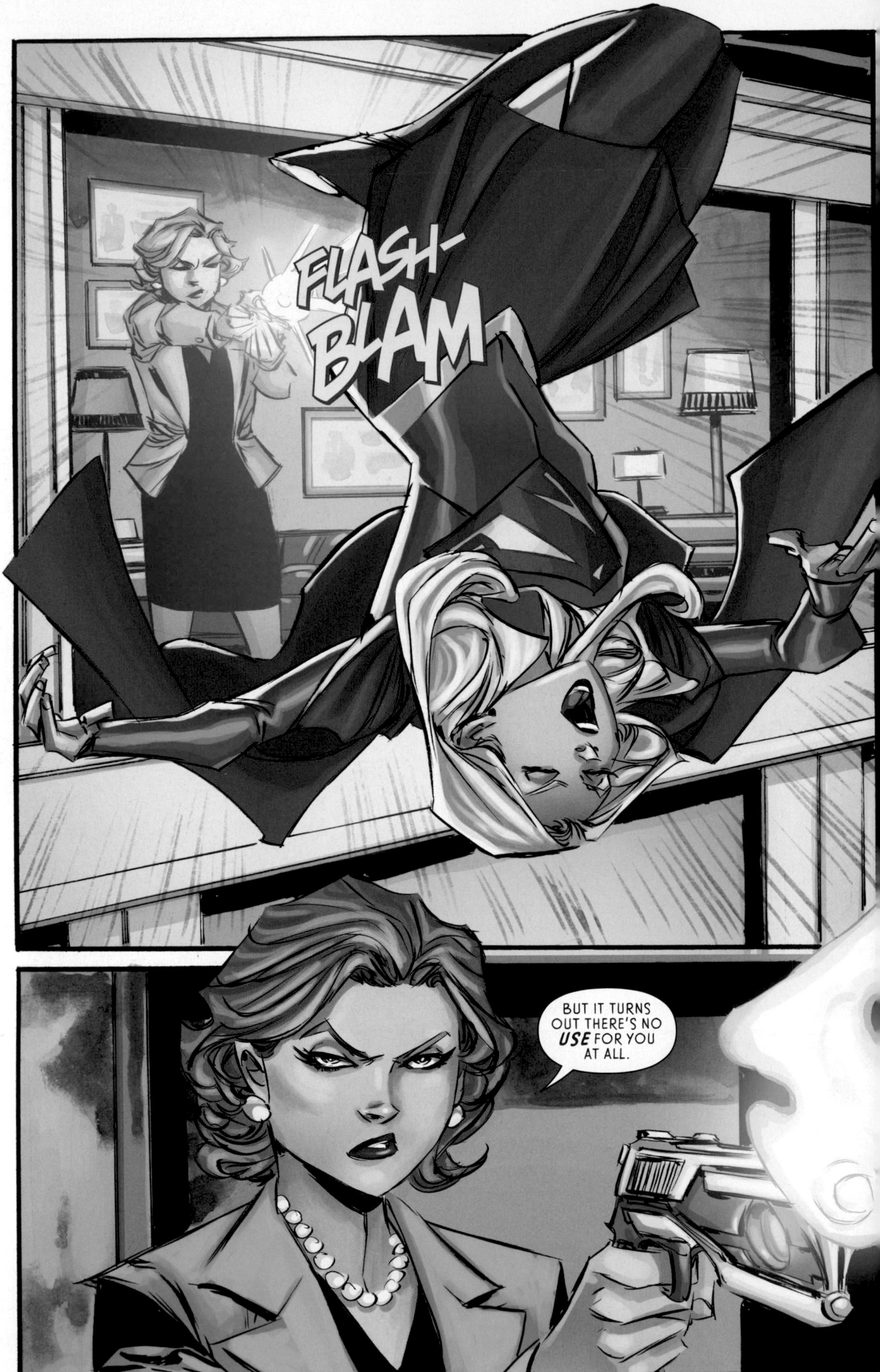
FLASH-
BLAM
BUT IT TURNS OUT THERE'S NO *USE* FOR YOU AT ALL.

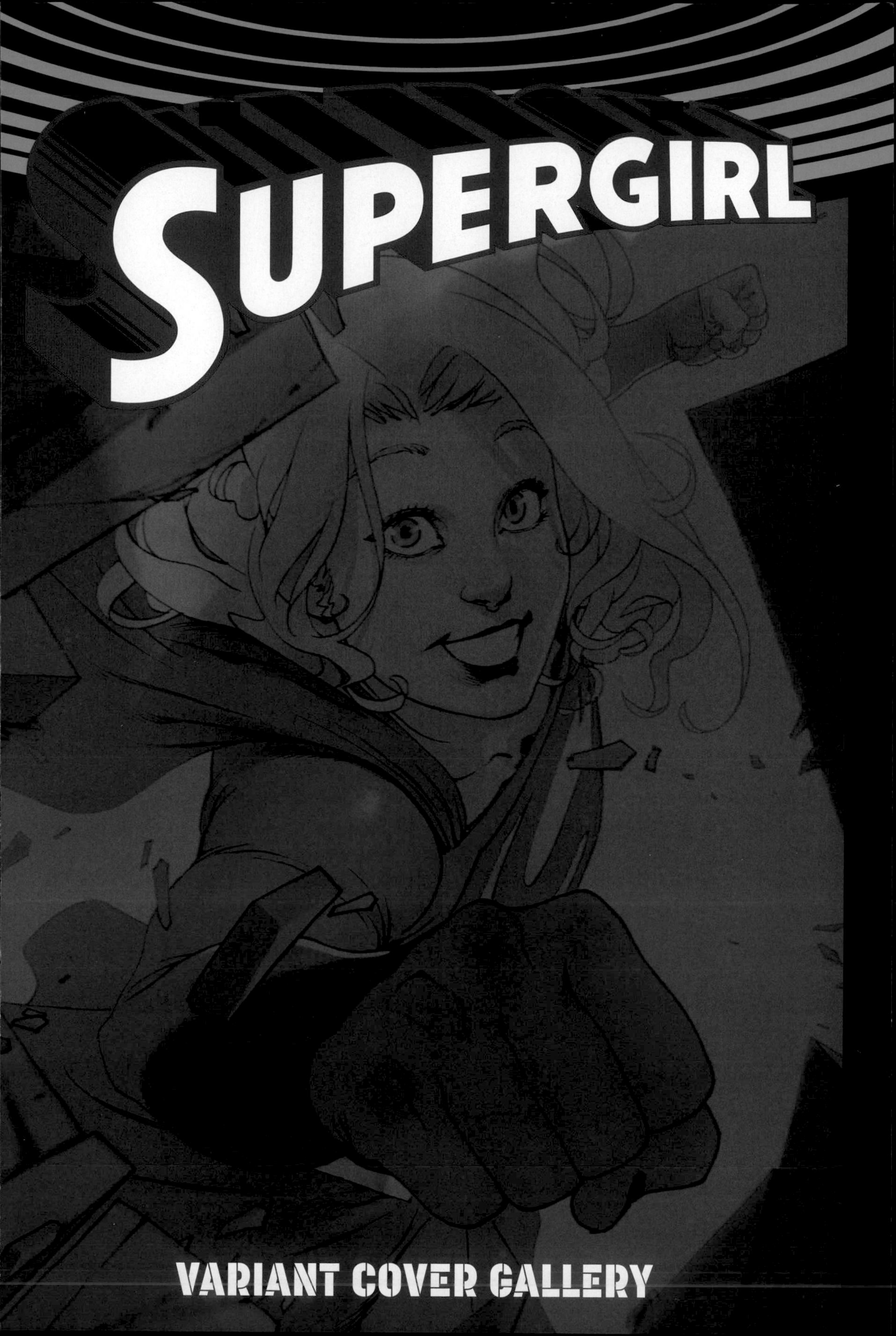
SUPERGIRL
VARIANT COVER GALLERY

SUPERGIRL #7 variant by BENGAL

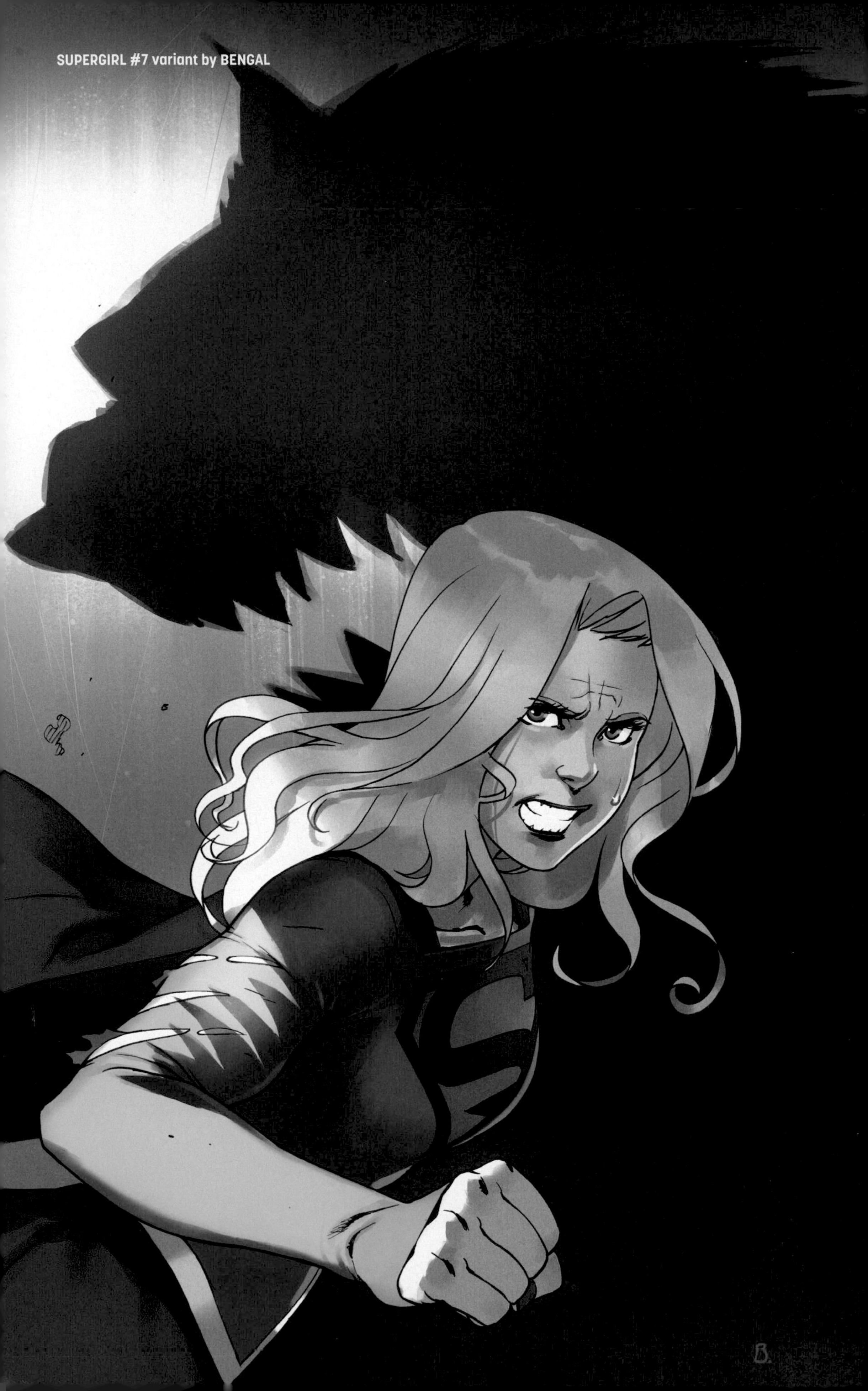

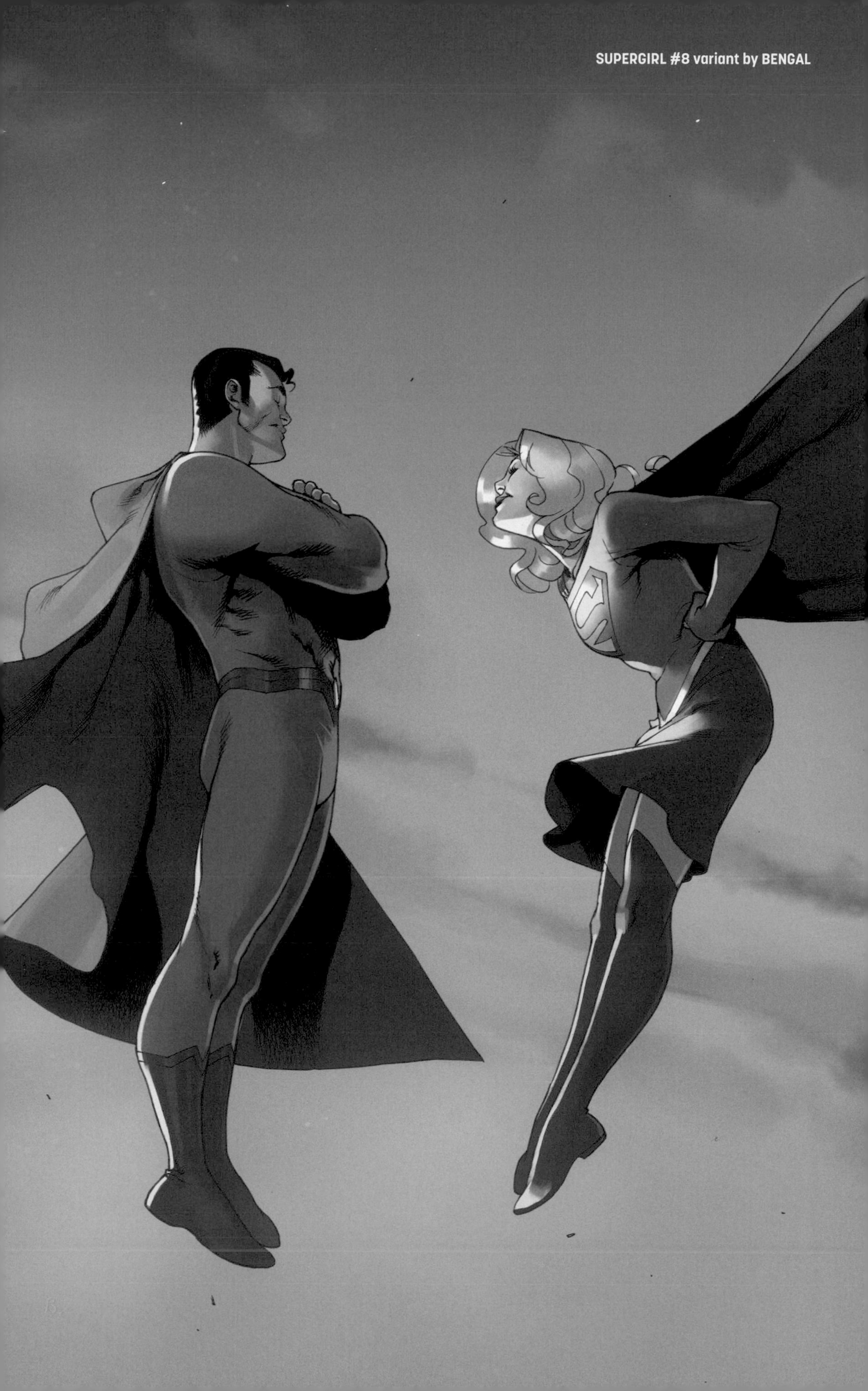
SUPERGIRL #8 variant by BENGAL

SUPERGIRL #9 variant by BENGAL

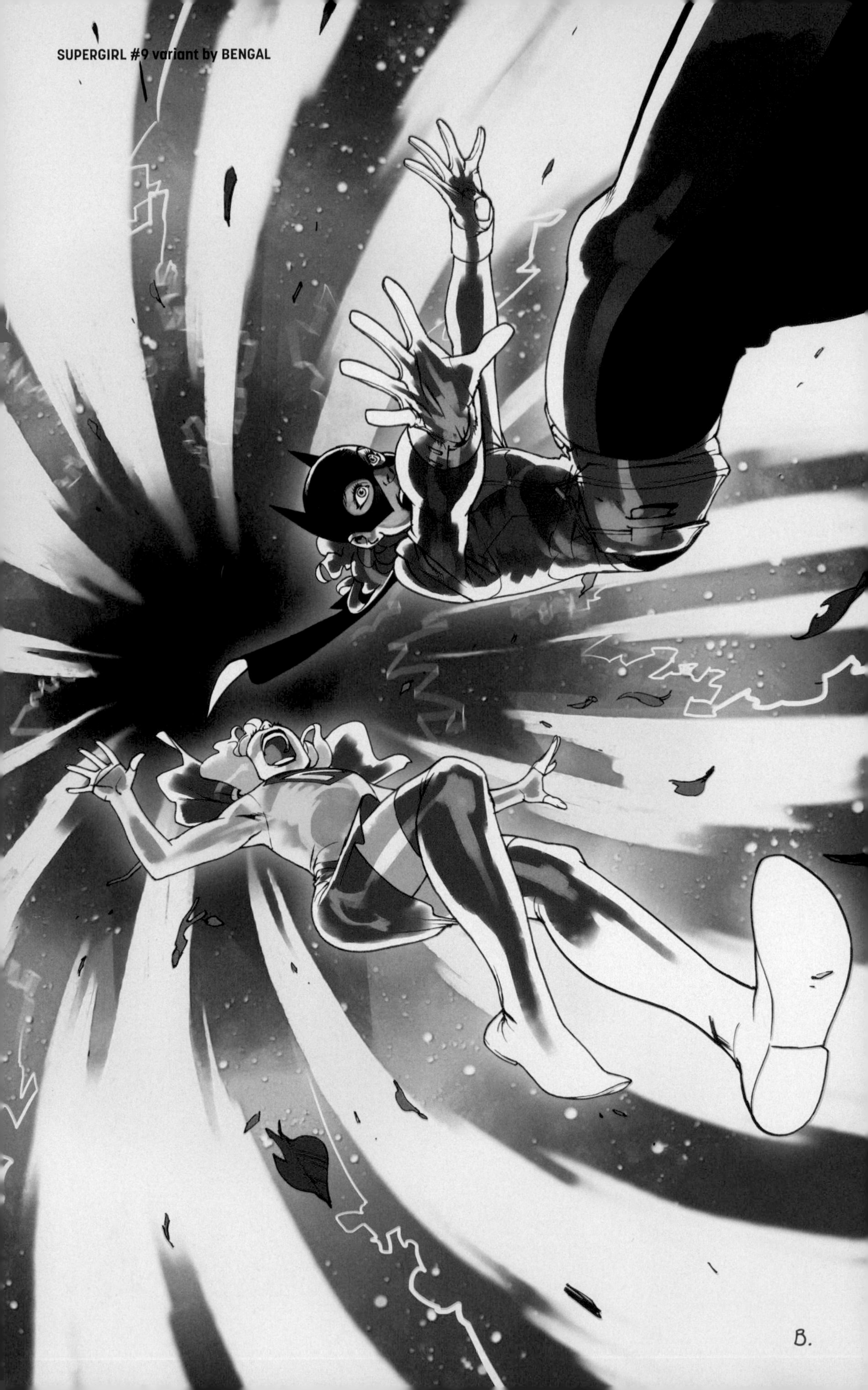

SUPERGIRL #10 variant by BENGAL

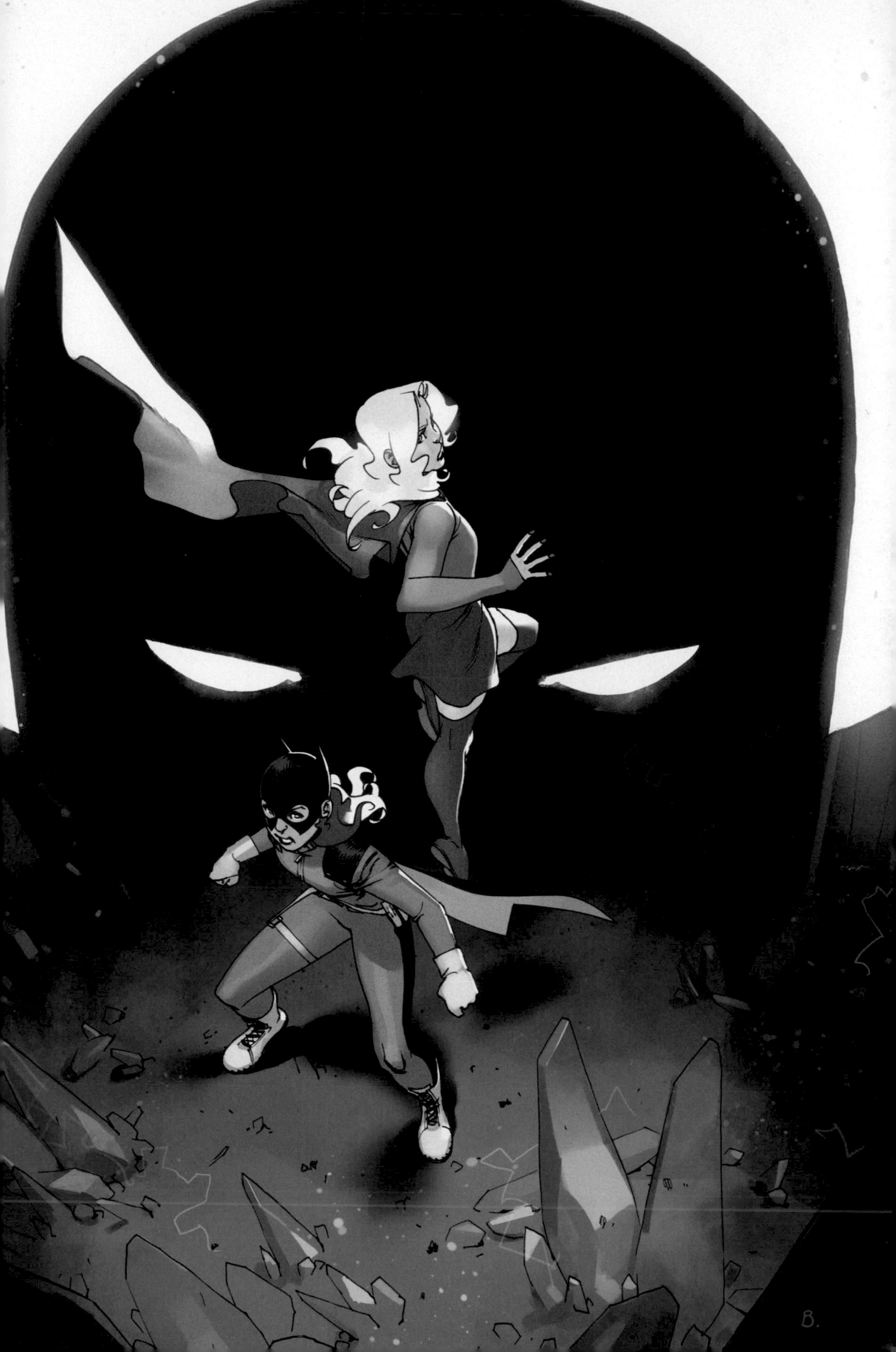
B.

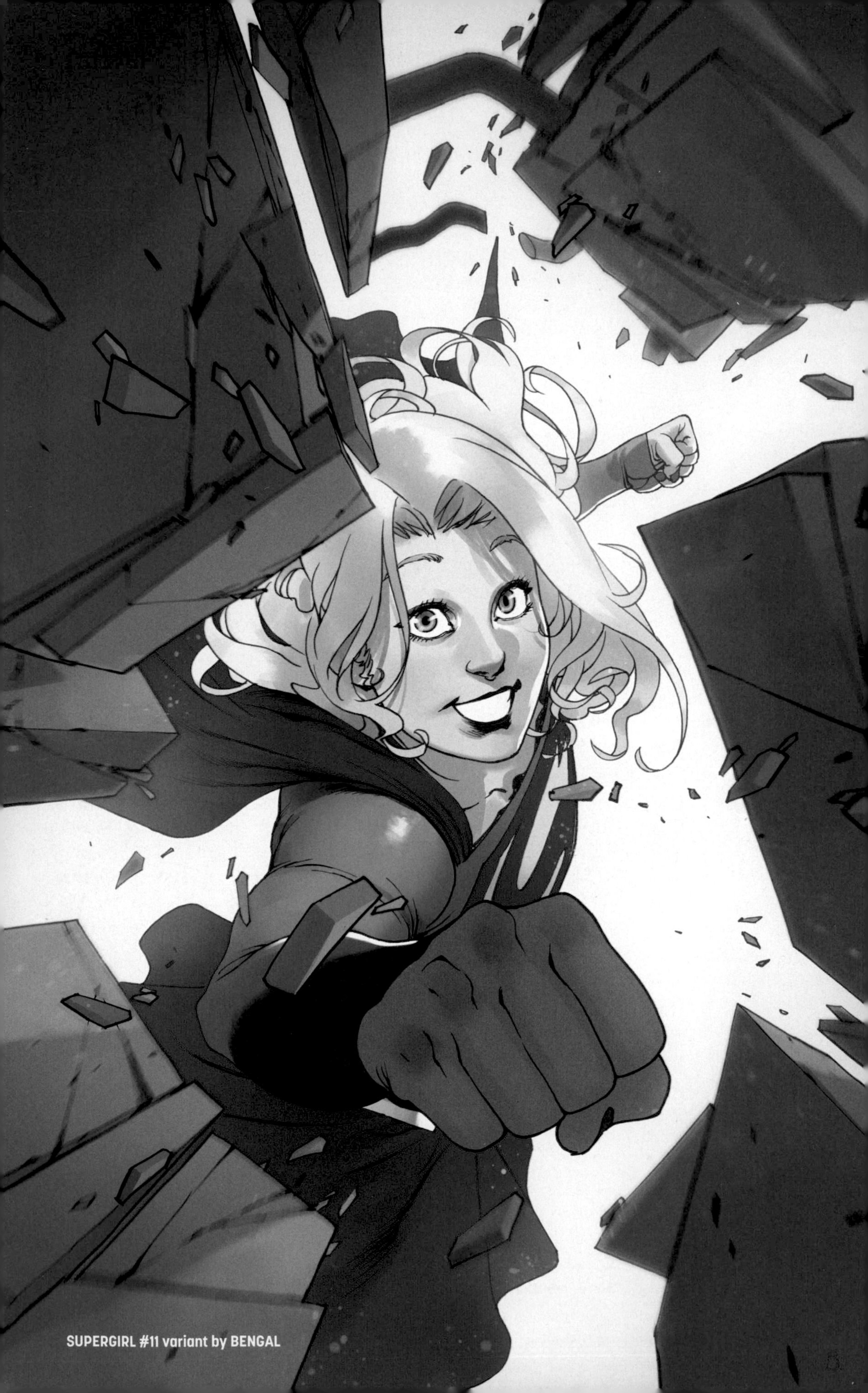

SUPERGIRL #11 variant by BENGAL

A brand-new take on a classic, and it looks
bsolutely, jaw-droppingly fantastic."
– **NEWSARAMA**

A whole lot of excitement and killer art."
– **COMIC BOOK RESOURCES**

ATGIRL

L. 1: BATGIRL OF BURNSIDE

AMERON STEWART &
RENDEN FLETCHER
ith BABS TARR

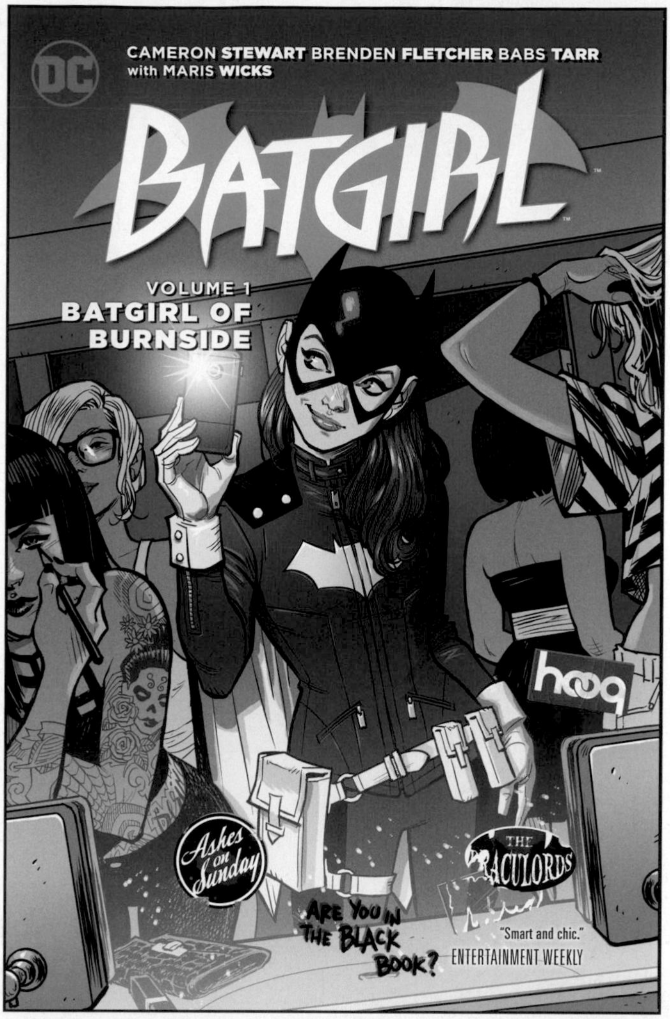
CAMERON STEWART BRENDEN FLETCHER BABS TARR
with MARIS WICKS
BATGIRL
VOLUME 1
BATGIRL OF BURNSIDE
hooq
Ashes on Sunday
ARE YOU IN THE BLACK BOOK?
"Smart and chic."
ENTERTAINMENT WEEKLY

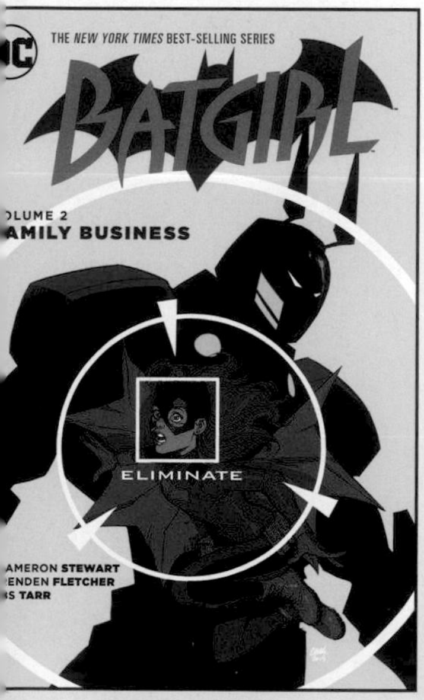
THE NEW YORK TIMES BEST-SELLING SERIES
BATGIRL
OLUME 2
AMILY BUSINESS
ELIMINATE
AMERON STEWART
ENDEN FLETCHER
S TARR

**BATGIRL VOL. 2:
FAMILY BUSINESS**

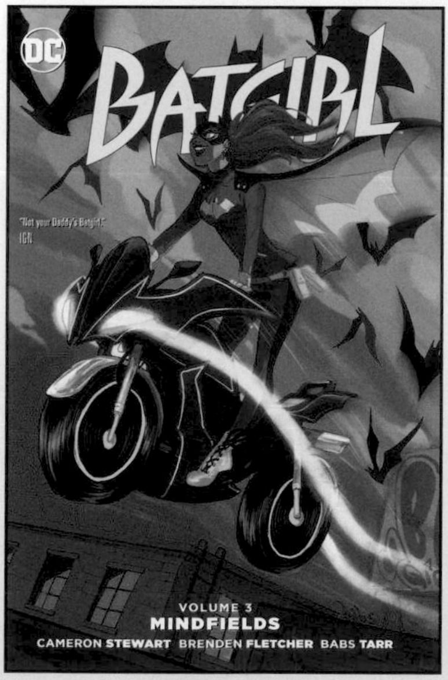
BATGIRL
VOLUME 3
MINDFIELDS
CAMERON STEWART BRENDEN FLETCHER BABS TARR

**BATGIRL VOL. 3:
MINDFIELDS**

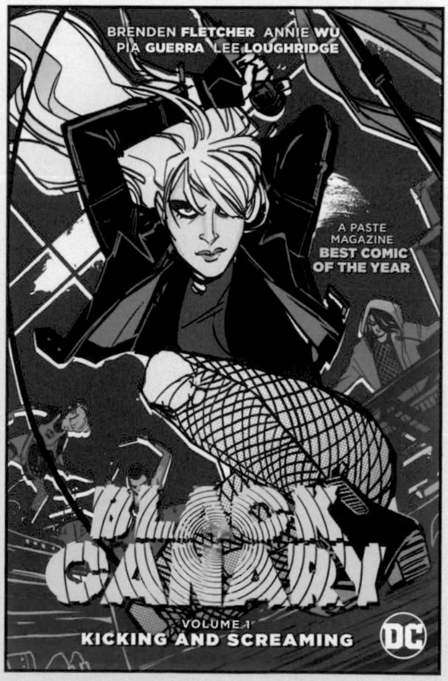
BRENDEN FLETCHER ANNIE WU
PIA GUERRA LEE LOUGHRIDGE
A PASTE MAGAZINE BEST COMIC OF THE YEAR
BLACK CANARY
VOLUME 1
KICKING AND SCREAMING

**BLACK CANARY VOL. 1:
KICKING AND SCREAMING**

Get more DC graphic novels wherever comics and books are sold!

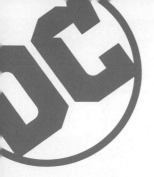

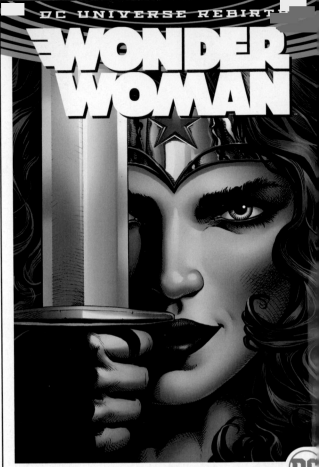